Strategic Media Planning

Kent M. Lancaster
Helen E. Katz

NTC Business Books
a division of *NTC Publishing Group* • Lincolnwood, Illinois USA

Published by NTC Business Books, a division of NTC Publishing Group.
© 1989 by NTC Publishing Group, 4255 West Touhy Avenue,
Lincolnwood (Chicago), Illinois 60646-1975 U.S.A.
All rights reserved. No part of this book may be reproduced, stored
in a retrieval system, or transmitted in any form or by any means,
electronic, mechanical, photocopying, recording or otherwise, without
the prior permission of NTC Publishing Group.
Manufactured in the United States of America.
Library of Congress Catalog Card Number: 88-62474

8 9 0 ML 9 8 7 6 5 4 3 2 1

Contents

Preface

This text and software provide users with state-of-the-art advertising media planning theories, concepts, and procedures that are accessible on a routine basis. They do this by combining several elements. These include syndicated advertising media audience, message, and cost data analyzed through four computer-based interactive advertising planning models. All procedures are demonstrated with numerous examples.

The material acquaints users with methods that help analyze marketing situations with implications for marketing, advertising, and media objectives and advertising appropriations. The situation analysis is facilitated through a competitive advertising spending analysis program called ADCOMP, while ADGOAL is an interactive program that enables users to analyze marketing situations and write measurable marketing, advertising, and media objectives and determine a reasonable advertising appropriation and monthly budget.

To assist you in developing optimum advertising media plans that contribute to advertisers' goals, there are several example computer runs for each media category on the program called ADPLAN. You will learn to communicate media plans effectively, in part, by learning how to summarize advertising budgets and develop media flowcharts using ADFLOW.

Material is also presented which allows users to develop and test their own models.

Acknowledgments

This project has spanned several years and has involved the energy of a number of faculty and students. Here is a partial list of contributors along with a brief description of the nature and scope of their input.

Kim B. Rotzoll deserves gratitude for providing encouragement and a first-rate teaching and research climate conducive to the development and funding of this text and software, and for his personal efforts in acquainting publishers with this material. Tom Galer-Unti, Mary Lowrey, and Kathy Mann should be recognized for patiently helping administer several aspects of this project over the past few years.

John D. Leckenby deserves recognition for sharing his model-building approach as an aspect of advertising education and for contributing several critical algorithms to the ADPLAN computer program. Without his generous solutions to very important problems, ADPLAN would be far less advanced.

Jack Klues, Chuck Quarnstrom, and Jayne Zenaty have provided a useful balance between theory and practice over the past several years by generously helping to keep the data and methods up-to-date, and by presenting substantive media planning material to students and faculty each semester.

Kevin C. Killion provided a thorough and detailed critique of a previous version of this text. His thoughtful comments and suggestions were most helpful in revising this material.

Thomas A. Bowers, James Kropp, Thomas C. Martin, and Ernest Larkin deserve thanks for spotting and carefully describing several problems in parts of the text or software, which are now better because of their help.

Over the past several years, a number of our colleagues have provided constructive suggestions and support for which we are most grateful. A partial alphabetical list includes: Arnold M. Barban, Martin Block, Marsha M. Boyd, Hugh

M. Cannon, Cathy J. Cobb, William R. Oates, John V. Pavlik, Frank Preissle, Roland T. Rust, Nancy Stephens, and George A. Wilcox.

Jung Sook Lee deserves recognition for preparing the glossary for the text, while Lori Boone helped with Chapter Seven.

Margaret A. Toomey not only helped edit previous versions of this manuscript, but she also worked diligently for nearly two years on earlier versions of programs included with this manual.

Sheryl A. Bahnks and Sheri Kramer were most helpful in preparing earlier versions of the text.

Jim Edfors and Dongseung Kim deserve recognition for developing equations speeding the iterative algorithms used in ADPLAN. Jim also deserves recognition for improving an earlier version of ADCOMP.

Lucy M. Wood and Kevin Weiberg helped program earlier versions of AD-PLAN, successfully converting mainframe programs to the personal computer.

Peggy J. Kreshel is one of four researchers involved in the surveys of media directors that are reported in the text and is a co-author of much of Chapter Three. We are grateful to her for allowing us to present some of that work here.

Marshall D. Rice shared his Fortran subroutines for combining exposure distributions which helped develop the Basic language version used here. He also shared a data base of network television cross-pair audience ratings which helped in the development of the cross-pair estimating equations used in ADPLAN.

Joya R. Harris deserves recognition for helping develop ADGOAL.

We especially are indebted to our students who endured endless experimenting as we tested the limits of our knowledge and of their patience. We hope that their lives are richer for the experience.

This manuscript is dedicated to our students and colleagues who are patient enough to endure the limitations of this effort. We hope they will help us make it better.

CHAPTER ONE

An Overview

More than $100 billion is spent yearly in the United States to advertise goods, services, and ideas to businesses, consumers, and the public. Clearly, advertising is an integral part of the economy and society. To help advertisers spend this sum efficiently, there is a staggering quantity and flow of product, media usage, and consumer behavior data available to researchers and planners. In such a setting, it is no longer sufficient to use traditional tools alone in preparing students for careers in advertising because these would simply overwhelm them. In short, instructional methods must facilitate as well as keep pace with worthwhile changes.

Most leading advertisers and their agencies acquire, at great expense, consumer product and media usage data through two major media software houses headquartered in New York and Chicago. The authors experimented with one of these systems, but found the classroom support cost simply prohibitive.[1] For example, an educational discount still requires a yearly outlay of several hundred dollars per data base for access rights, plus $65 per student connect hour. An alternative, increasingly popular in industry, involves leasing microcomputer software for approximately $1,000 per diskette per year, plus the access cost of downloading relevant portions of mainframe data bases. Furthermore, critical computational algorithms are proprietary or black box, which makes them of limited value as educational or research tools.

Consequently, over the past several years, the authors have developed this public media evaluation system for use on the microcomputer. This system is now being used by faculty and students in advertising, communications, and marketing departments at several major universities in the United States and abroad. Several commercial advertisers, agencies, and media organizations are also using it.

This package provides students and instructors of marketing, communications, advertising, and public relations, among others, with state-of-the-art advertising media planning theories, concepts, and procedures that are documented and easily accessible on a routine basis. Although such material has been available to practitioners for nearly 20 years, it is proprietary and there have been too few equivalent procedures for campus use.[2] The severe financial constraints that make state-of-the-art procedures inaccessible, combined with time constraints that often limit the scope of material that can be covered in the classroom, mean that the most sophisticated techniques are often bypassed for sheer expediency and the lack of the practical tools needed to implement them.

This text and software will greatly reduce obstacles to bringing the best available theories and techniques to those eager to learn and use them. The material attempts this by combining a number of elements, which include syndicated advertising media audience, message, and cost data through four microcomputer-based interactive advertising planning models. All procedures are demonstrated in the text through numerous simple examples.

STRUCTURE

This text and software are organized into four sections. Chapters One through Five introduce some fundamental media planning concepts such as basic media planning and research terminology; procedures for analyzing the marketing and advertising situation; writing marketing, advertising, and media goals; and setting advertising appropriations. This section also deals systematically with the complex nature of the media planning process and the large quantities of available data. This is achieved by introducing two interactive microcomputer programs, including their capabilities and sample interactions. ADCOMP facilitates a thorough competitive advertising spending analysis, while ADGOAL uses data from the situation analysis to develop and write measurable marketing, advertising, and media objectives to arrive at a reasonable advertising appropriation and monthly budget.

Chapters Six and Seven introduce strategic aspects of major print and broadcast media categories. They also describe sources of audience, cost, and message data.

Chapters Eight through Eleven outline approaches for developing media schedules and evaluating their likely advertising effects across a broad range of media categories and target groups. A microcomputer program called ADPLAN is introduced which helps develop and evaluate optimum advertising media schedules based on media audience, message impact, and vehicle cost data, which the user provides. It then presents estimates of advertising schedule reach, average frequency, effective reach, cost-per-thousand impressions, and an exposure distribution, among other heavily used media evaluation factors. Another program called ADFLOW provides a systematic summary which explains the advertising budget and facilitates an overview of the entire advertising media schedule in flowchart form.

Chapters Twelve through Fourteen are written for those who wish to study further media planning and research questions. Simple curve fitting techniques are introduced involving the use of multiple regression analysis to show how media models can function effectively in the face of limited, cross-sectional, media vehicle audience data.

BASIC programming is explained to provide a better understanding of how comprehensive media models function, particularly the four models included with the text. This knowledge enables the user to write his or her own media models that embody some aspect of media planning theory or practice.

Chapter Fifteen outlines a number of fundamental advertising media planning and research problems and suggests directions for further research. These questions will most likely be of interest to those concerned with advancing advertising media planning theory and practice.

SAMPLE ANALYSIS

What follows is a brief outline of several ways this text and software could be used, with example output based on the Kellogg's All-Bran case. First, one might do a thorough marketing situation analysis using standard secondary data sources. ADCOMP will help determine competitors' advertising expenditures, by media category, as well as share-of-voice, media mix, gross rating points, and percent changes over previous periods (see Figure 1.1). Where appropriate, many of these estimates can be adjusted for the effects of media cost inflation as well. The benefit of this program is that it allows users to focus on principles and concepts instead of data gathering and entry. Competitive advertising expenditures for a variety of product and media categories can be obtained from Leading National Advertisers *Class/Brand YTD $* and Media Records, among other services that might be available.

Second, users could analyze a situation, write marketing, advertising and media objectives, and determine an optimum advertising appropriation. Using AD-GOAL, they provide data on industry, brand, and competitive circumstances. The program then computes necessary sales, market share, communication, and media goals so that several alternatives can be tried, underscoring the integrated nature of the three levels of objectives (see Figure 1.2). ADGOAL will then help allocate a fixed advertising budget or develop an advertising appropriation based on monthly sales and communications goals.

Third, if one has access to appropriate audience and cost data, such as A.C. Nielsen, Arbitron, Simmons Market Research Bureau (SMRB), and Mediamark Research Inc. (MRI), it is then possible to obtain media vehicle data, for example, that would satisfy certain target audience reach requirements and cost constraints. From this subsample, users could compile a media schedule that maximizes preselected objectives within monthly, quarterly, and annual budget constraints. The ADPLAN program evaluates the various alternatives selected, providing estimates of critical and popular media evaluation factors (see Figure 1.3).

Fourth, the efforts and recommendations can be summarized, helped in part by ADFLOW, to provide comprehensive budget outlines and flow charts of proposed advertising campaigns (see Figures 1.4 and 1.5).

Finally, the last few chapters are designed to help develop one's own BASIC language, beta binomial exposure distribution (BBD) model for particular media categories. To tailor the BBD model to a particular media class requires that one develop self- and cross-pair audience estimating equations. Depending on the media category, it might be necessary to develop equations that estimate BBD parameters. This requires that microcomputer regression packages, such as LOTUS or SHAZAM,[3] be used to analyze large audience data sets to insure that equations can be generalized across a variety of broad target audiences, such as adults, males, females, and female homemakers, and across classes of vehicles within the chosen media category (e.g., women's versus general interest magazines; prime time versus daytime network television). These models must also be tested against tabulated data sets or against results from previously developed models.

PHILOSOPHY

This text and software is guided by a simple philosophy. It is that advertising plans should be developed, evaluated, and compared in terms of their likely *communications* impact on the target audience. The authors strongly believe that in most instances advertisers can estimate the likely magnitude of this effect. Consumer research should reveal the media usage patterns of the target audience, which planners must then use, along with data on the ability of advertising *messages* to communicate, and of *media vehicles* to deliver those messages, in order to develop a plan that best matches the target's need for information with the advertiser's potentially profitable offering to satisfy consumer needs and wants.

There is nothing new about these ideas. What is unique about this text and software, however, is that every effort is made to implement this communication impact philosophy of advertising planning, regardless of the difficulties involved.

If the objective of an advertising plan is to communicate effectively and efficiently, how can one tell in advance which plans are likely to be most effective? Both text and software are unique because they tackle this question by addressing a number of difficult planning issues.

For example, it is well known that media vehicle audiences are often larger than their advertising audiences. So how can media planners estimate advertising audiences? The value of a media plan is affected not only by the correct placement of ads in media vehicles, but by the quality or impact of the message. How can message impact, which will vary from one media category, consumer group, and product class to the next, be taken into account when evaluating media plans? Media categories, such as network television and consumer magazines, differ in terms of their value to consumers. How can planners evaluate the combined impact of several media categories taken together, given these inherent differences?

These are taxing problems. Recent research reveals that, more often than not, planners are inclined to ignore most of them largely because it requires considerable effort to deal with them intelligently and adds unacceptable levels of time, complexity, and expense to the media planning process.[4] Too often clients simply do not demand such sophistication.

Others, of course, attempt to handle the issues directly. This package attempts to acquaint users with important media planning problems and pose solutions from the many alternatives that might be offered. Furthermore, it attempts to do so in a way that is manageable. While the solutions offered are not necessarily the best, they are reasonable and readily available, and should therefore be considered and used.

The media planning process, however it is conducted, also involves a large number of decision points. Each of these is couched in a wide array of alternatives, and every one will probably lead to a different level of target impact. Estimating the likely effect of a media schedule can require thousands of calculations using various

FIGURE 1.1 Competitive Advertising Spending Analysis: Sample ADCOMP Output

```
-----------------------------------------------------------------------------
                    Bran Cereals Media Spending Analysis (1985 - 86)
-----------------------------------------------------------------------------

                              Advertising Expenditures
                              ------------------------
Brand/   7-Media   Magazns   N Paper   Network   Spot     Network   Outdoor   Cable
  Year     Total             Supplmt     TV        TV       Radio              TV
------   -------   -------   -------   -------   -------   -------   -------   -------
All-Bran
   85    11216.6      0.0       0.0   10195.6    950.2       0.0       0.0      70.8
   86    14923.9      0.0       0.0   13631.7   1176.1       0.0       0.0     116.1
Fruit & Fibre
   85    17154.1   2985.0     190.2   10913.4   2330.9       0.0       0.0     734.6
   86    15344.4   3234.8       0.0   10448.0   1219.8       0.0       0.0     441.8
Class Total
   85    70649.6   3402.7     190.2   56504.6   8294.5       0.0       0.0    2257.6
   86    71706.2   4375.4       0.0   58905.4   6660.5       0.0       0.0    1764.9

                              Advertising Media Mix
                              ---------------------
Brand/   7-Media   Magazns   N Paper   Network   Spot     Network   Outdoor   Cable
  Year     Total             Supplmt     TV        TV       Radio              TV
------   -------   -------   -------   -------   -------   -------   -------   -------
All-Bran
   85    100.0%      0.0%      0.0%     90.9%     8.5%      0.0%      0.0%      0.6%
   86    100.0%      0.0%      0.0%     91.3%     7.9%      0.0%      0.0%      0.8%
Fruit & Fibre
   85    100.0%     17.4%      1.1%     63.6%    13.6%      0.0%      0.0%      4.3%
   86    100.0%     21.1%      0.0%     68.1%     7.9%      0.0%      0.0%      2.9%
Class Total
   85    100.0%      4.8%      0.3%     80.0%    11.7%      0.0%      0.0%      3.2%
   86    100.0%      6.1%      0.0%     82.1%     9.3%      0.0%      0.0%      2.5%

                                 Share of Voice
                                 --------------
Brand/   7-Media   Magazns   N Paper   Network   Spot     Network   Outdoor   Cable
  Year     Total             Supplmt     TV        TV       Radio              TV
------   -------   -------   -------   -------   -------   -------   -------   -------
All-Bran
   85     15.9%      0.0%      0.0%     18.0%    11.5%      0.0%      0.0%      3.1%
   86     20.8%      0.0%      0.0%     23.1%    17.7%      0.0%      0.0%      6.6%
Fruit & Fibre
   85     24.3%     87.7%    100.0%     19.3%    28.1%      0.0%      0.0%     32.5%
   86     21.4%     73.9%      0.0%     17.7%    18.3%      0.0%      0.0%     25.0%

                              Gross Rating Points
                              -------------------
Brand/   7-Media   Magazns   N Paper   Network   Spot     Network   Outdoor   Cable
  Year     Total             Supplmt     TV        TV       Radio              TV
------   -------   -------   -------   -------   -------   -------   -------   -------
All-Bran
   85    3418.9%     0.0%      0.0%   3160.4%   225.6%      0.0%      0.0%     32.8%
   86    4558.6%     0.0%      0.0%   4225.6%   279.3%      0.0%      0.0%     53.8%
Fruit & Fibre
   85    5126.0%   828.2%     21.1%   3383.0%   553.5%      0.0%      0.0%    340.3%
   86    4630.5%   897.6%      0.0%   3238.7%   289.7%      0.0%      0.0%    204.6%

                     Advertising Expenditures Annual Changes
                     --------------------------------------
Brand/   7-Media   Magazns   N Paper   Network   Spot     Network   Outdoor   Cable
  Year     Total             Supplmt     TV        TV       Radio              TV
------   -------   -------   -------   -------   -------   -------   -------   -------
All-Bran
   86     33.1%      0.0%      0.0%     33.7%    23.8%      0.0%      0.0%     64.0%
Fruit & Fibre
   86    -10.5%      8.4%   -100.0%     -4.3%   -47.7%      0.0%      0.0%    -39.9%
Class Total
   86      1.5%     28.6%   -100.0%      4.2%   -19.7%      0.0%      0.0%    -21.8%
-----------------------------------------------------------------------------
```

FIGURE 1.2 Developing Marketing, Advertising and Media Goals: Sample ADGOAL Output

```
-------------------------------------------------------------------
All-Bran Projected Marketing Situation, Fiscal Year 1988
-------------------------------------------------------------------
Bran Cereal Unit Sales                                       Change
     1987                           =       557,134,270
     1988                           =       640,704,380      15.00%
All-Bran Sales Revenue
     1987                           =       $41,420,600
     1988                           =       $49,704,720      20.00%
All-Bran Unit Sales
     1987                           =        31,862,000
     1988                           =        38,234,400      20.00%
All-Bran Unit Sales Share
     1987                           =             5.72%
     1988                           =             5.97%       4.35%

Target Size (Female Homemakers)     =        69,719,000
-------------------------------------------------------------------


-------------------------------------------------------------------
Consumer   ---- Percent of Target Market To Be Affected Each Month (L =0.36)---
Hierarchy  JAN  FEB   MAR   APR   MAY   JUN   JUL   AUG   SEP   OCT   NOV   DEC
-------------------------------------------------------------------

Recall     6.1  10.8  10.2  32.6  24.6  24.6  24.6  24.6  24.6  0.6   9.2   9.2
Purchase   1.2  1.4   1.4   3.3   3.3   3.3   3.3   3.3   3.3   1.2   1.2   1.2
-------------------------------------------------------------------

Hierarchy      Percent of Target Market To Be Affected, APR, 1988 (L = .36)
---------
-------------------------------------------------------------------
 1. Recall      I              *
 2. Purchase    I *

+-------------+-------------+-------------+-------------+-------------+
              0%            25%           50%           75%          100%
-------------------------------------------------------------------
```

Marketing Goals:

Within fiscal year 1988, All-Bran should achieve
a market share of 5.97% in the Bran Cereal market
through marketing emphasis on Female Homemakers.
This should result in unit sales of 38,234,400 and sales
revenue of $49,704,720 assuming a manufacturer's price of
$1.30 per unit.

Advertising Goals:

Each month of 1988, All-Bran must achieve the following
Recall levels against Female Homemakers who use Bran Cereal.

```
    JAN =  6.1%        JUL = 24.6%
    FEB = 10.8%        AUG = 24.6%
    MAR = 10.2%        SEP = 24.6%
    APR = 32.6%        OCT =  0.6%
    MAY = 24.6%        NOV =  9.2%
    JUN = 24.6%        DEC =  9.2%
```

Messages will emphasize that All-Bran
is highest in fiber content.

Media Goals:

Each month of 1988, All-Bran must achieve the following
effective reach levels against Female Homemakers
who use Bran Cereal.

```
    JAN =  6.1%        JUL = 24.6%
    FEB = 10.8%        AUG = 24.6%
    MAR = 10.2%        SEP = 24.6%
    APR = 32.6%        OCT =  0.6%
    MAY = 24.6%        NOV =  9.2%
    JUN = 24.6%        DEC =  9.2%
```

Effective reach is the percent of the target audience
exposed to messages three to ten times per month.

FIGURE 1.3 **Developing and Evaluating Optimum Media Plans: Sample ADPLAN Output**

```
--------------------------------------------------------------------------

ADPLAN RESULTS:  CABLE TV

Name = Kent Lancaster          Target ID = Female Homemakers
Brand = All-Bran               Target Size =  69,405,000
Period = June 1988
```

Frequency (f) Distribution	Unweighted		Weighted	
f	% f	% f+	% f	% f+
0	65.33%	100.00%	78.33%	100.00%
1	16.06%	34.67%	10.04%	21.67%
2	7.65%	18.61%	4.78%	11.63%
3	4.23%	10.96%	2.64%	6.85%
4	2.49%	6.73%	1.56%	4.21%
5	1.53%	4.24%	0.95%	2.65%
6	0.96%	2.71%	0.60%	1.69%
7	0.61%	1.75%	0.38%	1.10%
8	0.39%	1.14%	0.25%	0.71%
9	0.26%	0.75%	0.16%	0.47%
10	0.17%	0.49%	0.10%	0.31%
11+	0.33%	0.33%	0.20%	0.20%

```
BBD Factors:  R1 = .003, R2 = .007, A = .3472942709, B = 100.0267791
Weight (Recall) = 62.5%
```

Summary Evaluation	Unweighted	Weighted
Reach (1+)	34.67%	21.67%
Effective Reach (3+)	10.96%	6.85%
Average Frequency	2.40	2.40
Gross Rating Points	83.04	51.90
Gross Impressions (000)	57,633.91	36,021.19
CPM/Gross Impressions	$3.11	$4.98
Cost Per Rating Point	$2,158.96	$3,454.34

Vehicle List	Rating	Cume	Ad Cost	CPM	Ads	Total Cost
ESPN	0.47	0.84	$578	$2.84	30	$17,340
CNN	0.44	0.80	$584	$3.03	30	$17,520
CBN	0.43	0.77	$1,318	$7.02	30	$39,540
MTV	0.37	0.67	$1,385	$8.56	30	$41,550
TNN	0.35	0.62	$1,075	$7.12	30	$32,250
LIFE	0.23	0.41	$500	$5.01	30	$15,000
A & E	0.14	0.25	$450	$7.36	30	$13,500
USA	0.33	0.59	$86	$0.60	30	$2,580
			Totals:	$4.98	240	$179,280

media models. Consequently, to make the process as accurate as possible given the limitations of the available data, the text is supported by a number of integrated, interactive advertising media planning computer programs. These help to deal systematically with a comprehensive range of important decisions, which are stored by the computer program and then used to estimate the likely impact on the marketplace of all of the choices combined. Without the use of such software, it is inconceivable

FIGURE 1.4   Summarizing the Advertising Budget: Sample ADFLOW Output

```
------------------------------------------------------------------
      Kellogg's All-Bran Budget Summary for Fiscal Year 1987-88
------------------------------------------------------------------
```

	Amount	Percent
Target Audience: Female Homemakers	------	-------
Target Audience Size: 69,405,000		
Advertising Appropriation	$13,791,667	100.0%
Media Budget	$12,412,500	90.0
Contingency	$1,379,167	10.0
Marketing Regions		
Northeast	$2,556,975	20.6
East Central	$1,849,462	14.9
West Central	$2,259,075	18.2
South	$3,624,450	29.2
Pacific	$2,122,537	17.1
	-----------	------
	$12,412,500	100.0%
Media Categories		
Consumer Magazines	$6,422,940	51.7
Network TV	$5,989,560	48.3
	-----------	------
	$12,412,500	100.0%
Quarterly Expenditures		
JAN-FEB-MAR	$3,103,125	25.0
APR-MAY-JUN	$3,103,125	25.0
JUL-AUG-SEP	$3,103,125	25.0
OCT-NOV-DEC	$3,103,125	25.0
	-----------	------
	$12,412,500	100.0%
Products		
Regular	$3,723,750	30.0
High Fiber	$3,723,750	30.0
Fruit and Almonds	$4,965,000	40.0
	-----------	------
	$12,412,500	100.0%

```
------------------------------------------------------------------
```

that numerous alternatives can be considered simultaneously and evaluated in a manner that maximizes consumer and advertiser benefit.

CONTINUITY: THE KELLOGG'S ALL-BRAN CASE

This text covers a broad range of complex advertising planning topics, which are often illustrated using realistic examples. One case, used throughout as the basis for examples, is that of Kellogg's All-Bran cereal; it serves as a familiar benchmark, providing a measure of continuity as the various topics are presented and analyzed.

The Kellogg's All-Bran case was selected because extensive marketing and advertising data are readily available in the public domain, a broad range of con-

FIGURE 1.5   Presenting an Advertising Media Schedule: Sample ADFLOW Output

```
---------------------------------------------------------------------------------------
                      Kellogg's All-Eran Media Schedule For Fiscal Year 1987-88
---------------------------------------------------------------------------------------
Target Audience:  Female Homemakers                    Advertising Media Budget:  $12,412,500  ( 90.0%)
Target Audience Size:   69,405,000                           Contingency:          $1,379,167  ( 10.0%)
```

Media Vehicles	Yearly Ads	Yearly Cost(000)	Number of Insertions per Month											
			JAN	FEB	MAR	APR	MAY	JUN	JUL	AUG	SEP	OCT	NOV	DEC
Consumer Magazines	72	$6,422.9	6	6	6	6	6	6	6	6	6	6	6	6
Reader's Digest	12	$1,305.6	1	1	1	1	1	1	1	1	1	1	1	1
TV Guide	48	$4,286.4	4	4	4	4	4	4	4	4	4	4	4	4
Good Housekeepin	12	$830.9	1	1	1	1	1	1	1	1	1	1	1	1
Network TV	96	$5,989.6	8	8	8	8	8	8	8	8	8	8	8	8
Young and Restle	24	$540.2	2	2	2	2	2	2	2	2	2	2	2	2
All My Children	24	$515.7	2	2	2	2	2	2	2	2	2	2	2	2
Dallas	24	$2,580.7	2	2	2	2	2	2	2	2	2	2	2	2
Bill Cosby Show	24	$2,353.0	2	2	2	2	2	2	2	2	2	2	2	2
Total		$12,412.5												

```
Consumer Magazines  ($000)  $535   $535   $535   $535   $535   $535   $535   $535   $535   $535   $535   $535
Network TV          ($000)  $499   $499   $499   $499   $499   $499   $499   $499   $499   $499   $499   $499
Monthly Totals      ($000)  $1034  $1034  $1034  $1034  $1034  $1034  $1034  $1034  $1034  $1034  $1034  $1034

Effective Reach             27.7%  27.7%  27.7%  27.7%  27.7%  27.7%  27.7%  27.7%  27.7%  27.7%  27.7%  27.7%
Gross Rating Points         169.8  169.8  169.8  169.8  169.8  169.8  169.8  169.8  169.8  169.8  169.8  169.8
CPM Impressions             $8.78  $8.78  $8.78  $8.78  $8.78  $8.78  $8.78  $8.78  $8.78  $8.78  $8.78  $8.78
```

sumers use the product category, product use by consumers is not often controversial, and the brand is top-of-the-line in terms of popularity and product quality. It also underscores the idea that advertising can be a factor of considerable value to segments of the economy and society.

At the time the case was selected, All-Bran was recognized as one of the most nutritious ready-to-eat (RTE) breakfast cereals on the market, a field which touches numerous sectors of society. Considerable data are also available on marketing and advertising aspects of this industry, on the Kellogg Company, and on All-Bran, as indicated by the additional reading listed at the end of this chapter.

Recent heavy publicity on the value of high-fiber content in the diet as a means of maintaining health and reducing the risk of certain types of cancer has added some genuine excitement to the case. So it would not be surprising if sales of bran cereals more than double over the next year or two. Furthermore, the ethics of using the advertising message to suggest that consumption of bran cereals can be a means of reducing the risk of certain types of cancer is certain to embroil this segment of the market in considerable controversy over the next several years. What follows, then, is some further information on the marketing situation facing Kellogg's All-Bran, which should enrich the meaning of the examples used throughout this text.

The RTE cereal industry consistently achieves more than $3 billion in annual sales. It is dominated by four major manufacturers: the Kellogg Company, General Mills, General Foods, and Quaker Oats. Together these four firms account for nearly 90 percent of RTE cereal sales. Other manufacturers in the industry include Ralston Purina, Nabisco, and Pet.

This industry is characterized by brand proliferation, with more than 50 major RTE cereal brands and close to 200 brands and sizes in all. The top brands of cold cereals include such well known products as Corn Flakes, Cheerios, Sugar Frosted Flakes, Raisin Bran, Chex, Shredded Wheat, Rice Krispies, Grape-Nuts, and Captain Crunch, among others. This group of cereals accounts for nearly 40 percent of all RTE cereal sales, with market shares ranging from three to nearly seven percent in both units and dollars.[5]

Brands typically are categorized into four major product segments: regular, pre-sweetened, bran, and natural cereals. The bran segment is experiencing rapid growth at the present time, estimated by some to be about 33 percent annually; it currently has a 17 percent share of the RTE cereal market.

The Kellogg Company of Battle Creek, Michigan, was founded in 1906. Since then, it has become the world leader in manufacturing and distributing RTE cereals. The company sells its products in more than 100 countries and has production facilities in more than a dozen of them. Kellogg's share of the RTE cereal market had been eroding steadily since the mid 1970s, but in 1986 it rebounded to take 48 percent of the market.

All-Bran is Kellogg's most important entry in the bran segment of the RTE cereal market, with an industry volume share of approximately 2.3 percent, including regular All-Bran, All-Bran Extra Fiber, and All-Bran Fruit and Almonds. Kellogg's also manufactures other bran products, such as Raisin Bran, Bran Flakes, Bran Buds, and Fruitful Bran. Bran products manufactured by other firms include Fiber One, 40% Bran, Fruit & Fibre, Post Raisin Bran, 100% Bran, Quaker Oat and Corn Bran, and Bran Chex. Most of these products appeal primarily to older segments of the population who are concerned about nutrition and health. However, All-Bran and other competitors are now placing additional emphasis on middle-age groups.

Kellogg's All-Bran was rated in 1981 and 1986 by *Consumer Reports* as one of the highest quality RTE cereals in terms of its nutritional value; regular All-Bran contains 9.9 grams of fiber per ounce.[6] After Fiber One was introduced, containing 12 grams of fiber per ounce, Kellogg's countered that with its Extra Fiber All-Bran, having 13 grams of fiber per ounce. Extra Fiber All-Bran and All-Bran Fruit and Almonds are currently in a national roll-out after test marketing in cities such as New York.

All-Bran is distributed intensively and has a retail price of approximately $1.80 per 13.8 ounce box. The product is supported by roughly $6 million in advertising and often offers a coupon on the package that has, on occasion, also featured recipes.

Both the All-Bran package and advertisements currently emphasize the high fiber content of the product and that fiber has been demonstrated to reduce the risk of certain kinds of cancer, and may make one healthier all around. The package also features "Preventative Health Tips From the National Cancer Institute." The present All-Bran advertising campaign is running on major television networks, in magazines, newspaper supplements, and news weeklies.

In contrast, General Mills is supporting Fiber One with nearly $14 million in annual advertising expenditures. Fiber One is being positioned against All-Bran and 100% Bran, manufactured by Nabisco. Meanwhile General Foods is supporting Fruit and Fibre with more than $13 million in annual advertising expenditures.

For additional details on Kellogg's All-Bran and the RTE cereal industry, the additional readings would be an excellent point of departure.

ENDNOTES

1. David R. Gusse and Kent M. Lancaster, "Using On-line Data Services Makes Course More Realistic," *Journalism Educator,* 38 (1983), pp. 6-10, 38.

2. Martin P. Block, Don E. Schultz and Bret Jacobowitz, "DONMAR: A Computer Simulation Media Buying Game," in Alan D. Fletcher, ed., *Teaching the Advertising Media Course: Organization, Content, Textbooks*, Proceedings, Advertising Division of the Association for Education in Journalism, 1976, pp. 46-66; Douglas J. Buffo, Margaret A. Toomey, Lucy M. Wood and Kent M. Lancaster, "ADPLAN: An Interactive Advertising Media Planning System," *Proceedings of the 1985 Conference of the American Academy of Advertising*, pp. NR165-NR170; and Kent M. Lancaster, John D. Leckenby and Judith A. Stern, "Teaching Advertising Media Planning Using Interactive Media Models," *Journal of Marketing Education*, (Spring, 1985), pp. 22-28.

3. Lotus Development Corporation, *123 Reference Manual* (Cambridge, Massachusetts: Lotus Development Corporation, 1985); and Kenneth J. White, *SHAZAM: An Econometrics Computer Program, Version 4.6*, Vancouver, B.C., Canada, University of British Columbia, Department of Economics, 1983.

4. Peggy J. Kreshel, Kent M. Lancaster, and Margaret A. Toomey, "How Leading Advertising Agencies Perceive Effective Reach and Frequency," *Journal of Advertising*, 14:3 (September 1985), pp. 32-38, 51; and Kent M. Lancaster, Peggy J. Kreshel, and Joya R. Harris, "Estimating the Impact of Advertising Media Plans: Media Executives Describe Weighting and Timing Factors," *Journal of Advertising*, 15 (September 1986), pp. 21-29, 45.

5. John C. Maxwell Jr., "Adults lead cereal boom," *Advertising Age*, July 7, 1986; John C. Maxwell Jr., "Cold cereals heating up," *Advertising Age*, August 5, 1985; and John C. Maxwell Jr., "Cereal milks '83 gains," *Advertising Age*, May 28, 1984, p. 32.

6. *Consumer Reports*, "Ready-to-eat cereals," October 1986, pp. 628-642; and *Consumer Reports*, "Which Cereal for Breakfast?" February, 1981, pp. 68-85.

ADDITIONAL READING

Advertising Age, "Kellogg appealing to adults," September 27, 1984.

Advertising Age, "Kellogg tells new strategy," February 28, 1983, pp. 1, 72.

Cleaver, Joanne, "Cereal picture stays sweet," *Advertising Age*, May 3, 1984.

Colford, Steven W., "Advertisers hunger for FDA word on Kellogg," *Advertising Age*, December 3, 1984, p. 97.

Colford, Steven W., "FDA policy targets food health claims," *Advertising Age*, October 28, 1985, pp. 4, 101.

Colford, Steven W., "Food health claims hit by GF's Ferguson," *Advertising Age*, June 17, 1985, pp. 3, 81.

Colford, Steven W., "All-Bran ads given praise of FTC exec," *Advertising Age*, December 6, 1984.

Colford, Steven W., "MDs move to halt Kellogg health ads," *Advertising Age*, November 1, 1984, pp. 1, 58.

Colford, Steven W., "Kellogg eyes long run for All-Bran ads," *Advertising Age*, January 7, 1985.

Dwyer, Paula, "A Turf Fight over Health Claims in Food Ads," *Business Week*, February 17, 1986.

Fannin, Rebecca, "Brand Report 66: Cereals," *Marketing and Media Decisions*, June, 1981, pp. 191-200.

Finn, Susan Calvert, "Fiber Is Hard to Ignore," *50/Plus*, March, 1985, pp. 37-39.

Fortune, "Madison Avenue's Cancer Sell Spreads," August 19, 1985, p. 77.

Franz, Julie, "Kellogg bran-ching out with new cereal," *Advertising Age*, July 7, 1986, pp. 40, 54.

Franz, Julie, "Kellogg's market share starting to flake," *Advertising Age*, January 1, 1986.

Franz, Julie, "Kellogg goes with the grain to be No. 1," *Advertising Age*, August 4, 1985, pp. 4, 42-44.

Franz, Julie, "Gen. Mills bran-dishes new cereal," *Advertising Age*, February 18, 1985.

Franz, Julie and Nancy Giges, "Fiber cereals in bran(d) shootout: Reagan news primes market," *Advertising Age*, July 22, 1985, pp. 1, 62.

Galanti, Dave, "Cold cereal becomes a hot commodity," *Advertising Age*, September 27, 1984, p. 30.

Giges, Nancy, "New GF raisin bran a natural," *Advertising Age*, September 9, 1985, pp. 1, 132.

Giges, Nancy, "Ads tie in to Reagan news," *Advertising Age*, July 22, 1985.

Johnson, Greg, "Who's Afraid of Generic Cereals?" *Industry Week*, May 16, 1983, p. 33.

Kanner, Bernice, "Kellogg's Hard Sell," *New York*, December 3, 1984, pp. 22-28.

Leading National Advertisers, *LNA Class/Brand YTD $*, F122 Cereals, January-December, 1983, pp. 224-26; 1984, pp. 337-39.

Meyers, Janet, "All-Bran ads avoid FDA's ire," *Advertising Age*, April 4, 1985.

MRI Mediamark Research, Inc., *Breakfast Cereals (Cold)*, Volume P-20, Spring, 1984, pp. 41-65.

Nieman, Janet, "Kellogg hungers to snap back with pop," *Advertising Age*, June 11, 1986, pp. 4, 92.

Neiman, Janet, "All-Bran ads may inspire health trend," *Advertising Age*, October 29, 1984, p. 6.

Schnorbus, Paula, "Brand Report No. 141: Adult Cereals; BRANTASTIC," *Marketing and Media Decisions*, April 1987, pp. 93-109.

SerVass, Cory, ''Dr. Vincent Devita Speaks Out on Cancer Prevention with Fiber,'' *The Saturday Evening Post*, July/August, 1984, pp. 51-55.

Sherrid, Pamela, ''Fighting Back at Breakfast,'' *Fortune*, October 7, 1985, pp. 126-130.

Simmons Market Research Bureau, *1985 Survey of Media and Markets*, ''Breakfast Cereals (Cold),'' Volume P-20, pp. 21-113.

Simon, Allen, ''High Fiber With a Southern Accent,'' *The Saturday Evening Post*, September, 1984, p. 12.

CHAPTER TWO

Basic Media Concepts

Advertising planning involves an array of media terms and concepts that must be mastered in order to understand the process and to develop and evaluate media plans effectively. Space constraints do not allow a comprehensive list of these concepts to be covered in this chapter. Instead, the focus is on a few of the more important, fundamental ideas that must be understood if the remainder of this text is to be useful.

For guidance as to which concepts are most relevant, recent surveys are useful starting points. They revealed that a number of media evaluation factors are used heavily by media directors of major U.S. advertising agencies.[1] This chapter will define these concepts and give examples as well as explore some industry practices.

Several fundamental media evaluation factors must be introduced. These are listed below.

1. Rating points
2. Households using television
3. Share
4. Gross rating points
5. Gross impressions
6. Cost-per-thousand impressions
7. Cost-per-rating point
8. Reach
9. Average frequency
10. Effective frequency
11. Effective reach
12. Exposure distributions
13. Time frame

Each of these concepts will be defined and supported with examples as the chapter unfolds.

RATING POINTS

In developing media plans, it is essential that media planners understand the nature and scope of audience measurement. There is a large number of corporations that monitor the size and characteristics of mass media audiences. Many of their names are familiar: Arbitron, A. C. Nielsen Company, Simmons Market Research Bureau (SMRB), Mediamark Research, Inc. (MRI), Birch, Mendelsohn Media Research, Inc., Scarborough, and RADAR.

The audience data provided by these firms cover the full range of mass media categories, demographic consumer groups, and product categories, among other breakdowns.

Yet, regardless of the method used by a particular service, each will detail audience data in terms of their sizes, usually expressed as a percentage of a particular segment of the population, such as adults, males, females, or female homemakers. The percentage of one of these groups that is estimated to be exposed to a particular media vehicle within a specified time frame is known as a vehicle *rating*. One rating point is equivalent to one percent of a particular population or base. For example, if SMRB (Volume P-20, 1985) were used as a source of audience data, and the media planner was interested in the top-rated magazines against all users of cold breakfast cereals (base = 69,405,000), three magazines stand out.

Magazine	Single-Issue Rating (%)
Reader's Digest (RD)	26.6
TV Guide (TV)	25.4
Good Housekeeping (GH)	20.8

Reader's Digest, for example, is read by 26.6 percent of the 69,405,000 users of cold breakfast cereals. This is the same as 26.6 rating points against the target.

Rating points, then, are the fundamental building blocks for developing and evaluating media plans. They are used to develop the important media evaluation factors mentioned earlier. Throughout the remainder of this text, the following notation will be used to indicate a rating for a particular vehicle:

$R_i = R_{RD} = 26.6\%$
where: R = vehicle rating,

i = subscript denoting vehicle i (*Reader's Digest* [RD] in this instance).

Where did the estimated rating points come from? SMRB and MRI are the most popular syndicated sources of consumer magazine audience data. The data shown here pertain to female homemakers who use cold breakfast cereal and come from the 1985 SMRB volume P-20, pages 36-41. Chapter Seven discusses SMRB methodology. The focus here simply will be how to find and interpret magazine audience ratings.

On page 39 of the SMRB data, the following information is extracted— including the page banner, the top row, and the five rows of data including the highest rated magazine, *Reader's Digest*—against the target audience of all users of cold breakfast cereals.

TABLE 2.1 Sample SMRB Magazine Audience Data

	All Users				
	TOTAL U.S. '000	A '000	B % DOWN	C ACROSS %	D INDEX
Total Female Homemakers	82273	69405	100.0	84.4	100
Prevention	4441	3967	5.7	89.3	106
Psychology Today	1643	1424	2.1	86.7	103
Reader's Digest	21346	18481	26.6	86.6	103
Redbook	8226	7080	10.2	86.1	102
Road & Track	**269	247	0.4	91.8	109

Source: SMRB, 1985, Volume P-20, p. 39.

Here's how one would read the data contained in Table 2.1, as well as most other SMRB and MRI data, which are largely presented in the same format. There are 82,273,000 U.S. female homemakers, 69,405,000 of whom (84.4 percent) use cold breakfast cereals. Since all users of cold breakfast cereals is our target audience, then 26.6 percent of that base regularly read *Reader's Digest*. That is, the rating of *Reader's Digest* against our target audience of 69,405,000 female homemakers who use cold breakfast cereals is 26.6 percent. The typical issue of *Reader's Digest* delivers 18,481,000 target audience members. The index number of 103 simply means that female homemakers who read *Reader's Digest* are three percent more likely to use cold breakfast cereals than are all female homemakers (that is, $103 = (86.6/84.4)(100)$).

Although there are numerous other uses for this data, the point made for now is that where media vehicles are involved, Column B (% down) presents rating points against the base shown in the first row (Column A) of the data on a given SMRB or MRI page.

One should remember that audience measurement is such an important and complex matter that it could easily require book-length treatment to be covered adequately. In this text it is covered in greater detail in Chapter Seven.

In television, there are two additional concepts that are applied usefully in media planning.

HOUSEHOLDS USING TELEVISION

This measure is self-explanatory. It tells what percentage of all U.S. households had their television sets on at any given time. It is often used to calculate the audience share (see below) to provide a net audience estimate, showing the potential audience coverage available. If, for instance, the objective is to reach 65 percent of all female homemakers who use cold breakfast cereal (69,405,000 x .65 = 45,113,250) through prime-time television and the Households Using Television (HUT) for that time period is 78 percent, then one could assume that only 78 percent of the target will have their sets on too and discount the initial number accordingly, to 35,188,335 (45,113,250 x .78 = 35,188,335).

SHARE

In the broadcast media, where competition occurs between only a few channels or stations within each market, advertisers are not only interested in the ratings of programs, but also the percentage of the total television viewing audience tuned to each show. This is provided in the audience share figure, which represents the percent of all homes watching television (or listening to radio) who were tuned to Station Y. It is calculated by dividing the rating points for a given program by the HUT figure. This allows one to compare two programs shown at different times of the day or week or follow a single program over several months. To make a decision solely based on ratings can sometimes lead to errors. As the table below shows, while a program's ratings may seem to decline over the year, its share may in fact improve.

Month	HUT Level	Rating	Share
January	70.1	25.3	36.1
June	65.4	21.4	32.7
October	55.6	20.6	37.1

You should remember that within a given time period, ratings will always add to the HUT and shares will always add to 1.0.

GROSS RATING POINTS

Gross rating points (GRPS) are, as the name implies, a crude or gross measure of audience potential. They are nothing other than the sum of the rating points delivered by a particular schedule. So rating points can be added together as long as the base (target size) is the same for each vehicle rating point. In other words, if one advertisement were placed in *Reader's Digest* and one in *TV Guide* this would give a schedule consisting of 52 GRPs against the target (i.e., 52 = 26.6 + 25.4).

There will be some overlap between the audiences of these two magazines. Some female homemakers who use cold breakfast cereals actually may subscribe to and read both of them. This overlap between audiences typically is referred to as audience duplication. Since GRPs do not account for duplication, they are considered a gross measure of audience potential.

Media planners often judge the weight of a schedule by estimating its GRPs. For example, Kellogg's All-Bran media planners may wish to obtain 500 magazine GRPs per month against female homemakers who use cold breakfast cereals.

GROSS IMPRESSIONS

Gross impressions (GIs) are similar to GRPs except that GIs express GRPs as the potential *number* of target impressions delivered. They are simply GRPs (divided by 100) multiplied by the target audience size. In the example, the GIs delivered are given by:

$$GI = (GRPs/100)(Target\ Size) \qquad (2\text{-}1)$$
$$= (52/100)(69,405,000)$$
$$= (.52)(69,405,000)$$
$$= 36,090,600$$

In other words, this small magazine schedule will deliver more than 36 million impressions to female homemakers who use cold breakfast cereals.

COST PER THOUSAND IMPRESSIONS

Media planners require a measure of vehicle and schedule efficiency in order to compare the cost effectiveness of alternatives. Cost per thousand impressions (CPM) is one method for doing so. In general:

$$CPM = Cost/GI(000) \qquad (2\text{-}2)$$
where: Cost = media vehicle or schedule cost.
GI(000) = Gross Impressions (in thousands) delivered by a vehicle or a schedule (for example, if GI = 1,000,000, then GI(000) = 1,000; just move the decimal three places to the left).

Now, in the example, a full-page, four-color ad in *Reader's Digest* costs $108,800 and in *TV Guide* it costs $89,300. And it was just determined that GI(000) = 36,090.6. Consequently, this gives:

$$CPM = (\$108,800 + \$89,300)/36,090.6$$
$$= \$5.49$$

In words, it costs $5.49 per thousand impressions using *Reader's Digest* and *TV Guide* to reach the target audience. Readers might want to make sure that they understand this by computing CPM for each magazine separately.

CPM based on gross impressions is not dependent on schedule size. Therefore, schedules of differing size can be compared using CPM based on gross impressions.

Cost data for vehicles or schedules can be obtained from numerous sources. One method is to contact magazines, newspapers, or television or radio stations directly to obtain a copy of their rate cards. Rate cards generally show the costs for various sizes and types of advertisements, including any available quantity or volume discounts. Standard Rate and Data Service (SRDS) publishes rates, among other important information, for vehicles in all major advertising media categories. The rates for each media category are contained in separate volumes and usually are published quarterly. Most major advertising agencies, as well as *AD Week* magazine, for example, publish summaries of rates and trends for all major media categories.

COST PER RATING POINT

Another popular efficiency measure used to compare schedules is cost per rating point (CPP). Although CPP would probably lead to the same conclusion regarding the relative merit of media vehicles and schedules as would CPM, it has the added advantages of facilitating the conversion of competitive advertising expenditures to GRPs, and it is useful in the advertising budgeting process, as will be shown in Chapters Four and Five. CPP can also be used to convert vehicle ratings to estimated vehicle cost. The formula for CPP is given by:

CPP = Cost/GRPs   (2-3)
where: Cost = media vehicle or schedule cost,
          GRPs = gross rating points for the schedule or vehicle.

In the example, CPP can be estimated for the entire schedule as follows:
CPP = ($108,800 + $89,300)/52
     = $3,810.

In words, it costs $3,810 per rating point to reach the target audience using *Reader's Digest* and *TV Guide*.

CPP is also handy when a media planner has some idea concerning needed schedule weight in terms of GRPs. The necessary total advertising expenditures can be estimated by multiplying required GRPs by an appropriate CPP.

REACH

More sophisticated procedures for estimating schedule reach will be presented in Chapter Eight. To begin with, however, the concept is introduced in its simplest form, involving a single insertion in each of two different vehicles.

If an estimate of duplication among two magazines were available, then it could be subtracted from GRPs, as a percentage of the target, to estimate reach. That is:

Reach = GRPs - duplication.   (2-4)

If one insertion were placed in *Reader's Digest* and one in *TV Guide*, that would deliver 52 GRPs (26.6 + 25.4) against the target. In fact, it turns out (as shown in Chapter Eight) that the duplication between these two vehicles is 8.4 percent. Therefore, the reach of one insertion in each vehicle is given by:

$Reach_{RD,TV}$ = 26.6% + 25.4% - 8.4%
         = 52% - 8.4%
         = 43.6%

Thus, this small magazine schedule will likely reach 43.6 percent of the target. These are target persons who are potentially exposed to *Reader's Digest* and/or *TV Guide*. The "and/or" is important, since reach here is the total percentage of different target persons exposed to *Reader's Digest* alone, or to *TV Guide* alone, or to both. Reach counts only one time those target persons who saw both vehicles. GRPs count those who saw both vehicles twice—once for each vehicle.

FIGURE 2.1 GRPs, Reach, and Duplication

Reach = 43.6% = 52% - 8.4%
GRPs = 52% = 26.6% + 25.4%

Figure 2.1 presents these concepts in a diagram that can be helpful in decomposing GRPs into reach and duplication where simple schedules are considered.

Reach is one of the most important evaluation factors for media planners to consider since it is an estimate of the total universe of individuals who may receive an advertiser's messages. Planners often like to maximize reach and avoid duplication in their schedules, exposing the greatest possible number of different target persons to advertising messages. Schedules that maximize reach and minimize duplication often use few insertions per vehicle, but a large number of vehicles and, possibly, several different media categories. A major concern of media planners, then, is estimating reach and duplication so that schedules can be fairly and accurately compared on the basis of audience delivery.

AVERAGE FREQUENCY

The concept of average frequency of a media schedule is also important since it indicates the average number of times those reached by a schedule are likely to have been exposed to the advertising campaign. Since advertising messages are often ignored by consumers, or even avoided, media planners strive for a certain level of impressions to insure that target members have ample opportunity for exposure to the campaign. High levels of average frequency are also one way of overcoming competitive messages. The formula for average frequency is often given by:

$$\bar{f} = GRPs/Reach. \tag{2-5}$$

In the example, using one insertion in *Reader's Digest* and one in *TV Guide*, this gives:

$$\bar{f} = 52/43.6$$
$$= 1.2$$

Therefore, the average frequency of this small schedule is estimated to be 1.2, meaning that those reached by the schedule are exposed an average of 1.2 times.

EFFECTIVE FREQUENCY

The concept of average frequency clouds the fact that target persons have either been exposed once or twice to the example magazine schedule. Experience with a target audience, brand advertising messages, and product category characteristics may indicate that some minimum level of frequency is required for most consumers in order for the message to have measurable impact. Media planners often consider the concept of effective frequency, which is the number of advertising exposures needed for a message to have its desired effect on individuals. At present, however, considerable judgment is required when determining what number of exposures maximizes advertising communication, or if there is a threshold effect in exposure frequency. There are many variables to consider, such as brand message strength, competitive message clutter, timing and spacing of the advertisements, campaign objectives, and the purchase cycle of the product.[2] Recent research has shown that the most common level of effective frequency used is three or more exposures (3+), followed by four or more (4+), and three to ten (3-10), among others.[3]

EFFECTIVE REACH

Using the concept of effective frequency, some advertisers define effective reach to be the percent of the target exposed to an advertising schedule some minimum number of times or more. Often the cutoff is set at 3+, 4+, or 3-10, for example. If 2+ is set as the cutoff for the small magazine schedule here, what would be the effective reach? Effective reach (2+) would be equal to GRPs - Reach (1+), or 8.4 percent (that is, 8.4% = 52% - 43.6%). It is clear from this example that effective reach (n+) is a much more conservative estimate of schedule reach than is reach (1+). This is because the concept of effective reach generally recognizes the need for a minimum level of effective frequency in addition to reach.

EXPOSURE DISTRIBUTIONS

As a practical matter, media schedules are much more complex than the simple example used here. In order to evaluate the effective reach of a complex schedule, media planners often estimate and evaluate exposure or frequency distributions. This indicates the percent of the target exposed to a schedule 0, 1, 2,..., N times, where N is generally set at 10+ or 11+ for large schedules, indicating the percentage of the target exposed 10, or 11, or more times. This is often called a *truncated exposure distribution* since it aggregates upper exposure levels.

Returning to the example, what would the exposure distribution look like? Given the schedule, it is known that target members can be exposed 0, 1, or 2 times.

Frequency	Percent of Target Exposed
0	?
1	?
2	?

One needs to know the percent of the target exposed at each frequency level. It stands to reason that the percent *not* exposed will be 100% of the target minus the percent reached by the schedule, 43.6%, for a total of 56.4% (that is, 100% - 43.6% = 56.4%). Also, it is known that duplication, or the percent of the target exposed twice, is 8.4%. Consequently, the percent of the target exposed exactly once must be 43.6% - 8.4% = 35.2%. Therefore, the exposure distribution looks like this:

Frequency	Percent of Target
0	56.4% = (100% - 43.6%)
1	35.2% = (43.6% - 8.4%)
2	8.4% = given, for now
Sum:	100.0%

Notice that the key to this analysis is that the sum of the percentages of the target exposed at each frequency level must add up to 100 percent.

The exposure distribution is an important tool in media plan analysis. Considerable time will be spent throughout the remainder of this text demonstrating how such exposure distributions can be estimated for each major media category and for combinations of media categories.

TIME FRAME

An important consideration in developing media evaluation factors is the time frame over which the factors are to be estimated. For example, if the magazine schedule were evaluated on both a monthly basis and a quarterly basis, the quarterly evaluation would lead to significantly higher levels of GRPs, GIs, reach (1+), effective reach (n+), and average frequency. Which time frame should be selected? The answer will depend on a number of factors, the principal ones being the desired communication goal in relation to target forgetting and competitive advertising. As a rule, it is probably better to provide management with conservative estimates of schedule weight. Selecting a reasonable time frame would do so effectively. Another approach would be to do some posttesting to measure target recall. The objective would be to compare media evaluation factors, particularly effective reach (n+), assessed on, say, a monthly or quarterly basis, in order to see which calculation of effective reach corresponds most closely to market impact or posttest recall.

Nevertheless, the time frame selected for evaluating media plans is related directly to the apparent size of estimated media evaluation factors. In general, the longer the time frame, the higher the levels of reach and frequency predicted. It is possible that management could reach a variety of conflicting conclusions regarding the value of a particular media schedule, depending on the time frame selected.

To learn which time frames are actually used in practice and what factors are taken into account, a survey was conducted of media directors of the top 225 advertising agencies in terms of worldwide gross billings.[4] Executives were asked

TABLE 2.2 Time Frames Used for Media Plan Evaluation
(N = 91 Media Directors)

Media Used	Time Frames Analyzed				
	Daily (%)	Weekly (%)	4 Weeks (%)	Quarterly (%)	Annual (%)
Newspapers	14.3	27.5	31.9	15.4	14.3
Network TV	3.3	16.5	50.5	19.8	15.4
Spot TV	3.3	24.2	64.8	19.8	15.3
Cable TV	1.1	13.2	40.2	17.6	9.9
Magazines	1.1	6.6	50.5	33.0	29.7
Network Radio	1.1	14.3	36.3	11.0	11.0
Spot Radio	1.1	18.7	49.5	18.7	9.9
Outdoor Posters	4.4	2.2	38.5	16.5	19.8

Note: Percentages exceed 100 due to the use of multiple media categories and multiple time periods within media categories.

which time frames actually were used, by media category, for a major product or service for which they had media planning responsibility. They were also asked which marketing factors they believed were the most important determinants of the chosen time frames. As a result, the survey shows which factors selected were, in fact, related to the time frames used.

Table 2.2 illustrates time frames most often used in each media category. Although all time periods are represented in each media type, four weeks is the most common. For example, 64.8 percent of the executives surveyed noted that a four-week interval is used when evaluating spot television media plans. At the other extreme, only 31.9 percent use four weeks when evaluating newspaper schedules. Quarterly and weekly evaluations alternate as the second choice, followed by annual evaluations, with daily evaluations generally coming in last place for all but two media categories. Logically, newspapers are most likely to be evaluated on a daily (14.3 percent) or weekly (27.5 percent) basis, while magazines are often evaluated on a quarterly (33.0 percent) or annual (29.7 percent) basis.

Based on their media planning experience in general, executives were asked to use a five-point scale to rate the importance of six factors believed to influence the choice of time frame (see Table 2.3). The nature of the product was rated as the most significant determinant of time frame choice, with a mean of 4.54 on the five-point scale. This was followed closely by consumer product repeat purchase frequency, with a mean of 4.49. Of course, the nature of the product and consumer repeat purchase frequency are related closely. One would expect narrower time frames to be used when product repeat purchase cycles are short, and broad time frames used when repeat purchase cycles are long.

Media categories used is third in importance with a mean of 4.28. This is also consistent with the results presented in Table 2.2, which show some relation between media categories used and the choice of time frame.

Executives wrote in several other factors that they believe influence the choice of time frame. The most frequently mentioned of these include product sales or

TABLE 2.3 Determinants of the Appropriate Time Frame for Media Plan Evaluation (N = 91 Media Directors)

| Determinants of Time Frame Choice | Factor Importance (%) | | | | | |
| | Not Important | | | Very Important | | |
	1	2	3	4	5	Mean
Nature of the Product (non-durable, durable, etc.)	6.6	3.3	13.2	24.2	52.7	4.54
Consumer Product Repeat Purchase Frequency	4.4	3.3	17.6	29.7	45.1	4.49
Media Categories Used	6.6	7.7	20.9	19.8	45.1	4.28
Media Budget Size	12.1	7.7	14.3	26.4	39.6	4.11
Geographic Coverage Required	27.5	15.4	16.5	13.2	26.4	3.25
Consumer Target Audience Size	29.7	18.7	19.8	14.3	17.6	2.99

advertising campaign seasonality, activities of competitors, message content, and communication objectives.

The study also examined the actual relation between product marketing characteristics and the choice of time frame for media plan evaluation. With few exceptions, and across all media categories, the monthly time frame was the favorite regardless of the nature of the product, geographic scope of the market, size of the advertising appropriation, number of consumers in the target audience, as well as consumer product repeat purchase frequency. Beyond that, the only additional pattern concerns the link between consumer product repeat purchase frequency and the time frame used. Products with daily or weekly repeat purchase frequency rates were just as likely to use daily and weekly media evaluation time frames as they were to use quarterly or monthly intervals. Products with six-month or longer repeat purchase rates were less likely to use daily or weekly media plan evaluations.

SUMMARY

This chapter has barely scratched the surface of factors that should be taken into account when evaluating advertising media plans, simply focusing on a few of the most important concepts. Learning them thoroughly will serve you well throughout the remainder of this text, giving a solid foundation to build upon. At this point, overwhelming you with more realistic detail may do more harm than good. There will be plenty of time and opportunity to enhance this background.

Chapter Three adds an important qualification to the concepts presented here—the distinction between media vehicle audiences and advertising audiences. All of the media evaluation factors discussed so far can be examined from either perspective. Since advertising audiences usually are significantly smaller than vehicle audiences, it is important for planners to distinguish clearly between them.

ENDNOTES

1. Peggy J. Kreshel, Kent M. Lancaster, and Margaret A. Toomey, "How Leading Advertising Agencies Perceive Effective Reach and Frequency," *Journal of Advertising*, 14 (3, 1985), pp. 32-38, 51; and John D. Leckenby and Shizue Kishi, "How Media Directors View Reach/Frequency Estimates," *Journal of Advertising Research*, 22 (June/July 1982), pp. 64-69.

2. For a thorough discussion of the question of effective frequency, see the Fall 1986 issue of the *Journal of Media Planning* (Volume 1, Number 1), edited by Jack Z. Sissors.

3. Kent M. Lancaster, Peggy J. Kreshel, and Joya R. Harris, "Estimating the Impact of Advertising Media Plans: Media Executives Describe Weighting and Timing Factors," *Journal of Advertising*, 15 (September 1986), pp. 21-29, 45.

4. Ibid.

ADDITIONAL READING

Beville, Hugh Malcolm, Jr., *Audience Ratings: Radio, Television and Cable* (Hillsdale, New Jersey: Lawrence E. Erlbaum Associates, 1985).

Hall, Robert W., *Media Math: Basic Techniques of Media Evaluation* (Lincolnwood, Illinois: NTC Business Books, 1986).

Kaatz, Ronald B., *Cable Advertiser's Handbook* (Lincolnwood, Illinois: NTC Business Books, 1985).

Leckenby, John D. and Nugent Wedding, *Advertising Management: Criteria, Analysis and Decision Making* (Columbus, Ohio: Grid Publishing, Inc., 1981).

McGann, Anthony F. and J. Thomas Russell, *Advertising Media*, 2nd Ed., (New York: Richard D. Irwin, 1988).

Rust, Roland T., *Advertising Media Models: A Practical Guide* (Massachusetts: Lexington Books, 1986).

Sissors, Jack Z. and Jim Surmanek, *Advertising Media Planning*, 2d ed. (Lincolnwood, Illinois: NTC Business Books, 1982).

Surmanek, Jim, *Media Planning: A Practical Guide* (Lincolnwood, Illinois: NTC Business Books, 1985).

CHAPTER THREE

Media Vehicle versus Advertising Audiences

EFFECTIVE REACH REVISITED

In Chapter Two a significant and highly controversial media planning problem was ignored because it was assumed that media vehicle audiences are valuable to advertisers. That is true to the extent that vehicle audiences deliver advertising audiences. But even a superficial study of advertising would lead to the conclusion that advertising audiences are generally smaller, substantially smaller, than vehicle audiences. Target members may not open a magazine at an advertiser's page. They may leave the room, or turn the channel, or "zap" during a television commercial. They may not pay full attention to a drive time radio spot. The opportunities for missing advertisements are great indeed. Most sophisticated advertisers, as this chapter will demonstrate, take this into account.

Research services such as Starch, Burke, and Gallup and Robinson provide advertisers with estimates of advertising recognition and recall. This information can be used to adjust, discount, or weight media vehicle audiences. For example, if Kellogg's All-Bran had its current campaign messages evaluated by Starch in *Reader's Digest* and *TV Guide*, or if it had averages from other publications for similar advertisements, the Starch "noted" score (that is, the percent of the Starch sample of readers of a given magazine that can recall having looked at a particular advertisement) could be used to approximate advertising audiences. If one assumes that the average All-Bran Starch "noted" score is 50 percent, which is probably high, then the estimate of the advertising audiences for *Reader's Digest* and *TV Guide* would be half the size of the vehicle audiences as reported by SMRB.

Magazine	SMRB One-Issue Rating (%)	X	Average Starch Noted Score for All-Bran (%)	=	Estimated Message Rating (%)
Reader's Digest	26.6		50		13.3
TV Guide	25.4		50		12.7

This procedure dramatically changes all of the estimated media evaluation factors, making them substantially more conservative. For practice, readers might see whether they can re-estimate all of the media evaluation factors explained in Chapter Two using the message audience estimates. Here is what would result:

Media Evaluation Factors	Vehicle	Message
GRPs	52.0%	26.0%
Gross Impressions (000)	36,090.6	18,045.3
CPM	$5.49	$10.98
CPP	$3,810	$7,620
Reach (1+)	43.6%	21.8%
Average Frequency	1.2	1.2
Effective Reach (2+)	8.4%	4.2%

The weight of 50 percent can be used to discount the magazine vehicle exposure distribution to estimate an advertising message exposure distribution. Here is how it can be done.

First, one discounts all exposure percentages for frequency levels greater than zero using the discount factor (50 percent in this instance). Next, the weighted exposure distribution for frequency levels greater than zero are summed. This sum is subtracted from 100 percent to estimate the weighted percent of the target not exposed to the schedule. This is what it would look like for the magazine example.

Adjusting a Magazine Exposure Distribution Using a Weight of 50%

f	%(Unweighted)	×	Weight	=	%(Weighted)
0	56.4		N/A		78.2 = 100 − 21.8
1	35.2	×	.5	=	17.6
2	8.4	×	.5	=	4.2
Total	100.0				100.0

Although there are numerous other weighting techniques space constraints prevent a demonstration of them here, so the procedure described will be used throughout the remainder of the text.

This method is not without its critics. Nevertheless, the problem of estimating advertising audiences versus vehicle audiences is one of the most fundamental questions facing media planners. To ignore the issue due to methodological difficulties does a disservice to advertising decision makers.

INDUSTRY PRACTICES

It is generally accepted that the gap between media vehicle audiences and advertising audiences is typically large. Less clear, however, is what to do about it in the media planning process. Consequently, the remainder of the chapter will deal with this highly controversial topic by illustrating the range of industry practices so that you will appreciate the equivocal nature of the topic.

☐ Use of Communication Effects

A survey of media directors of leading U.S.-headquartered, multinational advertising agencies investigated actual industry practices to show how media plan-

TABLE 3.1 How Communication Effects Are Used in Advertising Media Planning

Dimensions	Agency Size Groups			
	Large	Medium	Small	Total
A. Sample Size (Column Base)	42	23	29	94
B. Communication Effects Used	**85.7%**	**65.2%**	**79.3%**	**78.7%**
Recall	59.5	60.9	55.2	58.5
Advertising Exposure	57.1	52.2	44.8	52.1
Awareness	50.0	47.8	44.8	47.9
Attentiveness	64.2	39.1	17.2	43.6
Purchase	38.1	21.7	31.0	31.9
Recognition	28.6	30.4	13.8	24.5
Preference	19.1	30.4	6.9	18.1
Attitude Toward Ad	14.3	8.7	10.3	11.7
Pre-purchase Behavior	16.7	17.4	17.2	17.0
Comprehension	14.3	26.1	10.3	16.0
Effects *Not* Used	14.3	34.8	20.7	**21.3**
C. Communication Effect Source	**85.7**	**65.2**	**79.3**	**78.7**
Starch Inra Hooper	59.5	52.2	55.2	56.4
Executive Judgment	61.9	43.5	31.0	47.9
Burke Marketing Research	57.1	39.1	34.5	45.7
Custom Research	54.8	34.8	41.4	45.7
Gallup and Robinson	42.9	14.3	10.3	28.7
AdTel	40.5	14.3	10.3	27.7
BehaviorScan	50.0	17.4	3.4	27.7
Mapes and Ross	14.3	17.4	0.0	10.6
Effects *Not* Used	14.3	34.8	20.7	**21.3**
D. Media Categories Weighted	**61.9**	**34.8**	**51.7**	**52.1**
Magazines	59.5	34.8	37.9	46.8
Spot TV	47.6	21.7	44.8	40.4
Network TV	50.0	17.4	24.1	34.0
Spot Radio	28.6	21.7	31.0	27.7
Newspapers	28.6	13.0	27.6	24.5
Outdoor Posters	26.2	17.4	20.7	22.3
Network Radio	31.0	13.0	13.8	21.3
Cable TV	28.6	13.0	10.3	19.1
Sunday Supplements	28.6	8.7	13.8	19.1
Do *Not* Weight	38.1	65.2	48.3	**47.9**

ners evaluate media vehicle schedules in a way that predicts their likely communication effects.[1] Table 3.1 shows which communication effects and sources are most often used and which media categories typically are weighted. Because of the vast differences in the practices of the very large agencies and those agencies ranked considerably down the scale, this information is broken down by three agency-size groups organized in terms of gross billings. Small agencies are defined as having gross billings ranked less than or equal to $75 million, medium-size agencies are ranked above $75 million and less than or equal to $150 million, and large agencies are ranked above $150 million.

Section B of the table indicates that all three agency groups use a large array of communication effects, although there is a tendency for this practice to be more common among the largest agencies. The communication effects used most often include recall, advertising exposure, awareness, and attentiveness. The largest agencies are also likely to use purchase and recognition as well.

Section C shows that a variety of sources are used to measure communication effects. The most often mentioned of these are Starch, individual and group executive judgment, Burke, custom research, Gallup and Robinson, AdTel, and BehaviorScan. The larger agencies generally are more likely to use a particular source.

Section D reveals that all major media categories are weighted using the various sources of communication effects data, especially magazines, spot television, network television, and spot radio. Larger agencies are more likely to weight a given media category than are smaller agencies.

Equally important, 21.3 percent of the total respondents indicated that their agencies do not use communication effects in the media planning process and that 47.9 percent do not weight. Both of these percentages are understated because respondents whose agencies use communication effects or weight vehicle audiences do not do so for all accounts, all of the time. Also, there is likely to be some reluctance to admit that what are perceived to be the most sophisticated procedures are not used routinely.

A follow-up study provides further detail concerning how major agencies evaluate the effective reach of media schedules, what weights are used for which media categories, and how the weights are applied to media vehicle audiences.[2]

☐ Defining Effective Reach

The definition of effective reach applied in the media plan of a particular product or service can vary across a number of factors, including the media categories and time frames used. If multiple media categories are evaluated simultaneously, then, of course, the same definition of effective reach and time frame must be used for all of them. The survey found that 76.9 percent of the media plans described by respondents include evaluations of schedule reach, frequency, and GRPs for combinations of two or more media categories. When asked whether their agency uses the same definition of effective reach in evaluating all media categories for their selected product or service, 59.3 percent said "yes."

Executives were then asked to note the most representative definition of effective reach for the product or service that they selected. The results are displayed in Table 3.2.

Almost half (48.4 percent) of the agencies surveyed use vehicle audiences as a proxy of advertising audiences. Nearly one third (31 percent) attempt to estimate advertising exposures, while less than one fifth (16.5 percent) try to calculate likely advertising impact. However, regardless of the degree of message impact required, the majority of definitions of effective reach recognize the need for a *minimum* frequency level: 93.4 percent require that to be two or more, 87.9 percent require three or more, and 26.4 percent require four or more. Most (58.2 percent) definitions recognize no upper frequency limit to effective reach, while 28.6 percent set some kind of upper bound, ranging from four to 20.

TABLE 3.2   Representative Definitions of Effective Reach
(N = 91 Media Directors)

Message Impact Required	%	Number of Exposures Required Regardless of Message Impact Level			
		Lower Limit %		Upper Limit %	
Media Vehicle Exposure (e.g.,		1+	6.6	None	58.2
saw publication or program)	48.4	2+	5.5	9	4.4
Advertising Exposure (e.g., saw		3+	61.5	10	6.6
ad in publication or program)	31.9	4+	17.6	11	2.2
Advertising Impact (e.g.,		Other	8.8	Other	15.4
recall product message)	16.5			No Answer	13.2
No Answer	3.3				

The study also examined the actual relation between the marketing character-istics of the product or service selected by the respondents and the definition of effective reach that is used. All aspects of the definition appear to be independent of the nature of the product, geographic scope of the market, size of the advertis-ing appropriation, number of consumers in the target audience, as well as con-sumer product re-purchase frequency.

□ **Audience Weighting Procedures**

In order to implement definitions of effective reach that involve estimates of advertising exposure or impact, media vehicle audience estimates generally have to be adjusted or weighted, usually, but not always, downward. Nearly one third (30.8 percent) of all executives noted that their agency weights media vehicle au-diences. The percentage of media plans weighted ranges from 5 percent to 100 percent. On average, just over half (56.6 percent) of all of their agencies' media plans are weighted. That is, approximately one third of major agencies weight roughly half of their media plans.

Executives from agencies that weight media plans were asked to describe the procedures typically used in applying weights to media vehicle audiences. Variable weights applied to each vehicle rating are used by 82.1 percent of the 28 agencies that weight. One executive noted that a single weight was applied to the entire expo-sure distribution. Five (17.9 percent) executives report that their agencies apply dif-ferent weights to the percent of the target exposed at each frequency level of the schedule exposure distribution. Two of these noted that the exposure distribution weights had a convex shape, while two others said that their weights were s-shaped.

Respondents were also asked to note how weights were applied to the audience data of each media category. The results are listed in Table 3.3. It indicates that all major media categories are weighted. The most likely candidates include spot tele-vision, both daytime and prime time, with 82.1 percent each, magazines (75.0 percent), daytime (67.9 percent) and prime time (64.3 percent) network televi-sion, and spot radio (64.3 percent). Although 28 respondents indicated that their agencies weight, not all specified the range such weights typically cover. Some,

**TABLE 3.3 How Audience Weights Are Used by Media Category
(N = 28 Media Directors)**

Media Category	Use Weights (%)	Provided Weights (%)	Typical Overall Weights Given (%)		
			Low	High	Average
Newspapers	50.0	28.5	20	60	35.0
Network TV					
Daytime	67.9	39.3	20	100	54.7
Prime Time	64.3	35.7	20	100	80.0
Spot TV					
Daytime	82.1	50.0	20	100	50.0
Prime Time	82.1	50.0	10	120	71.8
Cable TV	46.4	25.0	30	105	63.2
Magazines	75.0	39.3	10	100	52.5
Network Radio	50.0	32.1	20	75	40.3
Spot Radio	64.3	35.7	20	75	37.8
Outdoor Posters	28.6	10.7	20	130	46.6

Note: the number of respondents that use weights in each media category is greater than the number who offered weight ranges due to confidentiality, among other reasons.

for example, indicated that the specific values of the weights used were confidential. Nevertheless, the table shows the range of the weights reported and their overall average, by media category.

Prime time network television audiences are discounted least heavily, with an average weight of 80.0 percent. This is followed by prime time spot television audiences, with an average weight of 71.6 percent. Cable television audiences are also well regarded with an average weight of 63.2 percent. Newspapers are the most heavily discounted, with an average weight of 35 percent. The maximum weight given newspaper audiences was 60 percent.

Several executives were careful to qualify the range of weights that they provided, noting that the weights varied by media category, product type, creative aspects, client, campaign objectives, message unit sizes, and audience importance.

When asked how the weights were derived, responses fell into the following categories. Several executives checked more than one category.

%(N=28)

1. Judgmental weights that are largely subjective, based upon a review of communication effects data (for example, exposure, recall, attitude change), and vary for each brand and product.   67.9

2. Formula weights that are based on a review of communication effects using some standard formula or procedure.   35.7

3. Standard set of weights which are established by the agency.   25.0

4. Other procedures.   10.7

The "other procedures" for deriving weights mentioned include specific types of audience research.

TABLE 3.4 Reasons for Not Always Using Weights
(N = 91 Media Directors)

Reasons Checked or Provided Size of Sample (column base)	Total (%) 91	Weight Ratings (%)		Agency Billings Rank (%)		
		Yes 28	No 63	75 or Less 30	76-150 29	Over 150 32
Lack of data to substantiate assumptions	72.5	53.6	81.0	76.7	82.8	59.4
Each media planning situation is unique	61.5	53.6	65.1	60.0	65.5	59.4
Clients don't require such sophistication	52.7	67.9	46.0	50.0	37.9	68.8
Overkill in the manipulation of numbers	44.0	25.0	52.4	53.3	55.2	25.0
Difficult to be accurate	38.5	17.9	47.6	30.0	41.4	43.8
Too judgmental	37.4	25.0	42.9	56.7	31.0	25.0
Too much time spent justifying weights	20.9	14.3	23.8	13.3	24.1	25.0
Other reasons given	17.6	17.9	17.5	16.7	17.2	18.8

Note: Percentages exceed 100 due to multiple responses.

In those situations where agencies do not use weights in evaluating consumer advertising media plans, executives were asked to indicate the major reasons. The results are displayed in Table 3.4.

The lack of data (75.0 percent) and the uniqueness (61.5 percent) of each media planning situation are the most common reasons given for not weighting. The fact that clients do not require such procedures is also offered by just over half (52.7 percent) of the executives. However, these results differ markedly by agency size and whether or not an agency weights media vehicle audiences. As Table 3.4 indicates, executives from large agencies, or those from agencies that weight media vehicle audiences, are significantly less likely than all other respondents to be critical of weighting procedures.

Because there is a lack of consensus as well as relatively little published literature on the use of communication effects and weighting in media planning, the next section of this chapter will further explore how media planners might weight media vehicle audience ratings to estimate more accurately potential communication effects or advertising exposures. The conclusion is that, despite data limitations, weighting procedures are likely to be substantially more useful to decision makers than using no weighting procedures at all.

POSSIBLE WEIGHTING PROCEDURES

A recent survey has shown that the most popular media evaluation models are based on the beta binomial exposure distribution (BBD).[3] Although there are several variations of this model, it generally requires three measures of vehicle audience. These include single-insertion plus self- and cross-pair audience ratings.

Given this type of BBD model, there are at least three ways to adjust or weight vehicle audiences to account for communication effects or advertising exposures.

1. *Method One:* weight all three audience ratings equally.
2. *Method Two:* weight available single-insertion audience ratings and use these to *estimate* weighted self- and cross-pair audience ratings.
3. *Method Three:* obtain unweighted exposure distributions based on all three unweighted audience ratings, and then weight the percent of the target exposed at each frequency level.

Each of these methods will lead to somewhat different estimates of media evaluation factors. In the absence of syndicated sources of advertising exposure data, there is no way to determine whether one method is more accurate than another or whether any of the methods are accurate or valid. Instead, it will be shown that all three procedures will provide more useful information to decision makers than will avoiding the problem because of data limitations.

Method three is probably the most sensible since it does not require a priori assumptions about duplication within and between vehicles. Weighting each exposure level uniformly does not affect the ''shape'' of the exposure distribution, only its ''intercept'' or magnitude at each exposure level. Method three also appears to be employed by some major advertising agencies using weights that differ for each frequency level and assuming either an s-shaped or a convex advertising-sales response function.[4]

WEIGHTING PROCEDURES COMPARED

Using a single hypothetical network television advertising schedule, the differences in the media evaluation factors provided by each of the methods can be highlighted. This will show that the differences in media evaluation factors from one weighting method to the next are inconsequential when compared to unweighted media evaluation factors.

One can imagine a situation in which a media plan calls for a monthly network television schedule to reach adult males throughout the U.S. Four programs are available including ''60 Minutes,'' ''Quincy,'' ''20/20,'' and ''Hart to Hart.'' The communication objective is to achieve substantial correct recall of the brand's major selling proposition among target members. Average Burke day-after-recall (DAR) scores for the messages in the campaign, it will be assumed, are 50 percent. This unusually high Burke score is used for ease of exposition (i.e., a ''typical'' Burke DAR score is about 25-30 percent).

A monthly schedule with three insertions in each of four programs leads to the estimates of media evaluation factors presented in Table 3.5. In addition to providing media evaluation factors based on unweighted audience ratings, the table also presents evaluation factors based on ratings adjusted by the three weighting methods.

TABLE 3.5 Four Evaluations of a Network Television Advertising Schedule

Media Evaluation Factors	Weighting Method (Ad Recall = 50%)			
	Unweighted	Method 1	Method 2	Method 3
GRPs	167.10	83.55	83.55	83.55
Gross Impressions*	127.25	63.63	63.63	63.63
Cost-per-rating Point	$5,599.64	$11,199.28	$11,199.28	$11,199.28
CPM Gross Impressions	$7.35	$14.71	$14.71	$14.71
Reach (1+)	66.20%	35.50%	43.70%	33.10%
Effective Reach (3+)	26.10%	11.80%	10.30%	13.05%
Average Frequency	2.52	2.36	1.91	2.52

*Note: Gross Impressions are measured in millions. This table assumes a target of 76.155 million adult males and three insertions in each of the following programs (SMRB 1982 program audience ratings are in parentheses): "60 Minutes" (18.7 percent), "Quincy" (12.6 percent), "20/20" (12.2 percent) and "Hart to Hart" (12.2 percent).

Several important points should be identified. First, in all cases, weighted media evaluation factors are less optimistic than the unweighted factors. Ratings and impressions are cut approximately in half, relative costs are doubled. Second, regardless of the weighting method used, GRPs, gross impressions, cost-per-rating point, and cost-per-thousand impressions are identical for each of the three weighting methods since they are not dependent upon assumptions concerning the amount of duplication within or between vehicles. Third, despite the differences in reach (1+), effective reach (3+) and average frequency across the three weighting methods, these differences are of a second order of magnitude when compared to the differences between weighted and unweighted estimates of reach and frequency. Consequently, the decision to weight or not is substantially more significant than the decision regarding which weighting method to use.

Method three, which weights the vehicle exposure distribution, appears to be the preferred method in the absence of further research, for several reasons. First, it makes no assumption about the amount of duplication within or between advertising audiences of particular vehicles. Second, it provides estimates that fall between those provided by methods one and two. Third, media planners can use multiple weights that assume convex or s-shaped advertising response functions.

Why are weighted media evaluation factors, despite their many limitations, potentially more valuable to managers than unweighted factors? As the next section of this chapter illustrates, weighted media evaluation factors are probably more closely related to advertising impact or effects in the market place than are unweighted factors. Furthermore, weighted factors have substantial implications for the size of the advertising appropriation.

USING WEIGHTS THAT PREDICT ADVERTISING IMPACT

Table 3.6 provides proprietary quarterly media evaluation factors and communication effects data related to a recent magazine advertising campaign. The proprietary nature of the data requires that the identity of the advertiser and indus-

TABLE 3.6 Defining Effective Reach to Predict Market Impact

Advertising Campaign/ Vehicle Weight (%)	Possible Definitions (%)		Actual** Market Impact (%)
	Reach (1+)	Effective Reach (3+)	
A. Corporate Theme			15.5
100	92.0	80.4	
20	42.1	21.9	
15*	33.7	16.5	
B. Product Headline			14.7
100	84.5	61.1	
45	55.1	26.3	
35*	45.9	20.3	

*Three-year average Starch "Noted" score for corporate themes and product headlines.
**This column shows target percent who correctly identified corporate theme or product headline.
Measurements were taken just after the heaviest quarter of magazine expenditures.

try not be disclosed. This is not a serious limitation since the logic of the table is more important than the source of the data. The procedures can be applied in almost any reasonable market situation involving any major media categories.

The last column shows the estimated percent of the company's target market that correctly identified its current corporate theme (15.5 percent) and the current headline of its major product (14.7 percent). These estimates were obtained from a representative survey of target market members that was conducted just after the heaviest advertising quarter of the year.

For each of the two campaigns, there are also six alternative evaluations of advertising media activity during the previous quarter, using three different weights and two definitions of reach (n+). Weights were then applied to magazine audience ratings using data and software available through Telmar, a popular media software house. A weight of 100 percent indicates that vehicle audiences were evaluated at full strength (that is, unweighted). The weights of 15 percent and 35 percent are three-year averages of Starch "noted" scores for corporate themes and for specific products respectively. The weights of 20 percent and 45 percent assume approximately a one-third increase over the average Starch scores for the corporate theme or the product headline respectively. These serve to illustrate the value, in media terms, of increasing message impact.

Before proceeding, it should be noted that some have criticized the use of Starch scores for media evaluation purposes because they are intended to be used as directional message indices.[5] Starch scores, as well as most other indices, leave much to be desired when used as media weights. But, as will be shown, if whatever weight is chosen can provide management with a realistic picture of the likely impact of advertising in the market place, the methodological difficulties inherent in the selected weight are of secondary importance.

As indicated, one of the company's objectives is that a significant percent of the target market correctly identify the current corporate theme and product headline. It is therefore instructive to ask which media evaluation method provides the best indication of the extent to which this goal is achieved. The resulting definition could then be used to evaluate proposed media plans with some confidence that the estimated media evaluation factors may be fairly close to the communication effects that result from running the schedule.

In this situation it is clear that the most conservative estimate of reach (that is, effective reach (3+)) and the most conservative media vehicle weights (that is, 15 percent and 35 percent, respectively) provide estimates of effective reach which are closest to the percent of the target who correctly identified the corporate theme or product headline. Moreover, both of these conservative estimates exceed the market place estimates of correct identification.

One implication of this example is that there is no purpose to be served by providing decision makers with optimistic media evaluation factors. More realistic estimates of likely advertising impact might instead highlight strengths or weaknesses in the advertising campaign leading to increases or decreases in advertising expenditures, to shifts in the amount allocated to particular media categories or, perhaps, to a reorganization of multiple product advertising campaigns.

For example, if managers of the situation outlined in Table 3.6 wanted 30 percent of the target to correctly identify the corporate theme and product headline, media planners could then search for a schedule and budget likely to yield a weighted effective reach (3+) that is close to 30 percent. To do so may require an increase in media expenditures or a shift in media strategy. Unweighted media evaluation factors would provide no clues as to which strategies and tactics are most likely to be successful.

If this type of analysis is undertaken routinely by decision makers, then it may also be possible to avoid the use of Starch or Burke scores, for example, by simply choosing weights to apply to media audiences that best predict market effects. Experience may lead to consistent rules of thumb. It is believed that the types of relationships depicted in Table 3.6 are available in the files of most major advertisers. Analyzing such data in the manner of Table 3.6 could allow decision makers to choose a definition of effective reach that fits their unique market circumstances and objectives.

USING GENERAL WEIGHTS

In many situations tracking study results will not be available, nor will there be corresponding media schedule evaluations to help planners choose predictive definitions of effective reach. In the face of limited data, judgment plays an important role in deciding on the relative value of various media categories and options within them. The decision rules are likely to change from one product to the next and, for the same product, from one creative execution to the next. Despite such potential complexity in selecting appropriate vehicle audience weights, you should nevertheless be exposed to some generalizations that will help you develop better media plans.

The objective here is not to expose you to a framework that will handle every conceivable situation, but rather to give some manageable rules of thumb. In the extreme, a post-buy analysis, such as Table 3.6, can be quite accurate, since the exact placement, sizes, and copy test results are available for much of the schedule. When planning, however, future schedules are proposed based on limited and dated information. Consequently, the recommendations will be more directional than conclusive.

Here are some suggestions for several important media categories including television, magazines, newspapers, and radio. You might use this information to identify strategic strengths and weaknesses of each media category and to assess the central tendencies of media schedules when selecting vehicle weights. This information can also be helpful when negotiating price with sales representatives of vehicles in a schedule.

Suggestions for using the indices presented are provided in the television section. Those indices listed for the other media categories can be used in a similar manner.

☐ Television Message Weights

Advertising message recall indices provided by Burke and Gallup and Robinson are readily available to subscribing agencies and their clients for a variety of products and services. While recall is not necessarily the best or only measure of message effectiveness, the extent of the data has made it an attractive basis for comparing identical and similar commercials in a variety of contexts. The observed differences can be used to highlight strategic implications of messages and positions and as a basis for weighting. The media research department at Leo Burnett has prepared such a summary titled "Beyond the Numbers: Factors Affecting Commercial Performance" (1978). This 18-page report highlights those dimensions that seem to matter, and sets aside those that do not.

Distilled here are some of the most actionable conclusions of that report. For each executional or positioning dimension, index numbers are given in comparison to the norm. One can simply choose a typical weight for television (see the last column of Table 3.3 for example), and adjust it up or down depending on what is known about message qualities or context. The indices presented below will be followed by an example showing how to use them.

Television Message/Context Dimension	Recall Index
Daypart	
Prime time	80
Late fringe	75
Prime access	70
Daytime	55
Early fringe	45
Commercial length	
60 seconds	100
30 seconds	85
20 seconds	68
15 seconds	61
10 seconds	54

Position in program	100
Billboard support	110
Before entertainment	87
Station breaks	85
Internal	100
External	75
Program type	
Novels/spectaculars	115
First seven weeks of a series	110
Music/variety shows	90
Sports half-time	80
Ethnic situation comedies	75
News informational	75
Others	100
Unprotected (within 30 minutes of competition)	90

As an example, one can imagine that the advertising agency asks its media buyers to put together a typical monthly daytime network television schedule with protected, 15-second commercials to appear within programs. The typical daytime weight given in the last column of Table 3.3 and presented above is 55 percent (54.7 percent). The index that would be applied to this weight is .61 for 15 seconds. All other indices would equal 1.00. Therefore, a weight of 33.5 percent would be used (33.5 percent = 55 percent x .61).

☐ Magazine Message Weights

Starch "noted" scores, a measure of attention, are available to subscribing agencies and their clients and can be summarized for individual brands or types of ads across brands. The Leo Burnett media research department has provided such a summary in a 44-page report titled "Beyond the Numbers: Factors Affecting Magazine Ad Performance" (1978). These results are further condensed here to provide directional factors for planning and strategy and a basis for adjusting vehicle weights.

Magazine Message/Context Dimension	Attention Index
Page size (4-color)	
2-page	128
1-page	100
2/3-page	84
1/2-page vertical	79
1/2-page horizontal	80
Digest	63
Horizontal spread	84
Checkerboard	97
Black and white (apply to 4-color page indices)	75
Presence of offers	
Coupon	109
Send-away	111

Contest	120
Recipes	115

Cover position
2nd cover	133
3rd cover	112
4th cover	127

Spread location
2nd cover	154
Center	127
Other inside	128

Inside position
Page 1	121
1st ten pages	110
1st third	104
2nd third	103
3rd third	93
Campbell's Soup position	121
Left page	94
Right page	102
Opposite page content	
Table of contents	112
Editorial	99
Ad	102
Editorial and ad	104

☐ Newspaper Message Weights

The Newspaper Advertising Bureau has recently completed an extensive study of "Newspaper Pages, Ads & Readers" (1984). The data obtained by this research allow planners to assess the likely readership of all types of ads and locations. A few of the most important dimensions are presented here. It is recommended that the indices presented below be applied to a typical ad readership of 12 percent of all target members who read a paper.

Newspaper Message/Context Dimension	Readership Index
Ad size	
Under ¼ page	75
¼ - under ½ page	106
½ - under full page	156
Full page or more	275
Color of ad	
Color	194
Black and white	94
Location	
Back page	150
First two interior spreads	88
Third and fourth interior spreads	103
First page of section	69
Back page of section	138

Average page opening	
Males	97
Females	103
Circulation	
100,000 and over	94
Under 100,000	107
Section	
General news	108
Women's pages	97
Food	85
Fashion	109
Society	112
Men's pages	92
Business/Finance	88
Sports	92
Editorials	104
Classified	81
Radio/TV	96
Comics	104
Amusements	103
Home/garden	74
Columnists	99
Agriculture/farm	106
Health/science	114
Area/local news	106
Other	92

☐ Radio Message Weights

Available evidence on radio advertising communication impact is limited and dated. What data exist have been summarized by the Leo Burnett media research department (1977). This evidence includes commercial recall by dayparts and formats.

Radio Message/Context Dimension	Recall Index
Daypart	
M-F 6:00 a.m. - 10:00 a.m.	117
M-F 10:00 a.m. - 3:00 p.m.	99
M-F 3:00 p.m. - 7:00 p.m.	97
S-S 7:00 p.m. - 12:00 a.m.	92
Station format	
Personality, middle of the road, talk, ethnic	115
Music, top 40, classical, adult contemporary, all news	100
Country music	127
Beautiful music	63

There is evidence that away-from-home listeners are twice as likely to recall advertising content than those listening at home. Radio has also been shown to be an excellent supporting medium for television through "imagery transfer." Four studies show that roughly 75 percent of radio listeners correctly describe television images when played matching radio sound tracks.

SUMMARY

This chapter, by focusing on some of the more important concepts and factors to account for in media planning and practice, gives a solid foundation on which to build for the remainder of the text. While advertising media planning theory urges decision makers to evaluate media plans on the basis of the effective reach of advertising messages as opposed to media vehicle audiences, media planners generally only have available media vehicle audience ratings. Advertising exposure ratings are unlikely to be readily available for most of the major media categories for several more years. Consequently, considerable judgment is required to evaluate media plans on the basis of advertising exposures or impact instead of media vehicle exposures. Methods for doing so are controversial. Nevertheless, a recent survey of media directors of leading advertising agencies indicates that there is some consensus as to the use of communication effects and weighting in the media planning process.

Thus despite the methodological difficulties involved, it is more useful to decision makers to overcome the problems and use realistic media evaluation factors than it is to avoid the issue entirely and use clearly inflated ones. If this line of reasoning serves to stimulate further discussion of these problems and opportunities, much will have been achieved.

ENDNOTES

1. Peggy J. Kreshel, Kent M. Lancaster and Margaret A. Toomey. "How Leading Advertising Agencies Perceive Effective Reach and Frequency," *Journal of Advertising*, 14 (3, 1986), pp. 32-38, 51.

2. Kent M. Lancaster, Peggy J. Kreshel and Joya R. Harris, "Estimating the Impact of Advertising Media Plans: Media Executives Describe Weighting and Timing Factors," *Journal of Advertising*, 15 (September 1986), pp. 21-29, 45.

3. John D. Leckenby and Shizue Kishi, "How Media Directors View Reach/Frequency Estimation," *Journal of Advertising Research*, 22 (June/July 1982), pp. 64-69.

4. William V. Behrmann. "Putting Effective Frequency Strategies to Work in Media Planning," *Proceedings of ARF Key Issues Workshop—Effective Frequency: The State of the Art, Current Media Applications, Next Steps From ARF* (New York: Advertising Research Foundation, 1982), pp. 103-128.

5. Guggenheim, Bernard, "Advertising Media Planning and Evaluation: Current Research Issues," *Current Issues and Research in Advertising*, 2 (1984), pp. 19-38.

6. Kent M. Lancaster, Peggy J. Kreshel and Margaret A. Toomey, "Estimating the Communication Impact of Advertising Media Plans," *Proceedings*, Atlantic Marketing Association 1986 Annual Meeting, Orlando, Florida, October 8-11, 1986; and Kent M. Lancaster, Peggy J. Kreshel and Margaret A. Toomey, "How Should Advertising Media

Planners Estimate Effective Reach and Frequency,'' presented at the 1985 McElroy Symposium on *Current Trends in Broadcast Advertising*, University of Northern Iowa, April 1985.

ADDITIONAL READING

Chook, Paul H. *ARF Model for Evaluating Media: Making the Promise a Reality* (New York: Advertising Research Foundation, Inc., 1983).

Joyce, Timothy, *Page Exposures* (New York: Mediamark Research, Inc., 1984.)

CHAPTER FOUR

Analyzing the Advertising Situation

Whenever a media planner is faced with a new advertising or media planning problem or assignment, it is vital to conduct a thorough situation analysis before recommending a course of action. A situation analysis, as the name implies, includes two parts, a description of the situation and an analysis of the descriptive material. This chapter then follows with the first of four interactive advertising media planning computer programs, ADCOMP. For more information on how to use personal computers and the appropriate terminology involved, you should consult the Appendix.

DESCRIBING THE SITUATION

In describing the situation, it is useful to have as much relevant data as possible. These can include elements of the media situation facing a brand as well as other elements of the advertising and marketing mixes. Here is a brief outline of the types of information that would be valuable to have concerning a brand and its market situation:

1. Company and brand history and recent activities.
2. Business objectives (such as profit goals, plans for expansion).
3. Marketing objectives (for example, sales, market share, growth).
4. Elements of the marketing mix.
   a. Target markets (for example, consumer, business, trade).
   b. Characteristics of products and/or services.
   c. Retail and manufacturer prices, costs and margins.
   d. Distribution channel characteristics.
   e. Promotion tools used.
5. Special corporate resources.
6. Market potential (for example, market definition, brand and competitors' sales (units and/or dollars), market shares, growth rates, geographic distribution, seasonality).
7. Economic, regulatory, and social factors and trends.

Focusing on the advertising situation in particular, it is useful to obtain as much data as possible on the following elements of the advertising mix for the brand in question and its principal competitors.

1. Actual (or inferred) target audiences.
2. Advertising appropriation and major budget items including targets, media categories, seasonality, geographic spending patterns and product lines.
3. Message content including consumer problems portrayed, selling points, benefits promised, competitive position.
4. Media mix including expenditures in individual media categories, seasonal variation, GRP levels, size of ads, and length of commercials.
5. Characteristics of the advertising agencies and departments associated with the major brands in the market.

ANALYZING THE SITUATION

A situation analysis can focus on any one of the elements of the marketing and advertising mix. For example, managers may focus on product characteristics with the objective of learning what improvements consumers may wish to see in the product or service. They may thus consider the advertising situation with particular emphasis on the advertising message. In this case, they might look at the copy platform in order to spot opportunities for improving the basic proposition, approach, appeal, theme, characters, copy, etc.

The concern in this chapter will be on the elements related to the media situation, showing how to conduct a *competitive advertising spending analysis* across media categories; the next chapter then shows how to develop *media goals* and budgets that are consistent with advertising and marketing goals. Whatever media element is to be the focus of attention, it must be analyzed in light of other elements of the marketing situation.

These are not necessarily the best approaches in all situations but rather two methods that are logical and that deal with as much relevant detail as is practical. The next section of this chapter acquaints readers with the process and goals of an advertising spending analysis.

COMPETITIVE ADVERTISING SPENDING ANALYSIS

There are many objectives for conducting a competitive advertising spending analysis. The overall goal is to learn how the brand's advertising activity stands against its competition. Competitive spending analysis can be broad in scope yet also include a great deal of depth. Consequently, some advertisers and agencies have personnel assigned to this task for various brands who do nothing but such analyses for weeks or months on end. The possibilities in terms of the nature and scope of competitive spending analysis are infinite. Therefore, this chapter can only deal with a few of the more important ones.

SOURCES OF COMPETITIVE MEDIA USAGE DATA

There are a number of syndicated sources that can be used to compile data on competitive media usage activity. The most important of these are listed here along with a brief description of their nature and scope. *Leading National Advertisers* (LNA) is probably the most vital source of competitive advertising expenditure data. LNA gives estimates of advertising expenditures by media category for most major national advertisers. The seven media categories cover magazines, newspaper supplements, network television, spot television, network radio, outdoor and cable television. Three reports are provided including a *Company/Brand $* report which lists expenditures by company and by brand within each company. The *Class/Brand YTD $* report lists year-to-date expenditures each quarter by product category, then by company within each category and by brand within each company. The *Ad $ Summary* provides an alphabetical list of brands and then identifies the parent company, product category, seven media expenditures and notes the principal media categories used.

The *Class/Brand YTD $* will probably be the most useful competitive spending resource in the context of this text. Here LNA classifies national advertising expenditures by product category, in thousands of dollars. Each class is first alphabetically subdivided by company, then by brand within each company. In turn, each brand's advertising expenditures are broken down into seven advertising media categories, preceded by the seven-media category total.

This is then followed by each of the seven categories: magazines, newspaper supplements, network television, spot television, network radio, outdoor, and cable television. One drawback to using LNA data is that they do not include newspapers, spot radio, or direct mail advertising expenditures. Also, some brand names are combined which can make it difficult, if not impossible, to differentiate them.

Broadcast Advertisers Report (BAR) provides data on the network television activity of national advertisers. The report provides product and parent company activity by dollar volume, time of day, network, and program used. BAR is the basis of the LNA network television expenditures.

A. C. Nielsen's report on *Brand Cumulative Audience* (BCA) offers detailed information on competitive network television advertising schedules for selected brands. For a given brand, the report provides network and program name, number of commercials used, average household rating, four-week reach and average frequency, gross rating points, time and talent costs, cost-per-thousand impressions, and exposure distributions detailed by combinations of six major dayparts. The BCA report is published three times a year covering the months of October, February, and July. Brands included subscribe to the NTI Complete Service.

BARCUME reports spot television advertising activity for national advertisers covering the top 75 U.S. markets. The report content and format are similar to the BAR network television report and it is also used by LNA.

BAR Network Radio Service is similar to the BAR network television report and is the basis for the network radio expenditures reported by LNA.

Radio Expenditure Report (RER) tracks national brand use of spot radio advertising activity.

LNA-PIB (Publishers Information Bureau) provides data on brand, product, and company expenditures by magazine and type of advertisement, including size, use of color and bleed, and favorable position, among others. LNA-PIB is the basis of the magazine expenditures reported by LNA.

Media Records provides extensive product and brand data on advertising volume and expenditures in major newspaper markets. If newspaper advertising is important in the product category at hand, then LNA data should be supplemented with *Media Records* figures.

Outdoor Advertising Expenditure Report provides outdoor advertising expenditures that are also included in LNA.

WHAT TO LOOK FOR

There are well over a dozen uses for competitive advertising spending analysis. These can be organized in terms of basic uses and planning uses. Klues[1] has identified nine basic uses.

1. Identifying firms and brands involved in the product category or segment.
2. Identifying dominant spenders.
3. Detailing seasonal advertising spending and/or sales patterns.
4. Identifying media types selected by major competitors.
5. Distinguishing between national and regional or local competitive pressure.
6. Describing differences in competitors' television daypart mixes.
7. Estimating GRP levels required to compete.
8. Learning whether funds are diverted by competitors' parent companies from period-to-period.
9. Identifying corporate fiscal limitations.

The planning uses singled out by Klues include:

1. Developing media appropriations and budgets.
2. Selecting and adjusting the media mix and daypart mix.
3. Estimating competitors' reach, frequency and GRPs.
4. Developing schedules and seasonal spending patterns.
5. Choosing regions and markets for particular emphasis.

Any one of these uses can be further enriched through the nature and scope of the data that support it.

POSSIBLE DATA REQUIREMENTS

It might help to organize the view of the potential data requirements by a study of Figure 4.1, which presents an outline of what can be incorporated into a competitive spending analysis. The possibilities are presented from the broadest to the narrowest including the level of aggregation, type of media, alternative measures, time series, and geographic dimensions.

Due to the large number of possible basic and planning uses of competitive spending analysis, and given the vast array of possible data requirements which might support a given use, the available approaches can become unwieldy. This is

FIGURE 4.1 Competitive Advertising Spending Analysis: Possible Data Requirements

Total Product Category
Total Market Segment within Product Category
Brand
Each Major Competitor
  Total Advertising
  Individual Media Category Advertising
    Expenditures
    Share-of-voice
    GRPs
    Media Mix
    Expenditures per Market Share Point
    Indices
    Advertising Content (Size, Length, Color, Benefits, Selling Points, Position)
      Time Series
        Yearly
        Semi-annually
        Quarterly
        Monthly
          Period-by-Period
          Average Across Periods
          Percent Changes Over Previous Periods
          Indices Versus Previous Periods
          Adjustment for Media Cost (CPM) Inflation
  Geographic
    National
    Regional (Census, Marketing)
    Market-by-market (ADI, DMA, SMSA)

simply a broad overview in order to appreciate the possibilities and to better position the more important concepts and types of analysis emphasized throughout the remainder of this text.

SOME BASIC CONCEPTS

The focus here is on several of the most basic concepts that typically support a competitive advertising spending analysis. These include analyses of advertising expenditures, media mixes, shares of voice, estimates of GRPs, and annual changes in advertising expenditures. These concepts and the most important uses of them will be demonstrated using the Kellogg's All-Bran case described in Chapter One.

☐ Advertising Expenditures

The first step for a media planner in a competitive advertising spending analysis is to gather relevant data on the advertising expenditures of the given brand and major competitive brands. Essentially, one must carefully define the market segment in which that brand competes and identify the particular brands within the segment. This is more difficult than it may at first appear. The following steps may help narrow the scope of the brand's market segment.

1. Identify all brands with similar physical characteristics.
2. From this broad group, identify all brands with similar advertising message content or position.
3. Further narrow the scope of the list by eliminating all brands that have marginal advertising expenditures and no evidence that they are likely to dramatically increase expenditures in the near future.
4. Using SMRB or MRI product volumes, eliminate brands that appear to be used by target markets dissimilar to the brand's selected target.

These steps require considerable judgment. The ideal approach, of course, is to survey the chosen target to determine which brands they use or prefer. The last step above approximates this method by giving insights into the brands they use. But, of course, SMRB and MRI data will not provide information on new brands until they have penetrated the market with substantial sales and the data will not allow for identification of psychographic segments within broader demographic or socioeconomic groups.

Returning to the Kellogg's All-Bran case, six brands can be identified that satisfy the four criteria described above. Rather than list all of them here, the focus will be on Kellogg's All-Bran, and Post Fruit & Fibre, as well as the bran cereal segment as a whole. From the 1986 LNA *Class/Brand YTD $* summary, comes Table 4.1.

You will recall that LNA expenditures reported for brands, firms, and industries are in thousands (000) and therefore the 1986 advertising expenditures of Kellogg's All-Bran total $14,923,900 in the seven media categories combined. The segment totals were computed by hand based on the expenditures of the two brands listed plus those of the four remaining segment brands whose expenditures are not shown.

From Table 4.1 the competitive advertising spending analysis can continue, focusing on basic and planning uses. Identification of the competitors together with the data listed make it clear that Post Fruit & Fibre is the dominant spender. Four advertising media categories are used by all brands in the segment. Network television is the major media category both for the whole segment and for the two brands listed.

☐ Media Mix

Table 4.1 is useful, but there are several additional ways to examine the data to

TABLE 4.1   1986 Bran Cereal Advertising Expenditures (000)

Brand	7-Media Total	Maga-zines	News Supp	Net TV	Spot TV	Net Radio	Out-door	Cable TV
All-Bran	14,923.9	0.0	0.0	13,631.7	1,176.1	0.0	0.0	116.1
Fruit & Fibre	15,344.4	3,234.8	0.0	10,448.0	1,219.8	0.0	0.0	441.8
Segment Total	71,706.2	4,375.4	0.0	58,905.4	6,660.5	0.0	0.0	1,764.9

gain insights into the competitive situation. For example, Table 4.1 provides awareness of the media mix used throughout the segment, but this is clouded by the differences in the scale of the various brands and the segment total. To remove such variation in order to compare media mixes across a large number of brands, media planners divide the seven-media total for the various brands and the segment as a whole into their respective media category expenditures.

$$M_{i,m} = E_{i,m}/E_{i,\Sigma m}$$

(4-1)

where: $M_{i,m}$ = percent of total media expenditures for brand i in media category m.

$E_{i,m}$ = expenditures for brand i in media category m.

$E_{i,\Sigma m}$ = expenditures for brand i across all m media categories, where, in this case, m = 1,2,...,7.

Using Equation 4-1 throughout Table 4.1 leads to Table 4.2.

For each brand and for the segment total, the sum of the individual media category percentages should equal 100 percent. Small differences from 100 percent may occur due to rounding.

As an example, the percent of Kellogg's All-Bran (AB) total media expenditures devoted to network television (NTV) was computed as follows, using Equation 4-1.

$$M_{AB,NTV} = E_{AB,NTV}/E_{AB,7M}$$
$$= 13,631.7/14,923.9$$
$$= .913$$
$$= 91.3\%$$

This procedure was used for all percentages reported in Table 4.2.

An inspection of Table 4.2 for planning implications shows that the dominant media category is network television with 82.1 percent of the segment total devoted to it. All-Bran spends a higher percentage of its total in network television with 91.3 percent, while Fruit & Fibre spends below average on this medium with 68.1 percent. If All-Bran were going to compete head on with Fruit & Fibre, management may wish to allocate its budget to media categories using the Fruit & Fibre proportions. On the other hand, All-Bran management may wish to avoid direct competition and reallocate expenditures in media categories for which competitive expenditures, as a percentage of the total, are relatively low. Whatever strategy emerges, considerable guidance can be obtained from media mix tables such as Table 4.2.

TABLE 4.2 1986 Bran Cereal Advertising Media Mix (%)

Brand Name	7-Media Total	Mags	News Supp	Net TV	Spot TV	Net Radio	Out-door	Cable TV
All-Bran	100%	0.0%	0.0%	91.3%	7.9%	0.0%	0.0%	0.8%
Fruit & Fibre	100	21.1	0.0	68.1	7.9	0.0	0.0	2.9
Segment Total	100	6.1	0.0	82.1	9.3	0.0	0.0	2.5

☐ Share of Voice

A common rule of thumb has it that, other things being equal, a brand should keep its share of voice (SOV) ahead of its market share if it expects to grow. This is especially true for new brands. There, it is argued that SOV should be kept 1.5 to 2.5 times larger than the desired market share at the end of the second year, a phenomenon often referred to as Peckham's rule.[2] Other research has shown that, again with other factors held constant, market share tends to follow advertising share or SOV. Thus it is important, regardless of the particular circumstances facing a brand, that management has a clear picture of the brand's SOV as well as the SOV of its major competitors.

SOV for a particular brand is derived by dividing the product category or segment total or separate media expenditures into the corresponding expenditures for all of the relevant brands in the segment. Applying this reasoning to Table 4.1 results in Table 4.3.

The sum of the columns for all segment brands, including the two in Table 4.3, should come close to 100 percent with slight differences due to rounding. Here's the equation that was used to generate Table 4.3.

$$SOV_{i,m} = E_{i,m}/E_{\Sigma i,m} \qquad (4\text{-}2)$$

where: $SOV_{i,m}$ = share of voice for brand i in media category(ies) m.

$E_{i,m}$ = expenditures of brand i in media category(ies) m.

$E_{\Sigma i,m}$ = product category or segment total advertising expenditures (i.e., the sum across all i brands) in media category(ies) m.

Equation 4-2 was applied throughout Table 4.1 to derive Table 4.3.

For example, All-Bran's share of voice for network television in 1986 can be calculated as follows:

$$\begin{aligned} SOV_{AB,NTV} &= E_{AB,NTV}/E_{\Sigma i,NTV} \\ &= 13631.1/58905.4 \\ &= 2.31 \\ &= 23.1\% \end{aligned}$$

Again, there are several planning implications to be drawn from Table 4.3. For example, Fruit & Fibre's SOV is slightly higher than that of All-Bran for all media categories combined. All-Bran dominates SOV in network television, whereas Fruit & Fibre is the clear leader in magazines and has a SOV four times higher for cable television.

TABLE 4.3 1986 Bran Cereal Share of Voice (%)

Brand Name	7-Media Total	Mags	News Supp	Net TV	Spot TV	Net Radio	Out-door	Cable TV
All-Bran	20.8	0.0	0.0	23.1	17.7	0.0	0.0	6.6
Fruit & Fibre	21.4	73.9	0.0	17.7	18.3	0.0	0.0	25.0
Segment Total	100.0	100.0	0.0	100.0	100.0	0.0	0.0	100.0

□ Gross Rating Points

Another use of competitive advertising expenditure data is to facilitate estimates of competitive GRP levels. This translates advertising expenditures into media weights which can be of value in assessing competitive reach and frequency in the market place.

The cost-per-rating point (CPP) varies by media category and subcategory and by target audience. Since each brand in a product category uses different vehicles against different target audiences, one might wonder how it is possible to estimate GRP levels for each brand in a segment without detailed information about their schedule and target. As a practical matter, it is possible to learn the details of competitors' schedules through the use of the information services which support LNA. In this text, a more general position will emphasize the logic behind the concepts and procedures, rather than focusing on more realistic details.

The approach here assumes that all of the major brands in a segment are positioned against the same and broadest possible demographic or product usage target. It is also supposed that the mix of vehicles within a media category is similar across brands such that each brand faces the same CPP. This will generate crude, though useful, estimates of GRP levels for each brand in a segment.

To convert advertising media expenditures to estimates of GRPs, Equation 4-3 will be used.

$$GRP_{i,m} = E_{i,m}/CPP_m \qquad (4\text{-}3)$$

where: $GRP_{i,m}$ = gross rating point estimate for brand i in media category m,
$E_{i,m}$ = advertising expenditures for brand i in media category m,
CPP_m = cost-per-rating point for media category m.

GRPs for all seven media categories combined for a particular brand, then, are simply the sum of the individual media category GRPs for the brand

$$(\text{that is, } GRP_i = \sum_{m=1}^{7} GRP_{i,m}).$$

Now, the problem is to develop estimates of CPP for each media category in the segment. To do this, it is recommended that you add together the cost of several "typical" vehicles used by advertisers in the product category and divide this total cost by the GRPs delivered by the vehicle combination. The example below is for *magazines*.

Magazine	Four Color Page Cost	Rating*
Reader's Digest	$108,800	26.6
TV Guide	89,300	25.4
Good Housekeeping	69,425	20.8
Family Circle	74,400 (Oct.-Dec.)	20.8
Better Homes & Gardens	88,950	20.4
Total	$440,695	114.0

*Base is female homemakers who use cold breakfast cereals. Source is SMRB, 1985, Volume P-20.

Dividing $440,965 by 114, the estimated CPP for magazines is $3,866. This CPP will be overstated for advertisers that use more efficient vehicles. But the objective here is to obtain a reasonable CPP cost for approximating GRP levels across brands. Using the same procedure for the top two prime time network television programs and the top two daytime network television programs, one gets the following estimates.

Prime Time Network Programs	Cost/:30	Rating*
Dallas	$123,189	23.8%
60 Minutes	82,298	15.9
	$205,487	39.7
Daytime Network Programs		
All My Children	$ 22,814	8.4
General Hospital	21,185	7.8
	$ 43,999	16.2

*Base is female homemakers who use cold breakfast cereals. Source is SMRB, 1985, Volume P-20.

Dividing $205,487 by 39.7 results in a prime time network television CPP of $5,176, while the same procedure leads to a daytime network television CPP of $2,716. Now, assuming that, on average, advertisers in this segment use a 50/50 mix of daytime/prime time television as a percentage of their network television budgets, then this means the weighted network television CPP is $3,946 (e.g., (.5)($2,716) + (.5)($5,176) = $3,946).

It will be worthwhile to spend some time explaining how the network television program costs were estimated. A media cost guide provides network television cost ranges by quarter. It is recommended that the upper cost limit be chosen to be conservative and to account somewhat for inflationary factors. For the winter quarter, the upper unit cost for prime time is $103,000 and for daytime it is $22,000.

Now a method is needed to account for differences in cost for daypart programs with different ratings. This can be done by averaging the ratings by daypart to derive a CPP by daypart to apply to the ratings. For example, the average prime time rating in this schedule is 19.9 percent (39.7 GRPs/two programs) while for daytime it is 8.1 percent (16.2 GRPs/two programs). Therefore, the prime time CPP is $5,176 ($103,000/19.9) and the daytime CPP is $2,716 ($22,000/8.1) as shown above. Program costs, then, are estimated to be the product of the rating and the daypart CPP. In the case of "Dallas," the figure is $123,189 = (23.8)($5,176). You might wish to check your understanding of this method by estimating the cost of the remaining programs in the schedule.

For *newspaper supplements* the following costs and ratings apply.

Newspaper Supplement	Four-Color Page Cost	Rating*
Sunday	$238,307	28.1
Parade	284,560	34.3
	$522,867	62.4

*Base is female homemakers who use cold breakfast cereals. Source is SMRB, 1985, Volume P-20.

The CPP for newspaper supplements is $8,379 (that is, $522,867/62.4 = $8,379).

Since the CPP figures presented are for various aggregates of top U.S. market groups, it will be necessary to make an assumption regarding the number of markets selected by spot television advertisers in the chosen segment. If the top 50 markets are used, the best estimate of CPP is $6,831 for prime time and $2,134 for daytime. If a 50/50 budget split between the two dayparts is again assumed, as in the case of the network television CPP, then the spot television CPP is $4,483 (that is, (.5)($6,831) + (.5)($2,134) = $4,483).

For *cable television*, the principle used is the same as for network television. Assuming 30-second spots in three of the most popular cable channels leads to the estimates below:

Cable Channel	Cost/:30	Rating*
ESPN	$578	1.6
MTV	1,385	1.4
CNN	584	1.3
	$2,547	5.7

*For a list of sources, see Table 10.4 of this text.

If the total cost of $2,547 is divided by the total rating points, 5.7, then the CPP for cable comes out as $446.80.

To summarize, here are the estimates of CPP for each of the four media categories used in the chosen market segment in 1986; the CPP for newspaper supplements is also included since it was used in 1985.

Media Category	CPP
Network Television	$3,946
Spot Television	4,483
Magazines	3,886
Newspaper Supplements	8,379
Cable Television	447

These CPP estimates can now be applied to the advertising expenditure data displayed in Table 4.1. Using Equation 4-3 in order to estimate GRP levels for each brand and media category in the market segment gives the results shown in Table 4.4.

TABLE 4.4 1986 Bran Cereal Gross Rating Points (%)

Brand Name	7-Media Total	Mags	News Supp	Net TV	Spot TV	Net Radio	Out-door	Cable TV
All-Bran	3,976.6	0.0	0.0	3,454.6	262.3	0.0	0.0	259.7
Fruit & Fibre	4,744.9	836.7	0.0	2,647.7	272.1	0.0	0.0	988.4

The GRP estimate for All-Bran in network television was estimated using Equation 4-3 as follows:

$$GRP_{AB,NTV} = E_{AB,NTV}/CPP_{NTV}$$
$$= \$13,631,700/\$3,946$$
$$= 3,454.6$$

This procedure was used for all relevant media categories for both brands. The 7-Media total GRPs for every brand are obtained simply by summing the media category GRPs for each one.

The value of estimated GRP levels, such as those contained in Table 4.4, can be better appreciated when viewed from the perspective of the possible planning uses. For instance, if it is assumed that each brand has monthly reach and frequency goals given the nature of the product (such as low price, intensive distribution, frequent purchase cycles), then dividing total GRPs for each brand by 12 will give an idea of monthly schedule weight.

Brand	Monthly GRPs
All-Bran	3,976.6/12 = 331.4
Fruit & Fibre	4,744.9/12 = 395.4

Taken alone, this information can be useful for planning purposes because it gives some idea of how many insertions each brand might use per month. For example, if one assumes that a "typical" vehicle has a rating of 15 percent against the target, then All-Bran is running about 22 advertisements per month (that is, 331.4/15 = 22.1) and Fruit & Fibre is placing about 26 (that is, 395.4/15 = 26.4).

Furthermore, if it is supposed that each brand reaches 50 percent of the target per month, then average frequency for All-Bran is about 6.6 (that is, 331.4/50 = 6.6) and for Fruit & Fibre it is 7.9 (that is, 395.4/50 = 7.9). This kind of analysis can be quite handy in the initial stages of developing a new media schedule, since it gives some indication in advance of how large a schedule might be in terms of number of insertions and what reach and frequency levels are likely to be achieved. There are also many other creative uses that could be made of the GRP data contained in Table 4.4. Readers should not be afraid to experiment.

☐ Annual Rate of Change

Another important dimension of competitive advertising spending analysis is describing how brand expenditures change from one year to the next. Do they increase or decrease, and by how much? One can amplify Table 4.1 to include advertising expenditures for 1985 as well as 1986.

Now, for the segment, each brand, and the media category, one needs to know the rate of change. This usually is measured as the percent change over the previous period. The easiest way to calculate this is by using the following simple formula:

$$\text{Rate of Change} = (\text{New Value - Old Value})/\text{Old Value.} \tag{4-4}$$

The rate of change for All-Bran 7-Media expenditures from 1985 to 1986 can be computed as follows, using Equation 4-4.

$$\text{Rate of Change}_{AB,85\text{-}86} = (\$14,923.9 - \$11,216.6)/\$11,216.6$$
$$= \$3,707.3/\$11,216.6$$
$$= 0.3305$$
$$= 33.05\%$$

That is, All-Bran advertising expenditures increased 33.1 percent from 1985 to 1986. Applying Equation 4-4 to all of the data contained in Table 4.5 leads to Table 4.6.

There are many planning implications to be derived from Table 4.6. The principal one is its ability to help predict what is likely to happen in a given segment next year. For example, how much will be spent on 7-Media advertising in that segment in 1987? If brands continue to increase spending at the same rate as in the past, one would expect only a 1.5 percent increase overall. Adding 1.00 to the previous rate of change yields 1.00 + .015 = 1.015. The prediction for 1987 would be 1.015 times the 1986 figure. That is:

$$\text{Segment Advertising}_{1987} = (1.015)(\text{Segment Advertising}_{1986})$$
$$= (1.015)(\$71,706.2)$$
$$= \$72,781.8$$

One would expect 1987 expenditures, therefore, to be around $73 million. The implications of this outcome are clear. For example, if a brand wishes to maintain its SOV under such circumstances it *must* increase its 7-Media total expenditures 1.5 percent or it will lose ground. To increase SOV under such circumstances would require an expenditure increase greater than 1.5 percent.

TABLE 4.5 1985-86 Bran Cereal Advertising Expenditures (000)

Brand Name	Year	7-Media Total	Mags	News Supp	Net TV	Spot TV	Net Radio	Out-door	Cable TV
All-Bran	85	11,216.6	0.0	0.0	10,195.6	950.2	0.0	0.0	70.8
	86	14,923.9	0.0	0.0	13,631.7	1,176.1	0.0	0.0	116.1
Fruit & Fibre	85	17,154.1	2,985.0	190.2	10,913.4	2,330.9	0.0	0.0	734.6
	86	15,344.4	3,234.8	0.0	10,448.0	1,219.8	0.0	0.0	441.8
Segment Total	85	70,649.6	3,402.7	190.2	56,504.6	8,294.5	0.0	0.0	2,257.6
	86	71,706.2	4,375.4	0.0	58,905.4	6,660.5	0.0	0.0	1,764.9

TABLE 4.6 1985-86 Rates of Change in Bran Cereal Advertising Expenditures (%)

Brand Name	Year	7-Media Total	Mags	News Supp	Net TV	Spot TV	Net Radio	Out-door	Cable TV
All-Bran	86	33.1%	0.0%	0.0%	33.7%	23.8%	0.0%	0.0%	64.0%
Fruit & Fibre	86	-10.5	8.4	-100.0	-4.3	-47.7	0.0	0.0	-39.9
Segment Total	86	1.5	28.6	-100.0	4.2	-19.7	0.0	0.0	-21.8

☐ Media Cost Trends

The high rates of change that are observed for the entire segment come from two sources. One is the effect of rising media costs relative to audience size, or media "cost inflation." The other is from real spending increases.

To give readers an intuitive feel for the role of inflation, one can expect that ten percent of any annual media expenditure increase will be due to the influence of inflation. This changes from month-to-month by media category, but ten percent would be a sensible yearly rule of thumb to use in the absence of better data. *Marketing and Media Decisions* regularly publishes media cost factors that can be used to adjust media expenditures to account for inflation. Analyzing data that have been adjusted for the variable effects of inflation across media categories is a sensible habit to get into.

As an example, one can look at Table 4.5 in terms of constant dollars. The cost indices shown generally use 1980 as the base, meaning that the costs for all subsequent years are divided by 1980 costs (multiplied by 100) to create the indices. It is best to use cost indices based on CPM, since they capture cost trends in relation to audience size. For example, in 1980, prime time network television CPM (homes) was $4.94. In 1981 it was $5.84. As 1980 is used as the base, the index for 1981 is 118 [that is, $118 = (5.84/4.94)(100)$].

For the example below, the cost indices used are those that appear in the AD-COMP program, which were derived using both *Leo Burnett 1985 Media Costs and Coverage* and *Marketing and Media Decisions* figures.

Now, Table 4.5 can be reconsidered in terms of constant 1980 dollars. To do so, all cost indices related to the appropriate years and media categories must be gathered together.

Media Category	1985	1986
Magazines	142	151
Newspaper Supplements	201	197
Network TV	153	156
Spot TV	159	178
Cable TV	153	156

It should be noted that the TV cost indices assume a 50/50 split between prime time and daytime dayparts. In general, one can use the following formulas to adjust advertising expenditures for the effects of inflation.

$$R_{i,m,t} = E_{i,m,t}/(C_{m,t}/100) \tag{4-5}$$

where: $R_{i,m,t}$ = real advertising expenditures for brand i in media category m for year t.

$E_{i,m,t}$ = nominal advertising expenditures for brand i in media category m for year t.

$C_{m,t}$ = cost index (preferably based on CPM) for media category m for year t.

Now, one can apply the above cost indices and Equation 4-5 to the data presented in Table 4.5. Using Kellogg's All-Bran cable expenditures (CTV) for 1986 as an example, this gives:

$$R_{AB,CTV,1986} = E_{AB,CTV,1986}/C_{CTV,1986}/100)$$
$$= \$116.1/(156/100)$$
$$= \$116.1/(1.56)$$
$$= \$74.4$$

In other words, in 1986 All-Bran spent $74,400 (in constant 1980 dollars) in cable television. Continuing this procedure for the remainder of Table 4.5 leads to Table 4.7.

Since cost inflation affects each media category at a different rate, the seven-media total column of Table 4.7 is obtained simply by adding up a brand's deflated expenditure in a year in each media category.

The data presented in Table 4.7 can now be used to generate most of the additional tables explained earlier in the chapter, including media mix, share of voice, and annual rate of change. Of course, these additional tables will be based on real or constant expenditures, removing the effects of inflation. Generating an appropriate GRP table based on Table 4.7, however, would require constant CPP figures, which are not readily available.

You should reason from inflation-adjusted tables in the same way as from the unadjusted ones, the only difference being that real figures are being used, in the sense that changes from one period to the next do not include the inflating effects of rising media costs.

PRACTICAL CONSIDERATIONS

This chapter has so far demonstrated a number of basic concepts associated with competitive advertising spending analysis and has done so using a rather simple example. One can imagine, on the other hand, a more realistic situation with a dozen major brands and five years of data. That involves 480 separate expenditures from which to analyze media mixes, SOVs, GRPs, rates of change, and the implications of media cost trends. To do so accurately by hand would probably require days of work and delay the decision making process. Through the interactive computer program called ADCOMP, most of the tedious work is done for the

TABLE 4.7 1985-86 Bran Cereal Advertising Expenditures (000) in Constant (1980) Dollars

Brand Name	Year	7-Media Total	Mags	News Supp	Net TV	Spot TV	Net Radio	Out-door	Cable TV
All-Bran	85	7,307.7	0.0	0.0	6,663.8	597.6	0.0	0.0	46.3
	86	9,473.4	0.0	0.0	8,738.3	660.7	0.0	0.0	74.4
Fruit & Fibre	85	11,275.8	2,102.1	94.6	7,132.9	1,466.0	0.0	0.0	480.1
	86	9,808.2	2,142.3	0.0	6,697.4	685.3	0.0	0.0	283.2
Segment Total	85	46,114.3	2,396.3	94.6	36,931.1	5,216.7	0.0	0.0	1,475.6
	86	45,530.7	2,897.6	0.0	37,759.9	3,741.9	0.0	0.0	1,131.3

planner using the principles discussed so far. All that the user has to do is carefully define the segment and provide the program with the necessary raw data.

Using ADCOMP, one could expect to complete a relatively thorough competitive spending analysis in a few hours, focusing on implications for decision making rather than on the tedious calculations involved. For those who have never used or appreciated computers before, they will certainly do so after completing this text. They will gain the freedom to do highly sophisticated and creative work, leaving the mechanical chores to a machine. Nevertheless, it is important to understand what that machine is doing with the data if it is to be used intelligently.

COMPETITIVE ADVERTISING SPENDING ANALYSIS USING *ADCOMP*

ADCOMP provides valuable reports for the competitive advertising spending analysis. It will calculate the media mix, share of voice, gross rating points, and the annual percent change in expenditures over the previous year, for each brand or company in the product category. It will also adjust expenditures for the influence of media cost inflation.

If you are using microcomputers or ADCOMP for the first time, you are encouraged to read the Appendix for an introduction on how to use these tools efficiently.

☐ Describing the Scope of the Analysis

Initially, the program asks for a description of the scope of the analysis. Some basic questions appear, including the name of the industry or segment; the number of brands involved; the number of years to be analyzed; whether to adjust the data for media cost inflation; the option of converting the expenditures to GRPs; and the choice of entering the total advertising expenditures of the industry, or have ADCOMP calculate them.

Industry or segment name

The title that is chosen for the industry or segment should provide the reader with a concise definition of the market, differentiate these results from others that may be run, and describe the industry or segment that is being analyzed. Throughout this chapter Kellogg's All-Bran will be used as an example.

Thus the segment name used is ''Bran Cereals.'' This label tells what the product is—a cereal; and the industry name—bran, as opposed to a presweetened or nutritional type. Since each label can only be up to 20 letters, including spaces, the label ''Bran Cereals'' was chosen without the frequently used name ''ready-to-eat.'' Of course, many different labels are possible for the analysis. Users should choose one that adequately describes the industry or segment they are handling.

Number of brands in the industry or segment

This section of ADCOMP deserves the most attention and will require careful time and thought since the decisions made here will determine which other brands will be compared. In order to perform a competitive media spending analysis, it is necessary to distinguish accurately the primary competitors. The other brands that are chosen should be of the same product type. For example, Kellogg's All-Bran competitors would be other "ready-to-eat" bran cereals. Of those that fit into this category, some can be eliminated on the grounds that they only have minimal media expenditures and are not any real threat to the client. In deciding on the competitive brands, the following were found to be All-Bran's closest competitors.

Kellogg's 40% Bran Flakes
Kellogg's Fruitful Bran
Kellogg's Raisin Bran
Post Fruit & Fibre
Post Raisin Bran

These five were chosen because of their bran cereal characteristics, the amount they spend on advertising media, and the similar nature of their consumer franchise. Once the competitive brands are identified, one can answer the first part of this question by simply adding the number of competitors found together with the given brand and entering the total.

Then the brands to be analyzed must be named. The first 12 letters of each brand name should be unique so that they can be distinguished in the abbreviated output of the final results tables. The new labels can be seen in Figure 4.2.

Number of years to be analyzed

The answers in this section affect the amount of data that must be provided, as well as the annual percent changes calculated. The more years used, the better idea planners will have of industry changes. Knowing these should allow better prediction of what is likely to happen in the next year. For the sake of time and space, 1985 and 1986 LNA data were used here (Fig. 4.3). Once again, one starts by entering the number of years to be analyzed. Then the computer will ask for each year in turn, starting from the lowest (e.g., 1985) to the highest (e.g., 1986). The entire year designation should be used (e.g., 1985 not 85).

Adjustments for media cost inflation

ADCOMP offers the option discussed earlier, of providing inflation adjustments based on 1980 dollars for that and subsequent years. If the analysis includes years prior to this, the base year must be provided by the user, and the appropriate price indices input for each media category. For the purposes of this example, 1985 and 1986 expenditures are used so the input would be "1," using 1980 as the base year with the default cost indexes that are built into the program.

Inflation adjustments will be seen in the output tables; each one that deals with

FIGURE 4.2

```
Number of brands (20 maximum)     ? 6

        Brand name 1              ? All-Bran
        Brand name 2              ? Fruit and Fibre
        Brand name 3              ? 40% Bran
        Brand name 4              ? Fruitful Bran
        Brand name 5              ? Raisin Bran
        Brand name 6              ? Post Raisin Bran
```

FIGURE 4.3

```
ADCOMP uses these media cost indices:
```

Media Category	1980	1981	1982	1983	1984	1985	1986	1987
Magazines	100	107	115	132	133	142	151	160
Supplements	100	113	137	163	181	201	197	197
Network TV	100	114	117	131	150	153	156	159
Spot TV	100	112	114	131	147	159	178	197
Network Radio	100	109	120	129	140	150	161	172
Outdoor	100	113	139	154	162	178	191	204
Cable TV	100	114	117	131	150	153	156	159

```
Your choice (1=use these, 2=enter others)? 1
```

expenditures is followed by an adjusted expenditure table that has taken the inflation rate into consideration.

Converting expenditures to GRPs

ADCOMP will also allow one to estimate the number of gross rating points (GRPs) that are achieved by each brand. To do so, the user must input the estimated average CPP for each media category used in the given industry. The program provides the following default CPP values (Fig. 4.4).

Calculating the industry totals

The prompt "Enter Class Totals (1=yes, 2=no)" is designed to help work out industry total advertising expenditures. The user can choose either to calculate

FIGURE 4.4

```
Estimate GRPs (1=yes, 2=no)? 1

ADCOMP cost-per-point (CPP):

        Magazines        $  3,604
        Supplements      $  9,027
        Network TV       $  3,226
        Spot TV          $  4,211
        Network Radio    $  1,964
        Outdoor          $  1,138
        Cable TV         $  2,159

Your choice (1=use these, 2=input others)? 1
```

the totals, then input them, or have ADCOMP compute them. Users may wish to analyze only a few of the major brands in a product category. In such an instance, it would be correct to input the industry totals as they appear in LNA, or some other reasonable totals that are estimated. To allow ADCOMP to compute industry totals based on just a few brands could seriously overstate share of voice (SOV) for the included brands, while understating industry total expenditures and GRPs. Figure 4.5 provides an example of market totals entered into the microcomputer.

Entering brand (and product class) totals for the first year

This particular section also is important. The numbers used here will be the basis for comparison for all of the results. Therefore, the user should check and recheck all figures for accuracy. After each is entered, one presses the carriage return key <CR>. Commas should not be used in an entry. And as each entry is read in $(000)s, if the total is 18,000,000, for example, then it is entered as 18000. The last three zeros will be included automatically. The categories MUST be entered in the following order: seven-media total, magazines, newspaper supplements, network TV, spot TV, network radio, outdoor, and cable. If any category has no expenditure, one enters a zero (or presses <CR>) for that medium. The brand totals are derived from LNA expenditure data for 1985, or for whatever first year is chosen. Each brand is located under the appropriate product class, in this case class F122. Then, all lines that have anything to do with that *brand*, not company, are summed. For example, media expenditures for Post 40% Bran Flakes and Post 40% Bran Flakes Sweepstakes are added together since they belong to the same brand. Again, one must make sure that the calculations are correct. A quick check can be made by adding up the individual media categories and making sure they equal the seven-media total. Figure 4.5 shows how the entries would look for Kellogg's All-Bran and the bran cereal market.

Segment totals can be obtained either from the LNA product category totals, which often include too many segments for relevant analysis, or by totalling the

FIGURE 4.5

Enter 1986 spending in 000s, NO COMMAS, press <RETURN> after each medium.

7-Media Total	Magazns	N Paper Supplmt	Network TV	Spot TV	Network Radio	Outdoor	Catv TV	1=OK 2=no
All-Bran								
? 14923.9	? 0	? 0	? 13631.7?	1176.1	? 0	? 0	? 116.1	? 1
Fruit and Fibre								
? 15344.4	? 3234.8	? 0	? 10448	? 1219.8	? 0	? 0	? 441.8	? 1
40% Bran								
? 7754.9	? 0	? 0	? 6905.8	? 769.5	? 0	? 0	? 79.6	? 1
Fruitful Bran								
? 1045	? 0	? 0	? 895.2	? 148.4	? 0	? 0	? 1.4	? 1
Raisin Bran								
? 19229.5	? 0	? 0	? 15357.0?	1631.3	? 0	? 0	? 241.2	? 1
Post Raisin Bran								
? 15408.5	? 1140.6	? 0	? 11667.7?	1715.4	? 0	? 0	? 884.8	? 1
Class Total								
? 71706.2	? 4375.4	? 0	? 58905.4?	6660.5	? 0	? 0	? 1764.9	? 1

expenditures of brands that have been selected as competitors. In the example, each media category is totaled for all six brands. Once again, one should check the results before they are entered. All seven categories for the industry should add up to the seven-media total for that industry. If they don't, then there is a mistake. The computer program is not designed to find this, so one should always check and recheck the figures.

ADCOMP will also ask if the user wishes to make any changes (1=OK, 2=no). If there is an error, the program will allow one to back up and correct it.

Second year product class and brand totals

Next, ADCOMP will ask the user to repeat the process for the second year of the analysis. It will continue until all years of data have been entered. After this, the computer will start calculating five basic tables, some of which are repeated, if desired, to illustrate the influence of media cost inflation.

ADVERTISING EXPENDITURE TABLE

Here one can see where the competitors are spending their money. The Class Total lines are of particular importance because they show where all brands combined are putting their expenditures. Trends can also be seen, helping planners to decide how to allocate the advertising appropriation.

One can move on to view the next table by pressing any key. However, the

FIGURE 4.6

Advertising Expenditures

Brand/ Year	7-Media Total	Magazns	N Paper Supplmt	Network TV	Spot TV	Network Radio	Outdoor	Cable TV
All-Bran								
85	11216.6	0.0	0.0	10195.6	950.2	0.0	0.0	70.8
86	14923.9	0.0	0.0	13631.7	1176.1	0.0	0.0	116.1
Fruit and Fibre								
85	17154.1	2985.0	190.2	10913.4	2330.9	0.0	0.0	734.6
86	15344.4	3234.8	0.0	10448.0	1219.8	0.0	0.0	441.8
40% Bran								
85	7106.6	0.0	0.0	6279.8	777.5	0.0	0.0	49.3
86	7754.9	0.0	0.0	6905.8	769.5	0.0	0.0	79.6
Fruitful Bran								
85	7243.9	0.0	0.0	6298.4	889.9	0.0	0.0	55.7
86	1045.0	0.0	0.0	895.2	148.4	0.0	0.0	1.4
Raisin Bran								
85	16016.9	0.0	0.0	13907.7	1769.7	0.0	0.0	339.5
86	19229.5	0.0	0.0	15357.0	1631.3	0.0	0.0	241.2
Post Raisin Bran								
85	11911.5	417.7	0.0	8909.7	1576.4	0.0	0.0	1007.7
86	15408.5	1140.6	0.0	11667.7	1715.4	0.0	0.0	884.8
Class Total								
85	70649.6	3402.7	190.2	56504.6	8294.5	0.0	0.0	2257.6
86	71706.2	4375.4	0.0	58905.4	6660.5	0.0	0.0	1764.9

"Press any key to continue" prompt will not be displayed on the screen so as not to clutter the output tables.

ADVERTISING EXPENDITURES ADJUSTED FOR INFLATION

This table shows the expenditures in 1980 dollars, taking into account the inflation rate. Figure 4.7 thus presents Figure 4.6 in constant dollars.

ADVERTISING MEDIA MIX TABLE

The purpose of Figure 4.8 is to see how strong the competitors are across media categories, removing differences in brand advertising scale. If they are dominant in a certain medium, then one can match them, become superior, or switch into and so dominate other media categories. This table will also give an invaluable idea of industry trends.

INFLATION-ADJUSTED MEDIA MIX

Now the media mix is shown after accounting for the effects of inflation. Figure 4.9 shows Figure 4.8 in constant 1980 dollars.

SHARE-OF-VOICE TABLE

Maximizing share-of-voice (SOV) is often a goal of major brands. The SOV table indicates who has how much share and in which medium. Once this is

FIGURE 4.7

Advertising Expenditures (1980 Dollars)

Brand/ Year	7-Media Total	Magazns	N Paper Supplmt	Network TV	Spot TV	Network Radio	Outdoor	Cable TV
All-Bran								
85	7307.7	0.0	0.0	6663.8	597.6	0.0	0.0	46.3
86	9473.4	0.0	0.0	8738.3	660.7	0.0	0.0	74.4
Fruit and Fibre								
85	11275.8	2102.1	94.6	7132.9	1466.0	0.0	0.0	480.1
86	9808.2	2142.3	0.0	6697.4	685.3	0.0	0.0	283.2
40% Bran								
85	4625.7	0.0	0.0	4104.4	489.0	0.0	0.0	32.2
86	4910.1	0.0	0.0	4426.8	432.3	0.0	0.0	51.0
Fruitful Bran								
85	4712.7	0.0	0.0	4116.6	559.7	0.0	0.0	36.4
86	658.1	0.0	0.0	573.8	83.4	0.0	0.0	0.9
Raisin Bran								
85	10424.9	0.0	0.0	9090.0	1113.0	0.0	0.0	221.9
86	10915.3	0.0	0.0	9844.2	916.5	0.0	0.0	154.6
Post Raisin Bran								
85	7767.6	294.2	0.0	5823.3	991.4	0.0	0.0	658.6
86	9765.5	755.4	0.0	7479.3	963.7	0.0	0.0	567.2
Class Total								
85	46114.2	2396.3	94.6	36931.1	5216.7	0.0	0.0	1475.6
86	45530.7	2897.6	0.0	37759.9	3741.9	0.0	0.0	1131.3

FIGURE 4.8

Brand/ Year	7-Media Total	Magazns	N Paper Supplmt	Advertising Media Mix Network TV	Spot TV	Network Radio	Outdoor	Cable TV
All-Bran								
85	100.0%	0.0%	0.0%	90.9%	8.5%	0.0%	0.0%	0.6%
86	100.0%	0.0%	0.0%	91.3%	7.9%	0.0%	0.0%	0.8%
Fruit and Fibre								
85	100.0%	17.4%	1.1%	63.6%	13.6%	0.0%	0.0%	4.3%
86	100.0%	21.1%	0.0%	68.1%	7.9%	0.0%	0.0%	2.9%
40% Bran								
85	100.0%	0.0%	0.0%	88.4%	10.9%	0.0%	0.0%	0.7%
86	100.0%	0.0%	0.0%	89.1%	9.9%	0.0%	0.0%	1.0%
Fruitful Bran								
85	100.0%	0.0%	0.0%	86.9%	12.3%	0.0%	0.0%	0.8%
86	100.0%	0.0%	0.0%	85.7%	14.2%	0.0%	0.0%	0.1%
Raisin Bran								
85	100.0%	0.0%	0.0%	86.8%	11.0%	0.0%	0.0%	2.1%
86	100.0%	0.0%	0.0%	79.9%	8.5%	0.0%	0.0%	1.3%
Post Raisin Bran								
85	100.0%	3.5%	0.0%	74.8%	13.2%	0.0%	0.0%	8.5%
86	100.0%	7.4%	0.0%	75.7%	11.1%	0.0%	0.0%	5.7%
Class Total								
85	100.0%	4.8%	0.3%	80.0%	11.7%	0.0%	0.0%	3.2%
86	100.0%	6.1%	0.0%	82.1%	9.3%	0.0%	0.0%	2.5%

FIGURE 4.9

Brand/ Year	7-Media Total	Magazns	N Paper Supplmt	Media Mix (1980 Dollars) Network TV	Spot TV	Network Radio	Outdoor	Cable TV
All-Bran								
85	100.0%	0.0%	0.0%	91.2%	8.2%	0.0%	0.0%	0.6%
86	100.0%	0.0%	0.0%	92.2%	7.0%	0.0%	0.0%	0.8%
Fruit and Fibre								
85	100.0%	18.6%	0.8%	63.3%	13.0%	0.0%	0.0%	4.3%
86	100.0%	21.8%	0.0%	68.3%	7.0%	0.0%	0.0%	2.9%
40% Bran								
85	100.0%	0.0%	0.0%	88.7%	10.6%	0.0%	0.0%	0.7%
86	100.0%	0.0%	0.0%	90.2%	8.8%	0.0%	0.0%	1.0%
Fruitful Bran								
85	100.0%	0.0%	0.0%	87.4%	11.9%	0.0%	0.0%	0.8%
86	100.0%	0.0%	0.0%	87.2%	12.7%	0.0%	0.0%	0.1%
Raisin Bran								
85	100.0%	0.0%	0.0%	87.2%	10.7%	0.0%	0.0%	2.1%
86	100.0%	0.0%	0.0%	90.2%	8.4%	0.0%	0.0%	1.4%
Post Raisin Bran								
85	100.0%	3.8%	0.0%	75.0%	12.8%	0.0%	0.0%	8.5%
86	100.0%	7.7%	0.0%	76.6%	9.9%	0.0%	0.0%	5.8%
Class Total								
85	100.0%	5.2%	0.2%	80.1%	11.3%	0.0%	0.0%	3.2%
86	100.0%	6.4%	0.0%	82.9%	8.2%	0.0%	0.0%	2.5%

known, one can see where to increase or decrease expenditures for maximum effect. Industry trends also can be spotted. See Figure 4.10.

GROSS RATING POINT TABLE

The GRP table provides excellent guidance as to the media weight that rivals have achieved. GRP data can be used for reach and frequency analysis and assist in working out monthly or quarterly media schedules in terms of the number of vehicles and insertions necessary to compete. Figure 4.11 includes an example of a GRP table for the Kellogg's All-Bran case.

ADVERTISING EXPENDITURE ANNUAL CHANGES TABLE

Users can see how much money, as a percent change over the previous year, each brand is allocating to the different media categories (Fig. 4.12). Obviously, by following industry trends, one can know where to advertise in order to compete. Shifts in advertising from year to year should be highlighted to optimize the brand's media mix.

ANNUAL CHANGES ADJUSTED FOR INFLATION

Inflation can also be taken into consideration when analyzing annual changes. The table is displayed in Figure 4.13, showing how brands have shifted their expenditures in real terms, or in terms of constant 1980 dollars.

FIGURE 4.10

Brand/ Year	7-Media Total	Magazns	N Paper Supplmt	Network TV	Spot TV	Network Radio	Outdoor	Cable TV
All-Bran
85	15.9%	0.0%	0.0%	18.0%	11.5%	0.0%	0.0%	3.1%
86	20.8%	0.0%	0.0%	23.1%	17.7%	0.0%	0.0%	6.6%
Fruit and Fibre
85	24.3%	87.7%	100.0%	19.3%	28.1%	0.0%	0.0%	32.5%
86	21.4%	73.9%	0.0%	17.7%	18.3%	0.0%	0.0%	25.0%
40% Bran
85	10.1%	0.0%	0.0%	11.1%	9.4%	0.0%	0.0%	2.2%
86	10.8%	0.0%	0.0%	11.7%	11.6%	0.0%	0.0%	4.5%
Fruitful Bran
85	10.3%	0.0%	0.0%	11.1%	10.7%	0.0%	0.0%	2.5%
86	1.5%	0.0%	0.0%	1.5%	2.2%	0.0%	0.0%	0.1%
Raisin Bran
85	22.7%	0.0%	0.0%	24.6%	21.3%	0.0%	0.0%	15.0%
86	26.8%	0.0%	0.0%	26.1%	24.5%	0.0%	0.0%	13.7%
Post Raisin Bran
85	16.9%	12.3%	0.0%	15.8%	19.0%	0.0%	0.0%	44.6%
86	21.5%	26.1%	0.0%	19.8%	25.8%	0.0%	0.0%	50.1%
Class Total
85	100.0%	100.0%	100.0%	100.0%	100.0%	0.0%	0.0%	100.0%
86	100.0%	100.0%	0.0%	100.0%	100.0%	0.0%	0.0%	100.0%

FIGURE 4.11

Brand/ Year	7-Media Total	Magazns	N Paper Supplmt	Network TV	Spot TV	Network Radio	Outdoor	Cable TV
All-Bran								
85	3418.9%	0.0%	0.0%	3160.4%	225.6%	0.0%	0.0%	32.8%
86	4558.6%	0.0%	0.0%	4225.6%	279.3%	0.0%	0.0%	53.8%
Fruit and Fibre								
85	5126.0%	828.2%	21.1%	3383.0%	553.5%	0.0%	0.0%	340.3%
86	4630.5%	897.6%	0.0%	3238.7%	289.7%	0.0%	0.0%	204.6%
40% Bran								
85	2154.1%	0.0%	0.0%	1946.6%	184.6%	0.0%	0.0%	22.8%
86	2360.3%	0.0%	0.0%	2140.7%	182.7%	0.0%	0.0%	36.9%
Fruitful Bran								
85	2189.5%	0.0%	0.0%	1952.4%	211.3%	0.0%	0.0%	25.8%
86	313.4%	0.0%	0.0%	277.5%	35.2%	0.0%	0.0%	0.6%
Raisin Bran								
85	4888.6%	0.0%	0.0%	4311.1%	420.3%	0.0%	0.0%	157.2%
86	5259.5%	0.0%	0.0%	4760.4%	387.4%	0.0%	0.0%	111.7%
Post Raisin Bran								
85	3718.8%	115.9%	0.0%	2761.8%	374.4%	0.0%	0.0%	466.7%
86	4750.4%	316.5%	0.0%	3616.8%	407.4%	0.0%	0.0%	409.8%
Class Total								
85	21496.0%	944.1%	21.1%	17515.4%	1969.7%	0.0%	0.0%	1045.7%
86	21872.8%	1214.0%	0.0%	18259.6%	1581.7%	0.0%	0.0%	817.5%

Gross Rating Points

FIGURE 4.12

Brand/ Year	7-Media Total	Magazns	N Paper Supplmt	Network TV	Spot TV	Network Radio	Outdoor	Cable TV
All-Bran								
86	33.1%	0.0%	0.0%	33.7%	23.8%	0.0%	0.0%	64.0%
Fruit and Fibre								
86	-10.5%	8.4%	-100.0%	-4.3%	-47.7%	0.0%	0.0%	-39.9%
40% Bran								
86	9.1%	0.0%	0.0%	10.0%	-1.0%	0.0%	0.0%	61.5%
Fruitful Bran								
86	-85.6%	0.0%	0.0%	-85.8%	-83.3%	0.0%	0.0%	-97.5%
Raisin Bran								
86	20.1%	0.0%	0.0%	10.4%	-7.8%	0.0%	0.0%	-29.0%
Post Raisin Bran								
86	29.4%	173.1%	0.0%	31.0%	8.8%	0.0%	0.0%	-12.2%
Class Total								
86	1.5%	28.6%	-100.0%	4.2%	-19.7%	0.0%	0.0%	-21.8%

Advertising Expenditures Annual Changes

FIGURE 4.13

Brand/ Year	7-Media Total	Magazns	N Paper Supplmt	Network TV	Spot TV	Network Radio	Outdoor	Cable TV
Advertising Expenditures Annual Changes (1980 Dollars)								
All-Bran								
86	29.6%	0.0%	0.0%	31.1%	10.6%	0.0%	0.0%	60.8%
Fruit and Fibre								
86	-13.0%	1.9%	-100.0%	-6.1%	-53.3%	0.0%	0.0%	-41.0%
40% Bran								
86	6.1%	0.0%	0.0%	7.9%	-11.6%	0.0%	0.0%	58.4%
Fruitful Bran								
86	-86.0%	0.0%	0.0%	-86.1%	-85.1%	0.0%	0.0%	-97.5%
Raisin Bran								
86	4.7%	0.0%	0.0%	8.3%	-17.7%	0.0%	0.0%	-30.3%
Post Raisin Bran								
86	25.7%	156.8%	0.0%	28.4%	-2.8%	0.0%	0.0%	-13.9%
Class Total								
86	-1.3%	20.9%	-100.0%	2.2%	-28.3%	0.0%	0.0%	-23.3%

WHAT NEXT?

All that remains is to decide which of the following options to use:

1. Review tables on screen
2. Create new tables
3. Modify tables
4. Save raw data on disk file
5. Save tables on disk file
6. Print tables
7. Return to DOS
8. Stop, and return to DOS

CONCLUSION

The importance of developing a thorough situation analysis cannot be overstated. The material provided in this chapter attempts to provide some guidelines for developing such an analysis. It is merely a starting point, however, since practical situations often are complex. Thus, you should continually build upon this base and adapt the material given here to suit each unique problem or opportunity encountered.

ENDNOTES

1. Jack M. Klues, "University of Illinois Presentation: Use of Competitive Ad Expenditures in Media/Marketing Strategy," Leo Burnett U.S.A., April 26, 1985.

2. James O. Peckham, "Can We Relate Advertising Dollars to Market Share Objectives?" in *How Much to Spend for Advertising?*, edited by Malcolm A. McNiven (New York: Association of National Advertisers, 1969), pp. 23-30.

ADDITIONAL READING

Aaker, David A. and John G. Myers, *Advertising Management* (Englewood Cliffs: Prentice-Hall, Inc., 1987).

Leckenby, John D. and Nugent Wedding, *Advertising Management: Criteria, Analysis and Decision Making* (Columbus: Grid Publishing Inc., 1982).

Nylen, David W., *Advertising: Planning, Implementation & Control*, 3rd Ed. (Cincinnati: South-Western Publishing Co., 1986).

Ray, Michael L., *Advertising and Communication Management* (Englewood Cliffs: Prentice-Hall, Inc., 1982).

CHAPTER FIVE

Marketing, Advertising, Media Goals, and Budgets

Once the competitive marketing situation facing the product has been analyzed, the next logical step in the media planning process is to develop measurable media goals which will direct the overall media plans. They are, of course, developed as a complement to business, marketing, and advertising goals. While marketing objectives deal with sales and the market share of the product, the advertising objectives are concerned with the communication effects that are required to help achieve marketing goals. Finally, media objectives consider the effective reach of the media plan needed to achieve advertising goals.

The objective of *business* activity at its most basic level is to make a profit, strategically mixing together elements of production, finance, and marketing. *Marketing* activity aims to move goods and/or services from the point of production to the point of consumption or use. Marketing goals usually are stated in terms of sales and market share. To accomplish these objectives, marketers strategically combine particular product characteristics at an optimum price, using the right kind of distribution channels and promotional techniques. This effort is directed at a target market that research has shown desires this particular synthesis of marketing elements.

The promotion mix, as an element of the marketing mix, can consist of personal selling, sales promotion, public relations, publicity, and advertising. *Advertising* is, therefore, only one element in promotion; it can play a relatively minor role or it can completely dominate, depending on the nature of the product and on the consumer and trade needs for information. When the role of advertising is important to the success of the brand, its objective is to facilitate certain communication effects. These effects generally focus on moving the consumer from a point of complete lack of information about a brand, to awareness of particular product characteristics, for example, to taking some sort of action, such as clipping a coupon. To achieve advertising goals, planners strategically mix creative, media and budget elements that are in harmony with the information needs of consumers and the cost constraints of the firm.

One should notice that sales and market share goals are not the complete responsibility of advertising; price, distribution, and other promotional elements are also contributors. As a practical matter, however, it often happens in industry that when sales for a brand are up, the advertising personnel associated with the brand will tout the direct effects of advertising. When sales are down the same people are likely to remember that the role of advertising is limited to communication effects; research will usually show that advertising is doing its job, but that other elements of the marketing mix or competitive environment are conspiring to diminish sales. In either situation, it must be remembered that the objective of advertising is *to communicate in order to facilitate sales or market share goals*.

Media objectives are best stated in terms of effective reach of the target market or audience. To accomplish advertising communication goals, media planners strategically mix together media vehicles that are consistent with the brand image and that are used heavily by the target market or audience.

All business, marketing, advertising, and media activities take place in an uncontrollable environment that includes the similar activities of competitors, the state of the economy, regulatory factors and other cultural and sociological elements and trends. It is important that these also be taken into account, by conducting a thorough situation analysis, if brand objectives and strategies are to work properly.

The major premise of this chapter is that planners can develop measurable marketing, advertising, and media objectives and advertising appropriations and budgets that are integrated tightly and linked to other elements of the marketing situation. Because there are numerous dynamic marketing factors and relations to be taken into account, a microcomputer program called ADGOAL has been developed to show how they can be considered simultaneously. The theoretical basis for the model will be outlined according to marketing, advertising, media planning and budgeting areas, followed by ADGOAL examples based on hypothetical data. Given the complexity of the proposed framework, it would be useful to consider Figure 5.1 which contains the essential elements to be analyzed and integrated.

This chapter elaborates on each of the items contained in Figure 5.1. These elements are chosen to advance a general framework that can be applied in many marketing circumstances, particularly those facing frequently purchased, heavily advertised brands. Numerous other possibilities exist, of course, and will also be noted. You can use the framework and adapt it to suit your unique circumstances. The goal is to communicate effectively the essential framework, while stimulating the reader to make further connections. Each of the areas discussed are the main lines of a vast literature. The focus will therefore be multifaceted and integrative.

MARKETING GOALS

Marketing objectives should specify the time period over which sales to a particular target are to be achieved, along with supporting evidence and reasoning. To write marketing objectives that are consistent in terms of both projected sales and projected market share, one begins by examining industry and brand annual *unit* sales trends as a percent change over previous years to get a reasonable benchmark. Why unit sales? Unit sales reflect real growth, whereas dollar sales must be adjusted for product category inflation.

First, one considers product category or segment growth. High real category growth suggests that brand sales growth is possible without necessarily carving

FIGURE 5.1   Framework for Developing Integrated Marketing, Advertising and Media Goals and Advertising Budgets

Marketing Factors
> Macro time-frame unit sales goal (e.g., annual unit sales)
> Appropriate micro time-frame (such as, weekly, monthly, or quarterly periods)
> Projected unit sales per period
> Typical consumer product purchase rate per period
> Target market size

Marketing Goals: percent of target needed to purchase at typical rate per period to achieve unit sales goals

Advertising Factors
> Past communication percentages against the target (e.g., awareness, recall, recognition)
> Ratio of past target communication percentages to past target purchase rates
> Projected communication levels needed per period to support projected target purchase rates
> Advertising carry-over effects

Advertising Goals: percent of the target at each communication level per period required to support unit sales goals

Media Factors
> Message values (such as recall, recognition or noted scores)
> Effective message frequency necessary to achieve each communication level against the target (for instance, 3+, 3-10) per period
> Effective reach, defined as required percent of the target exposed to messages at effective frequency

Media Goals: effective reach necessary to accomplish each communication level per period
Advertising Budget: amount of money required per period to sustain effective reach goals

sales or market share points from competitors. Low real category growth, on the other hand, suggests that brand sales growth must probably come directly from competitors, that is, from increased market share. Therefore, it is important to track segment or product category sales growth trends, and to estimate future sales levels and trends, if marketing objectives are to be realistic.

Now one turns to brand growth. In light of segment or product category sales growth, how fast are brand sales likely to grow over the next fiscal or calendar year? If one is dealing with a new brand, then, as a benchmark, one might assess how rapidly the sales of new brands have grown in that product category in the past. An average sales growth rate can be assigned to the brand based on the previous pattern among similar new brands in the product category. If the brand is more well established, one could average its recent sales growth rates as a starting point for predicting the future rates of growth.

Sales forecasting is a more complex operation than the procedures described here would indicate. There are highly sophisticated techniques and factors that can, and should, be taken into account if forecasts are to be reasonable. Even the best techniques can be misleading. The objective at this point is to acquaint you with what is reasonable in the chosen product category or segment to give a clear understanding of the size of the product category and of the brands within it, and of the typical sales growth rates that the category and brands have experienced in the

FIGURE 5.2 Relationships among Brand and Category Sales Growth and Brand Market Share Growth

Category Sales Growth	Brand Sales Growth		
	High	**Average**	**Low**
High	Constant Share	Drop in Share	Fast Drop in Share
Average	Rise in Share	Constant Share	Drop in Share
Low	Fast Rise in Share	Rise in Share	Constant Share

recent past. This approach will be of help in writing measurable and reasonable goals.

To put all of this together, one can consider the relationships among the growth rates of market share and of category and brand sales. Figure 5.2 illustrates these relationships assuming high, average and low unit sales growth rates for the category and a given brand.

The point of Figure 5.2 is that the growth rates of brand and category sales and of brand market share can be quite different. And in order to write reasonable marketing objectives, these separate growth rates must be taken into consideration.

Here is an example. Assume that Kellogg's All-Bran is projected to achieve sales of 31,862,000 units in 1987 and that it is expected that All-Bran unit sales will grow 20 percent in 1988 over 1987 levels. The bran segment of the cold cereal industry is forecast to account for 557,134,250 units in 1987 and is expected to grow at the rate of 15 percent in 1988. Since All-Bran sales growth should exceed bran segment sales growth, it is clear that, if these sales projections are accurate, All-Bran market share will increase in 1988 over the 1987 figure. What are All-Bran's projected 1987 and 1988 market shares and what is the projected rate of growth of market share?

Market share, of course, is simply brand sales divided by industry or segment sales. In 1987, All-Bran's market share is projected to be 5.7 percent (31,862,000/557,134,250 = .057). In order to determine the 1988 market share for All-Bran, it is necessary to estimate 1988 All-Bran and segment unit sales. If 1.00 is added to the growth rates of All-Bran and the segment, this gives 1.20 for All-Bran and 1.15 for the segment. These ratios indicate that 1988 unit sales for All-Bran and the segment will be 1.2 and 1.15 times what they were respectively, in 1987. All-Bran's 1988 sales, then, are estimated to be 38,234,400 units ((1.2)(31,862,000) = 38,234,400). Likewise, 1988 category sales are estimated to be 640,704,390 units ((1.15)(557,134,250) = 640,704,390). The All-Bran 1988 market share is thus projected to be 6.0 percent (38,234,400/640,704,390 = .05967).

What is the 1987-88 rate of growth of market share for the brand? Using Equation 4-4, the percentage comes out to be 5.3 percent ((6.0-5.7)/5.7 = .0526)). This may seem low at first, but Figure 5.2 showed that when there are high brand and segment unit sales growth rates, market share growth will be relatively low.

The next step is to state concisely realistic unit sales and market share goals for the brand that are to be achieved within a specified time period. Using the Kellogg's All-Bran case as an example leads to the following measurable marketing objectives.

> Within calendar year 1988, Kellogg's All-Bran should achieve a market share of 6.0% of the bran segment of the cold breakfast cereal market through marketing emphasis on female homemakers who use cold breakfast cereals. This should result in unit sales of 38,234,400 and sales revenue of $49,704,720 at an average manufacturer's price of $1.30 per unit.

Of course, in a marketing, advertising, or media plan, the rationale for these objectives should be restated briefly. The reasoning leading to the marketing goal statement provided above is an example of the kind of justification one might wish to provide.

Since communication goals are typically stated with reference to a time-frame of less than one year,[1] such as monthly recall or awareness objectives, it is useful to consider marketing goals in the same way. This allows planners to link the two relatively directly. A brand's own monthly sales records will prove useful. In addition, a typical brand often has excellent monthly sales data through Selling Areas Marketing, Inc. (SAMI) or the A.C. Nielsen Food and Drug Index. This information, along with industry and brand unit sales trends and growth rates, can be used to forecast future sales patterns. Marketers should also have clear target market definitions in terms of their sizes and various demographic, geographic, and socio-economic factors.

It would be useful, therefore, for marketers to extend their monthly sales forecasts one step by expressing them in relation to target market size, taking into account the typical consumer monthly purchase rate. Consumer purchase rates are usually available from Simmons Market Research Bureau (SMRB) or Mediamark Research, Inc. (MRI). Using these data, monthly sales goals can be simply expressed as follows.

$$PR_t = SU_t \,/\, CPR_t \,/\, TGTSIZE \qquad\qquad (5\text{-}1)$$

where:

t	= appropriate time frame (such as weekly or monthly),
PR	= percent of target market purchasing average unit sales per period t,
SU	= sales units per period t,
CPR	= average consumer purchase rate per period t,
TGTSIZE	= target market size.

As an example, one may assume here a brand has average monthly sales of 1,000,000 units, and that the average monthly consumer purchase rate is two units. This means that the brand must be used at the typical rate by 500,000 consumers. With a target market of 10,000,000 consumers, five percent of the target must purchase the brand at the average rate. Clearly, to support monthly unit sales goals, the brand must achieve communication levels higher than five percent of the target. The question is, which communication effects are required, and just how much higher must they be?

ADVERTISING GOALS

Like marketing goals, advertising goals should be measurable. Unlike the former, however, these are effects attributable directly to exposure to advertising. In developing a rationale for advertising objectives, the following steps can be taken.

1. State the advertising problem or opportunity, (for example, a brief recap of relevant aspects of the marketing and advertising situation),
2. Describe who and how many target persons are to be affected, (e.g., a percentage of the target audience),
3. State the desired and measurable communication effects. These should include identification of both *general* and *specific* effects.
   a. The general effect is based on the hierarchy of communication effects that is presumed to operate for the majority of consumers in the target market. Borrowing from the learning hierarchy,[2] for example, general communication effects might include awareness, knowledge, liking, preference, conviction and purchase. Numerous other effects might be used as well.
   b. The specific communication effect refers to the actual message content in strategic terms. What is it that target members should be aware or knowledgeable of, for instance?
4. Estimate the time necessary to accomplish communication goals, (e.g., each month of the fiscal or calendar year).
5. Provide evidence and reasoning supporting each objective.

There is considerable theoretical and empirical work supporting the notion of communication hierarchies and goals. These include, for example, DAGMAR, high and low involvement hierarchies, and dissonance attribution models.[3] These frameworks typically assume that advertising influences one or more intervening variables, which facilitate some desired behavior. Intervening variables can include brand awareness, knowledge of brand attributes, knowledge of new applications, knowledge about the company, associating the brand with user types, brand attitude, associating feelings with the brand, among others. Behavior objectives can include, for example, trial purchase, loyalty, increased usage, and sales leads.

The choice as to which intervening and behavior variables should be the focus of advertising is beyond the scope of this chapter. Such decisions depend, of course, on the nature of the product category, competition, brand characteristics, consumer product shopping and mass media habits, and so on. Rather, the focus here will be on procedures to follow once the appropriate intervening and behavior variables have been selected as the objective of advertising. It is argued that the analytical procedures will be similar, regardless of the communication philosophy guiding management.

As a practical matter, advertisers often focus attention on a few broad communication goals in order to enhance the marketing climate facing a brand. These include advertising recall; awareness, or exposure, for example.[4] Advertisers often monitor these communication factors against their targets on a quarterly, semi-annual, or annual basis. For example, the brand described above may have had a recent quarterly brand awareness of 40 percent of its target. If previous sales rates against the target (PR) were four percent per month, on average, and assuming that the quarterly brand correct recall level of 40 percent is typical of all three months of the quarter, then the brand's past performance yields a ten-to-one (40 percent/4 percent) brand recall-to-purchase ratio. Ratios like these can be used to estimate minimum communication levels required to support future sales growth.

In the example, if the brand requires five percent of its target to purchase an average of two units per month, then it would need 50 percent correct brand recall to support that level of sales. This is determined by multiplying the sales goal expressed as a percent of the target (5 percent), by the brand's historical recall-to-purchase ratio (10). Assuming that other elements of the marketing mix are satisfactory, and that environmental and competitive activities are approximately typical of the past, then sales objectives should be achievable.

In deciding on the appropriate general communication effects to focus on during the advertising campaign, one would normally want to identify weaknesses in the hierarchy. These would be evident as communication effects that have relatively low percentages. In the case of new brands, however, the desired effects are usually quite general; often the focus is on awareness or knowledge of specific product attributes, for example. In the case of established brands, broad goals may also be appropriate if the brand is being reintroduced or repositioned, for instance.

Advertising has also been shown to have cumulative effects, meaning that its impact lingers from one period to another.[5] A "typical" monthly advertising carry-over or retention rate might be somewhere around 36 percent, meaning that just over one third of previous monthly advertising influence continues to exist among target members in subsequent months. This will reduce the amount of additional advertising a brand would have to provide each month to maintain its sales goals. Consequently, using the previous example, if the brand were to maintain the same level of communication against the target two months in a row (for example, 50 percent correct recall), the second month would require additional advertising recall impact equal to only 32 percent (that is, $32\% = 50\% - (36\%)(50\%)$). This relation can be expressed in general terms using Equation 5-2.

$$AC_t = TC_t - (CO)(TC_{t-1})$$ (5-2)

where:

t = appropriate time frame (such as weekly, monthly or quarterly period),

AC = additional communication impact required in period t to support marketing goals (e.g., 32 percent correct recall),

TC = total communication impact required to support marketing goals in period t (such as 50 percent correct recall),

CO = advertising carry-over or retention rate (for instance, 36 percent).

In situations where the advertising carry-over rate is unknown, it is probably safer to assume that it is zero, so that under-advertising will not occur.

Once the appropriate general and specific communication effects are settled, and the general communication effect expressed as a percentage of the target audience, the advertising goal statement can be written. Using the reasoning and data generated in the Kellogg's All-Bran example, the following advertising goal is offered.

Each month of calendar year 1988, Kellogg's All-Bran advertising will attempt to make 50% of all U.S. female homemakers who use cold breakfast cereals aware that All-Bran has more fiber content than any other popular bran cereal.

This advertising goal statement contains all of the necessary elements required to make it operational, including a time frame and general and specific communication effects expressed as a percentage of the target audience.

MEDIA GOALS

Media objectives usually involve desired levels of reach, frequency and continuity against the selected target audience. These are often combined in one statement concerning desired monthly or quarterly levels of effective reach.

Broad or cognitive advertising communication goals, such as attention, awareness, and knowledge, usually require high levels of reach. On the other hand, attitudinal and behavioral goals, such as liking, preference, conviction, and trial, usually require high levels of frequency.

High reach goals demand media strategies that achieve low duplication within and between vehicles and media categories. This results in the broad use of media categories, subcategories, and vehicles. High frequency goals, in contrast, need media strategies that achieve high duplication within and between vehicles and media categories, leading to a media strategy that focuses on the continuous use of a fixed group of media categories, subcategories, and vehicles.

In writing a media goal statement, one should consider the following elements.

1. Target audience definition. This is usually the same as the target audience selected for marketing objectives.
2. Creative requirements (e.g., size of ads, use of color and bleed, length of commercials, editorial environment).
3. Effective reach goals including the percentage of the target audience to be exposed "n" or more times.
4. Timing patterns (that is, macro and micro schedules).
5. Geographic coverage (for instance, local markets, SMSAs, ADIs, DMAs, regions, national).
6. Special marketing and advertising problems (such as the use of toll-free telephone numbers or coupons).
7. Reasoning and evidence supporting each objective.

Once planners know which communication effects and their magnitudes are necessary to support unit sales goals per period, they must decide what levels of message frequency are needed to maintain those levels among consumers. Recent survey research has shown that most advertisers opt for three or more exposures to vehicles or messages. Many are careful to choose other frequency levels (such as 4+, 3-10) to suit circumstances and objectives, and to require estimates of message frequency, not just vehicle frequency.[6]

To evaluate schedules based on message frequency, planners must have some quantitative appraisal of the communication values of the advertisements in the campaign. Depending on the communication goals, such values can be obtained from Starch, Burke, Gallup and Robinson, BehaviorScan, and AdTel, among others. The survey just mentioned showed that media planners use such tools, leading to the following average weights for reducing the size of vehicle audiences.

Media Category	Weight
Newspapers	35.0%
Network TV	
Daytime	54.7
Prime time	80.0
Spot TV	
Daytime	50.0
Prime time	71.8
Cable TV	63.2
Magazines	52.5
Network radio	40.3
Spot radio	37.8
Outdoor posters	46.6

These weights are listed here only to provide a view of the severity with which approximately one third of media directors discount the audiences of major media categories. Such weights are applied to vehicle audience measures to estimate advertising audiences for further schedule evaluation.

Once planners have chosen a message-based effective frequency level needed to achieve communication goals, the next step is to define effective reach as the percentage of the target so exposed. Thus, the effective reach goal, as defined, should be set equal to the required communication levels.

Returning to the example, one can assume that 50 percent correct recall of advertising content will support desired sales levels, that three or more exposures to ads per period are sufficient for the typical consumer, and that the typical advertisement in the campaign has a recall value of 45 percent. Then the brand should fashion a schedule each period that will effectively reach 50 percent of its target, exposing them three or more times to the advertisements in the message pool.

You will recall that for the Kellogg's All-Bran example, the *monthly* advertising goal was to make 50 percent of all female homemakers who use cold breakfast cereals aware that All-Bran has more fiber content than any other popular bran cereal. The connection between the advertising goal statement and the media goal statement is immediately obvious. For example, it is clear that in media terms at least 50 percent of the target must be *reached* at least once per month in order to accomplish the advertising goal. Furthermore, 50 percent of the target must become aware of All-Bran's principal selling point.

How many impressions will it take, on average, for target members to get that message? Pretesting might provide some clues, but often such research evidence is not readily available and management must rely on previous experience and judgment. Since this is a broad objective with relatively simple message content, one can assume that it will take at least three advertising exposures for the typical target audience member to recall correctly the All-Bran selling point. Therefore, the media goal statement would include an effective reach objective of 50 percent of the target, where effective reach is defined as the percentage of the target exposed three or more times to advertising messages. You should remember the distinction here between vehicle and advertising exposure, with the former sometimes known as opportunities-to-see. This reasoning leads to the following measurable media objective statement.

Each month of calendar year 1988, Kellogg's All-Bran advertising media schedule will attempt to effectively reach (3+) 50% of all U.S. female homemakers who use cold breakfast cereals. Emphasis will be placed on high quality print and broadcast vehicles that are consistent with All-Bran's top-of-the-line image.

This simple goal statement has addressed all of the criteria mentioned previously. And it makes it clear what media planners and buyers must accomplish with their advertising media plan.

THE ADVERTISING BUDGET

The media goal statement also has very important implications for the size of the advertising appropriation. In one or two hours media planners could develop and evaluate a media plan that achieves this media objective. In doing so, however, the plan is likely to exceed the initial advertising appropriation, particularly if weights are used to discount the size of the media vehicle audiences. Under these circumstances, the media plan becomes an excellent document for justifying an increased advertising appropriation. This is consistent with the task-objective method of budgeting, which has been shown to be used by 80 percent of leading U.S. advertisers.[7] If an increase in funds is not possible, then media planners can show management what impact insufficient funding is likely to have on the achievement of media objectives and, as a result, advertising objectives.

Another useful feature of the procedures described in this chapter concerns allocating the advertising appropriation among time periods. If it is known what effective reach goals are required from one month to the next, then it makes sense to allocate expenditures among months in proportion to the requirements for each one. An example will help clarify this.

Once the advertiser knows what levels of effective reach, as defined, are required each period, the amount of advertising expenditures necessary to achieve them can be determined accurately. This is accomplished by dividing the effective reach points required in a particular micro-period (such as a selected month) by the total required for the macro-period (such as the entire fiscal year). For example, if All-Bran required 50 effective reach points in July and 500 total for the year, management should plan to allocate approximately 10 percent (for instance, 50/500) of its total appropriation to the month of July. The actual allocation may vary, of course, depending on how radically the media mix changes from one month to the next.

The total advertising appropriation for the macro-time frame can be determined in a number of ways. The two most common are the task-objective method and the percent of anticipated sales.[8] Using the task-objective method is straightforward. Each media category will have its own efficiency structure given the nature of the target and schedule. In effect, there will be an effective reach point cost plateau for each schedule. Consequently, planners using this method will be developing budgets based on the cost of effectively reaching the target audience. Any restrictions on the budget below those required to meet effective reach goals can be shown to diminish the likely impact of the campaign. The magnitude of any communication deficit can be seen quite clearly.

The total advertising appropriation can also be determined by multiplying an amount to be spent per sales unit by total anticipated unit sales. The appropriation can be further subdivided in proportion to the level of effective reach required each month. A fixed advertising appropriation, arrived at using other methods, can also be allocated across months using this method.

AN EXAMPLE

ADGOAL is an interactive advertising planning model that quickly and easily operationalizes the framework described here. The program allows planners to concentrate on the overall picture, without getting bogged down in endless details, and to go through various "what if ... ?" scenarios toward an optimum solution. The program will be demonstrated from the hypothetical Kellogg's All-Bran case shown in Table 5.1, which will be used to illustrate the minimum data requirements needed to develop and integrate marketing, advertising, and media goals and the advertising budget. Appendix 5-A contains the complete interaction with the ADGOAL program, showing how it requests and analyzes the information contained in Table 5.1. The most important aspects of this interaction are discussed in the sections that follow.

☐ Summary of Marketing Situation

Using the information provided in Table 5.1, ADGOAL will print out the product's projected marketing situation as shown in Figure 5.3. This figure is based on brand and industry sales and projected growth rates.

Figure 5.4, generated by ADGOAL, shows the percent of total yearly unit sales and the actual unit sales that should occur each month in order to reach yearly unit sales and revenue goals. It also gives the percent of the target that should be

TABLE 5-1 Hypothetical Case: Kellogg's All-Bran Cereal

Macro time frame:	Fiscal year 1988
Micro time frame:	Monthly
Target market:	69,405,000 female homemakers who use cold breakfast cereals
Market sales (1987):	557,134,300
Expected market growth:	15%
Brand sales (1987):	31,862,000
Expected brand growth:	20%
Brand unit price:	$1.30
Consumer purchase rate:	Two units per month

Monthly sales pattern:			
January	4.5%	July	12.0%
February	5.0	August	12.0
March	5.0	September	12.0
April	12.0	October	4.5
May	12.0	November	4.5
June	12.0	December	4.5

Advertising carry-over rate:	36%
Communication levels (1987):	Quarterly correct recall of brand features = 35%
Target purchase rate (1987):	Percent of target purchasing two units per month = 3%
Advertising Budget Method:	Advertising as a percent of anticipated sales revenue = 17.6% (i.e., $0.23 per unit of anticipated sales)

purchasing the product at the specified purchase rate. Figure 5.4 is an example.

☐ Marketing Goals Statement

ADGOAL next generates a marketing goals statement, which combines the data provided from Table 5.1 with additional estimates that the program has calcu-

FIGURE 5.3

```
-----------------------------------------------------------------------
All-Bran Projected Marketing Situation, Fiscal Year 1988
-----------------------------------------------------------------------
                                                            Change
Bran Cereal Unit Sales
      1987                          =      557,134,270
      1988                          =      640,704,380       15.00%

All-Bran Sales Revenue
      1987                          =      $41,420,600
      1988                          =      $49,704,720       20.00%

All-Bran Unit Sales
      1987                          =       31,862,000
      1988                          =       38,234,400       20.00%

All-Bran Unit Sales Share
      1987                          =            5.72%
      1988                          =            5.97%        4.35%

Target Size (Female Homemakers)     =       69,719,000
-----------------------------------------------------------------------
```

FIGURE 5.4

Month	----Monthly Sales---- %	Units	Percent of Target Purchasing 2 Units/Month
JAN	4.5	1,720,548	1.23 %
FEB	5.0	1,911,720	1.37 %
MAR	5.0	1,911,720	1.37 %
APR	12.0	4,588,128	3.29 %
MAY	12.0	4,588,128	3.29 %
JUN	12.0	4,588,128	3.29 %
JUL	12.0	4,588,128	3.29 %
AUG	12.0	4,588,128	3.29 %
SEP	12.0	4,588,128	3.29 %
OCT	4.5	1,720,548	1.23 %
NOV	4.5	1,720,548	1.23 %
DEC	4.5	1,720,548	1.23 %
Total	100.0	38,234,400	

lated. For the Kellogg's All-Bran example, the marketing goals statement looks like Figure 5.5.

You should notice that the goal statement is measurable and 1) contains a time frame within which goals are to be obtained; 2) identifies the brand and product category; 3) specifies internally consistent market share, sales units and sales revenue goals; and 4) identifies the primary target market.

☐ Creating Advertising Goals

Advertising objectives generated by ADGOAL are based on communication-purchase ratios. It is assumed that brand awareness or recall, for example, are conducive to sales when other marketing elements are satisfactory. ADGOAL offers a choice of different communication hierarchies—learning, low-involvement, and custom. Users can opt for the default percentages for the various hierarchies, or provide their own (see Appendix 5-A).

Figure 5.6 provides example output generated by ADGOAL based on the communication-purchase ratio (for example, 11.66 = 35%/3%, see Table 5.1) and the advertising carry-over rate (36 percent).

Using the month of February as an example, ADGOAL estimates that 16 percent of the target must correctly recall brand attributes in order to stimulate 1.4 percent (actually 1.37 percent, according to Figure 5.4) of the target to purchase

FIGURE 5.5

```
Marketing Goals:
----------------
Within fiscal year 1988, All-Bran should achieve
a market share of 5.97% in the Bran Cereal market
through marketing emphasis on Female Homemakers.
This should result in unit sales of 38,234,400 and sales
revenue of $49,704,720 assuming a manufacturer's price of
$1.30 per unit.
```

FIGURE 5.6

Consumer	---- Percent of Target Market To Be Affected Each Month (L =0.36) ---											
Hierarchy	JAN	FEB	MAR	APR	MAY	JUN	JUL	AUG	SEP	OCT	NOV	DEC
Recall	6.1	10.8	10.2	32.6	24.6	24.6	24.6	24.6	24.6	0.6	9.2	9.2
Purchase	1.2	1.4	1.4	3.3	3.3	3.3	3.3	3.3	3.3	1.2	1.2	1.2

two units during the month. From this is subtracted the correct recall carry-over of 5.2 percent from January (that is, $5.2\% = (36\%)(11.66)(1.23\%)$). This leaves a balance of 10.8 percent additional correct recall to be obtained during the month of February.

☐ **Advertising Goal Statement**

ADGOAL uses the information contained in Figure 5.6 to generate an advertising goal statement. The necessary general communication percentages are reproduced for each month, along with the specific communication effects, in strategic terms, that messages will emphasize. Here is an example (Fig. 5.7).

You should notice that the statement specifies the time frame for achieving each advertising goal and also identifies the target audience.

☐ **Creating Media Goals**

ADGOAL will generate media goals, showing the desired effective reach levels for each month against the target audience. The media goals statement for Kellogg's All-Bran appears in Figure 5.8.

Notice that the user must specify the definition of effective reach, based on knowledge of the marketing-communications situation facing the brand and, in particular, of message quality and frequency levels required to communicate with the target audience.

☐ **Summary of Marketing, Advertising, and Media Goals**

The next section of ADGOAL output presents in one figure all three objectives

FIGURE 5.7

```
--------------------------------------------------------------
Advertising Goals:
------------------
Each month of 1988, All-Bran must achieve the following
Recall levels against Female Homemakers who use Bran Cereal.

        JAN =  6.1%      JUL = 24.6%
        FEB = 10.8%      AUG = 24.6%
        MAR = 10.2%      SEP = 24.6%
        APR = 32.6%      OCT =  0.6%
        MAY = 24.6%      NOV =  9.2%
        JUN = 24.6%      DEC =  9.2%

Messages will emphasize that All-Bran
is highest in fiber content.
--------------------------------------------------------------
```

FIGURE 5.8

```
Media Goals:
------------
Each month of 1988, All-Bran must achieve the following
effective reach levels against Female Homemakers
who use Bran Cereal.

        JAN =  6.1%        JUL = 24.6%
        FEB = 10.8%        AUG = 24.6%
        MAR = 10.2%        SEP = 24.6%
        APR = 32.6%        OCT =  0.6%
        MAY = 24.6%        NOV =  9.2%
        JUN = 24.6%        DEC =  9.2%

Effective reach is the percent of the target audience
exposed to messages three to ten times per month.
```

---

to help insure that they are logical and internally consistent. Such a summary is shown in Figure 5.9.

At this point, users of the program can return to any previous steps to modify input and output in an effort to obtain optimum goals or to evaluate other alternatives.

☐ **Developing an Advertising Appropriation**

ADGOAL helps develop an advertising appropriation and budget using the monthly communication goals. This can be based either on a total fixed budget arrived at outside the model, or as an amount per unit of anticipated sales. In each case, ADGOAL calculates and prints the monthly ad budget, along with the effective reach point cost that must be maintained to achieve media goals. It then lists the effective reach for each month, and that figure as a percentage of the yearly total effective reach points. The Kellogg's All-Bran example is shown in Figure 5.10. This information helps users to decide what media schedules are affordable in a particular month while still meeting marketing, advertising, and media goals.

The total advertising appropriation of $8,793,912 was obtained by multiplying the $0.23 advertising expenditure per unit by 38,234,400 unit sales anticipated in 1988. To determine how much of this total should be allocated to the month of October, for example, required effective reach points (0.58 percent) are divided by the yearly total (201.59 percent) to obtain 0.29 percent of the yearly total appropriation. The total of $25,119 allocated to October, then, is simply 0.29 percent of $8,793,912. This low monthly budget underscores the importance of accounting for advertising carry-over effects. The strong residual advertising impact from September apparently is sufficient to support almost completely the relatively low sales goal of October.

The effective reach point budget is obtained by dividing the total appropriation by 201.59 yearly total effective reach points to arrive at the amount of $43,623. This is the target effective reach point cost which must be achieved to reach com-

FIGURE 5.9

Summary of Marketing, Advertising, and Media Objectives

Marketing Goals:

Within fiscal year 1988, All-Bran should achieve
a market share of 5.97% in the Bran Cereal market
through marketing emphasis on Female Homemakers.
This should result in unit sales of 38,234,400 and sales
revenue of $49,704,720 assuming a manufacturer's price of
$1.30 per unit.

Advertising Goals:

Each month of 1988, All-Bran must achieve the following
Recall levels against Female Homemakers who use Bran Cereal.

JAN =	6.1%	JUL =	24.6%
FEB =	10.8%	AUG =	24.6%
MAR =	10.2%	SEP =	24.6%
APR =	32.6%	OCT =	0.6%
MAY =	24.6%	NOV =	9.2%
JUN =	24.6%	DEC =	9.2%

Messages will emphasize that All-Bran
is highest in fiber content.

Media Goals:

Each month of 1988, All-Bran must achieve the following
effective reach levels against Female Homemakers
who use Bran Cereal.

JAN =	6.1%	JUL =	24.6%
FEB =	10.8%	AUG =	24.6%
MAR =	10.2%	SEP =	24.6%
APR =	32.6%	OCT =	0.6%
MAY =	24.6%	NOV =	9.2%
JUN =	24.6%	DEC =	9.2%

Effective reach is the percent of the target audience
exposed to messages three to ten times per month.

---

munication goals. Any proposed schedule can be checked for this kind of efficiency by dividing the total schedule cost by the weighted (message) effective
reach delivered by the schedule.

SUMMARY

The framework embodied in the ADGOAL model also presents several other
important possibilities not explored here. Users can rapidly test a number of
"what if ... ?" scenarios to see other tradeoffs and opportunities. These could
involve experimenting with different monthly sales patterns, industry and brand
growth rates, consumer purchase rates, broader or narrower targets, single and

FIGURE 5.10

```
-------------------------------------------------
Monthly Advertising Budget, Fiscal Year 1988
-------------------------------------------------
          Effective    % of Yearly    Monthly Ad
Month      Reach         Total          Budget
-----     ---------    -----------    ----------
 JAN        6.06%         3.01%         $264,514
 FEB       10.81%         5.36%         $471,685
 MAR       10.24%         5.08%         $446,565
 APR       32.63%        16.19%       $1,423,427
 MAY       24.57%        12.19%       $1,071,757
 JUN       24.57%        12.19%       $1,071,757
 JUL       24.57%        12.19%       $1,071,757
 AUG       24.57%        12.19%       $1,071,757
 SEP       24.57%        12.19%       $1,071,757
 OCT        0.58%         0.29%          $25,119
 NOV        9.21%         4.57%         $401,909
 DEC        9.21%         4.57%         $401,909
-----     ---------    -----------    ----------
Total     201.59%       100.00%       $8,793,912

Effective reach point budget      =     $43,623
-------------------------------------------------
```

multiple communication levels, advertising carry-over rates, message values, effective reach and frequency, and budgeting approaches. Such experimentation is of enormous value to planners and would be severely limited without software designed to take the tedium out of the process.

This chapter has provided a general framework for developing and integrating marketing-communication goals and the advertising budget, with the purpose of communicating the main lines of reasoning and showing how they can be implemented. Most marketing-communication situations, of course, are considerably more complex than those shown here. Nevertheless, the outline provided can accommodate additional complexity.

ENDNOTES

1. Kent M. Lancaster, Peggy J. Kreshel and Joya R. Harris, "Estimating the Impact of Advertising Media Plans: Media Executives Describe Weighting and Timing Factors," *Journal of Advertising*, 15 (September 1986), pp. 21-29, 45.

2. David A. Aaker and John G. Myers, *Advertising Management*, (Englewood Cliffs: Prentice Hall, 1978); Peggy J. Kreshel, Kent M. Lancaster and Margaret A. Toomey, "How Leading Advertising Agencies Perceive Effective Reach and Frequency," *Journal of Advertising* 14 (3, 1986), pp. 32-38, 51; Michael L. Ray, *Advertising and Communication Management* (Englewood Cliffs: Prentice Hall, Inc., 1982).

3. Ibid.

4. Peggy J. Kreshel, Kent M. Lancaster and Margaret A. Toomey, op. cit.

5. D. G. Clarke, "A Reply to Weinberg and Weiss," *Journal of Marketing Research*, 19 (1982), pp. 592-94; D. G. Clarke, "Measuring the Cumulative Effects of Advertising," *Journal of Marketing Research*, 13 (1976), pp. 345-57; Charles B. Weinberg and

Doyle L. Weiss, "On the Econometric Measurement of the Duration of Advertising Effect on Sales," *Journal of Marketing Research*, 19 (1982), pp. 585-91; Doyle L. Weiss, Charles B. Weinberg and Pierre M. Windal. "The Effects of Serial Correlation and Data Aggregation on Advertising Measurement," *Journal of Marketing Research,* 20 (1983), pp. 268-79.

6. Kent M. Lancaster, Peggy J. Kreshel and Joya R. Harris, op. cit.

7. Kent M. Lancaster and Judith A. Stern, "Computer-Based Advertising Budgeting Practices of Leading U.S. Consumer Advertisers," *Journal of Advertising*, 12 (December 1983), pp. 4-9.

8. Ibid.

ADDITIONAL READING

Lancaster, Kent M. and Lisa Kay Slabon, "Developing and Integrating Marketing, Advertising and Media Objectives and the Advertising Budget Using *ADGOAL* on the Microcomputer," *1987 Proceedings of the American Academy of Advertising*, Las Vegas, Nevada, March 1987, pp. NR 127-32.

APPENDIX 5-A SAMPLE *ADGOAL* INTERACTION

This appendix demonstrates the ADGOAL interaction that was described in Chapter Five, showing all input and output. For instructions on how to run AD-GOAL on the microcomputer, see the Appendix at the end of this text.

```
(C) Copyright 1988, Kent M. Lancaster and Joya R. Harris
                  Department of Advertising
            University of Illinois at Urbana-Champaign
                  Urbana, Illinois  61801

              Compiled using Micorsoft QuickBASIC 4.0
          (C) Copyright Microsoft Corporation, 1985, 1986

                      Press any key to continue.

What output do you want printed?

      1 = Entire interaction
      2 = Final tables only
      3 = None

Your choice? 3

What next?

      1 = Review introductory material
      2 = Develop marketing goals

Your choice? 1
```

INTRODUCTION

ADGOAL is designed to help you create measurable marketing, advertising, and media objectives. The program is divided into four parts:

1. Marketing Objectives
2. Advertising Objectives
3. Media Objectives
4. Setting the Advertising Budget

You must begin by creating marketing objectives, and proceed to the advertising and media objectives. You also have the option of developing an advertising budget. You may return to re-evaluate any section you choose once one or all sections are completed.

Press any key to continue.

1. Creating Measurable Marketing Objectives

You are required to input the following information:

a. The specific time period, general information about the product and the target market and its size
b. Industry and brand unit sales for last year
c. Projected industry and brand growth rates
d. Manufacturer's price per unit
e. Consumer product purchase rate
f. Monthly sales pattern

ADGOAL will utilize this information to calculate future industry and brand unit sales, current and future market share and sales revenue, and the percentage of the target that must purchase the product in order to achieve marketing objectives.

Press any key to continue.

2. Creating Measurable Advertising Goals

You can input the following information or have ADGOAL do it for you:

a. Hierarchy of General Effects (e.g., awareness, knowledge)
b. Percentage of the target market required to purchase in order to achieve sales goals

You have a choice of three hierarchies--(1) Learning, (2) Low-involvement and (3) Custom.

Then, an advertising objective statement is created.

Press any key to continue.

The Learning Hierarchy

The Learning or Lavidge-Steiner hierarchy assumes that
there is an ordered series of reactions consumers go through
when making purchase decisions as they are exposed to product
advertising.

This hierarchy contains three levels: 1) COGNITIVE (attention,
awareness, comprehension, recall), 2) AFFECTIVE (interest,
feeling, evaluation, conviction), and 3) CONATIVE (intention,
trial, action, adoption, behavior). Cognitive reactions must
precede affective, which must precede conative, in a stairstep
fashion. In other words, the model assumes that learning comes
before attitude change, which leads to behavior. Also, when
consumers are involved with a product category, they are
thought to see differences among alternatives.

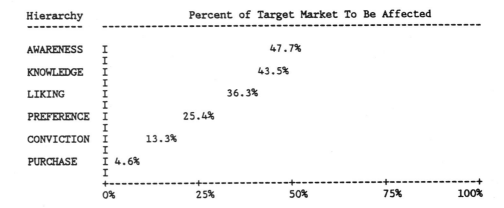

```
Hierarchy                Percent of Target Market To Be Affected
---------    ------------------------------------------------------------

AWARENESS    I                        47.7%
             I
KNOWLEDGE    I                      43.5%
             I
LIKING       I                  36.3%
             I
PREFERENCE   I          25.4%
             I
CONVICTION   I    13.3%
             I
PURCHASE     I 4.6%
             I
             +-------------+--------------+--------------+-------------+
            0%            25%            50%            75%          100%
```

The Low-involvement Hierarchy

The Low-involvement hierarchy attempts to explain why television
advertising seems to have a strong aggregate effect on consumers.
Sometimes television viewers are not initially involved with either
a product or its advertising. This means that there is little
perceptual defense against the projected messages. Therefore,
television ads may not directly change attitudes, but then
repetition may lead to shifts in cognitive structure. Thus,
consumers may be better able to recall advertised product names
and messages at the time of purchase.

This model assumes that learning leads directly to purchase behavior,
which ultimately influences attitudes. Like the Learning hierarchy,
the Low-involvement hierarchy contains three levels: 1) COGNITIVE,
2) CONATIVE, and 3) AFFECTIVE.

```
Hierarchy                  Percent of Target Market To Be Affected
---------      ------------------------------------------------------------

AWARENESS      I                        36.3%
               I
KNOWLEDGE      I               25.4%
               I
CONVICTION     I       13.0%
               I
PURCHASE       I  4.␣%
               I
LIKING         I 3.5%
               I
PREFERENCE     I.52%
               I
               +-------------+-------------+-------------+-------------+
               0%            25%           50%           75%          100%
```

3. Creating Measurable Media Goals

One is not required to input any data. ADGOAL will analyze the
situation and generate a media objective.

4. Setting the Advertising Budget

ADGOAL will help to set and/or allocate the advertising budget.
To do so, one must have an annual ad budget or provide ad
expenditures per unit of anticipated sales.

Press any key to continue.

What next?

    1 = develop marketing objectives
    2 = review introduction

Your choice? 1

```
--------------------------------------------------------------------
PART 1:  CREATING MEASURABLE MARKETING OBJECTIVES
--------------------------------------------------------------------
```

```
Fiscal year for marketing goal (e.g., 1986)      ? 1988
Brand name (e.g., All-Bran)                       ? All-Bran
Product category name (e.g., Bran Cereal)         ? Bran Cereal
Target market (e.g., Female Homemakers)           ? Female Homemakers
Target market size (e.g., 69719000)               ? 69719000
1987 industry unit sales (e.g., 360000000)        ? 557134300
1987 - 88 industry growth rate (e.g., .15)        ? .15
1987 brand unit sales (e.g., 6000000)             ? 31862000
1987 - 88 brand growth rate (e.g., .2)            ? .2
Manufacturer's unit price (e.g., 1.30)            ? 1.3
Consumer monthly purchase rate (e.g., 2)          ? 2
Do you want to make changes (1=Yes, 2=No)         ? 2
```

Monthly brand sales pattern:

```
1 = constant
2 = seasonal
```

Your choice? 2

When does the fiscal year begin?

```
1 = January
2 = July
```

Your choice? 1

For the first 11 months of fiscal year 1988, one should note the
percent of yearly sales that are likely to occur each month.
The sum of all 12 months must equal 100 (e.g., JAN = 10, FEB = 10).

```
JAN    ? 4.5
FEB    ? 5
MAR    ? 5
APR    ? 12
MAY    ? 12
JUN    ? 12
JUL    ? 12
AUG    ? 12
SEP    ? 12
OCT    ? 4.5
NOV    ? 4.5
```

All-Bran Projected Marketing Situation, Fiscal Year 1988

Bran Cereal Unit Sales			Change
1987	=	557,134,270	
1988	=	640,704,380	15.00%
All-Bran Sales Revenue			
1987	=	$41,420,600	
1988	=	$49,704,720	20.00%
All-Bran Unit Sales			
1987	=	31,862,000	
1988	=	38,234,400	20.00%
All-Bran Unit Sales Share			
1987	=	5.72%	
1988	=	5.97%	4.35%
Target Size (Female Homemakers)	=	69,719,000	

        Press any key to continue.

Month	%	----Monthly Sales---- Units	Percent of Target Purchasing 2 Units/Month
JAN	4.5	1,720,548	1.23 %
FEB	5.0	1,911,720	1.37 %
MAR	5.0	1,911,720	1.37 %
APR	12.0	4,588,128	3.29 %
MAY	12.0	4,588,128	3.29 %
JUN	12.0	4,588,128	3.29 %
JUL	12.0	4,588,128	3.29 %

```
        AUG       12.0       4,588,128      3.29 %
        SEP       12.0       4,588,128      3.29 %
        OCT        4.5       1,720,548      1.23 %
        NOV        4.5       1,720,548      1.23 %
        DEC        4.5       1,720,548      1.23 %
        -----     -----     -----------
        Total    100.0      38,234,400
```

        Press any key to continue.

Marketing Goals:

Within fiscal year 1988, All-Bran should achieve
a market share of 5.97% in the Bran Cereal market
through marketing emphasis on Female Homemakers.
This should result in unit sales of 38,234,400 and sales
revenue of $49,704,720 assuming a manufacturer's price of
$1.30 per unit.

        Press any key to continue.

What would you like to do next?

        1 = Develop Advertising Goals
        2 = Revise Marketing Goals

Your Choice? 1

  PART 2:   CREATING MEASURABLE ADVERTISING OBJECTIVES

    Which communication hierarchy would you like to use?

        1 = Learning
        2 = Low Involvement
        3 = Custom
        4 = Need more background first

Your choice? 3

How many levels in your custom hierarchy? 2

Name each of the 2 levels in your hierarchy (e.g., Recall)

        Level 1? Recall
        Level 2? Purchase

For your Custom hierarchy, input the percentage of the target
affected for each general effect level (e.g., Awareness ? .85).

        Recall   ? .35
        Purchase   ? .03

What monthly advertising retention or carry-over rate should be used?
(e.g., 0 = no ad carry-over, .36 = typical ad carry-over)

Monthly ad retention rate? .36

```
--------------------------------------------------------------------------
Consumer   ---- Percent of Target Market To Be Affected Each Month (L =0.36) ---
Hierarchy  JAN   FEB   MAR   APR   MAY   JUN   JUL   AUG   SEP   OCT   NOV   DEC
--------------------------------------------------------------------------
Recall     6.1  10.8  10.2  32.6  24.6  24.6  24.6  24.6  24.6   0.6   9.2   9.2
Purchase   1.2   1.4   1.4   3.3   3.3   3.3   3.3   3.3   3.3   1.2   1.2   1.2
--------------------------------------------------------------------------
```

  Press any key to continue.

What next?

  1 = Graph monthly hierarchies
  2 = Write advertising goals
  3 = Use another carry-over rate
  4 = Use another hierarchy

Your choice? 1

Which monthly communications hierarchies would you like to graph?

  1 = No graphs
  2 = Plot one or more months
  3 = Plot every month

Your choice? 2

Enter the number of the month you would like to graph
(e.g., JAN = 1, FEB = 2, JUL = 7, AUG = 8).

Graph month number? 4

```
--------------------------------------------------------------------------
Hierarchy           Percent of Target Market To Be Affected, APR, 1988 (L = .36)
---------           ------------------------------------------------------------
 1. Recall          I                        *
 2. Purchase        I *
                    +-------------+-------------+-------------+-------------+
                    0%           25%           50%           75%          100%
--------------------------------------------------------------------------
```

  Press any key to continue.

Which monthly communications hierarchies would you like to graph?

  1 = No graphs
  2 = Plot one or more months
  3 = Plot every month

Your choice? 1

Input the general effect that you wish to emphasize in your
advertising campaign (e.g., 1 = Awareness).

  1 = Recall
  2 = Purchase

Your choice? 1

Describe the specific communication effect desired
(e.g., is highest in fiber content).

Specific effect? is highest in fiber content

Advertising Goals:

Each month of 1987, All-Bran must achieve the following
Recall levels against Female Homemakers who use Bran Cereal.

JAN =	6.1%	JUL =	24.6%
FEB =	10.8%	AUG =	24.6%
MAR =	10.2%	SEP =	24.6%
APR =	32.6%	OCT =	0.6%
MAY =	24.6%	NOV =	9.2%
JUN =	24.6%	DEC =	9.2%

Messages will emphasize that All-Bran
is highest in fiber content.

What next?

      1 = Create media goals
      2 = Revise marketing goals
      3 = Revise advertising goals
      4 = Review introduction

Your choice? 1

How do you wish to define monthly effective message frequency?
(e.g., three or more, three to ten)

Describe effective frequency? three to ten

   PART 3: CREATING MEASURABLE MEDIA OBJECTIVES

Media Goals:

Each month of 1988, All-Bran must achieve the following
effective reach levels against Female Homemakers
who use Bran Cereal.

JAN =	6.1%	JUL =	24.6%
FEB =	10.8%	AUG =	24.6%
MAR =	10.2%	SEP =	24.6%
APR =	32.6%	OCT =	0.6%
MAY =	24.6%	NOV =	9.2%
JUN =	24.6%	DEC =	9.2%

Effective reach is the percent of the target audience
exposed to messages three to ten times per month.

       Press any key to continue.

Summary of Marketing, Advertising, and Media Objectives

```
Marketing Goals:
----------------
Within fiscal year 1988, All-Bran should achieve
a market share of 5.97% in the Bran Cereal market
through marketing emphasis on Female Homemakers.
This should result in unit sales of 38,234,400 and sales
revenue of $49,704,720 assuming a manufacturer's price of
$1.30 per unit.

Advertising Goals:
------------------
Each month of 1988, All-Bran must achieve the following
Recall levels against Female Homemakers who use Bran Cereal.

        JAN =  6.1%        JUL = 24.6%
        FEB = 10.8%        AUG = 24.6%
        MAR = 10.2%        SEP = 24.6%
        APR = 32.6%        OCT =  0.6%
        MAY = 24.6%        NOV =  9.2%
        JUN = 24.6%        DEC =  9.2%

Messages will emphasize that All-Bran
is highest in fiber content.

Media Goals:
------------
Each month of 1988, All-Bran must achieve the following
effective reach levels against Female Homemakers
who use Bran Cereal.

        JAN =  6.1%        JUL = 24.6%
        FEB = 10.8%        AUG = 24.6%
        MAR = 10.2%        SEP = 24.6%
        APR = 32.6%        OCT =  0.6%
        MAY = 24.6%        NOV =  9.2%
        JUN = 24.6%        DEC =  9.2%

Effective reach is the percent of the target audience
exposed to messages three to ten times per month.

-----------------------------------------------------------------------
        Press any key to continue.
-----------------------------------------------------------------------
    PART 4:  SETTING THE ADVERTISING APPROPRIATION
-----------------------------------------------------------------------

Would you like to develop an advertising appropriation
or budget based on these results (1=Yes, 2=No)? 1

ADGOAL will divide your fiscal year 1988 advertising appropriation
among months based on your monthly communication goals.

How is your appropriation to be determined?

    1 = Given, fixed amount
    2 = Amount per unit of anticipated sales

Your choice? 2

Enter the amount to be spent per unit sold during fiscal year 1988
(e.g., .50 = $.50 per unit, 1.25 = $1.25 per unit)? .23
```

```
--------------------------------------------------
Monthly Advertising Budget, Fiscal Year 1988
--------------------------------------------------
           Effective      % of Yearly    Monthly Ad
Month        Reach          Total         Budget
-----      ---------      -----------    ----------
 JAN         6.06%          3.01%          $264,514
 FEB        10.81%          5.36%          $471,685
 MAR        10.24%          5.08%          $446,565
 APR        32.63%         16.19%        $1,423,427
 MAY        24.57%         12.19%        $1,071,757
 JUN        24.57%         12.19%        $1,071,757
 JUL        24.57%         12.19%        $1,071,757
 AUG        24.57%         12.19%        $1,071,757
 SEP        24.57%         12.19%        $1,071,757
 OCT         0.58%          0.29%           $25,119
 NOV         9.21%          4.57%          $401,909
 DEC         9.21%          4.57%          $401,909
-----      ---------      -----------    ----------
Total      201.59%        100.00%        $8,793,912

Effective reach point budget    =          $43,623
--------------------------------------------------
```

Now, please type:

    1 = Return to introduction
    2 = Create new marketing goals
    3 = Create new advertising goals
    4 = List media goals
    5 = Analyze the advertising budget
    6 = Stop

Your choice? 6

CHAPTER SIX

Strategic Aspects of Advertising Media

After looking at what the main competitors are doing in terms of advertising, determining the marketing, advertising and media goals for the brand and setting the advertising appropriation, the next step in the planning process is deciding which media to use. This procedure usually is a logical extension of the previous steps, for the media objectives that are determined include a statement of the desired levels of reach, frequency, and continuity against the chosen target audience. Although those are some of the most common measures utilized for making media decisions, they are by no means the only ones. This chapter will provide guidelines for making strategic decisions on which advertising media categories to select. The media to be considered here include:

Television: Network, Spot, Cable
Radio: Network, Spot
Newspapers: National, Local, Supplements
Magazines: Consumer, Farm, Business
Outdoor
Direct Mail

As is seen in Table 6.1, the various criteria for making specific media decisions can be broken down into three dimensions. *Audience factors* include the interaction of the medium with the viewer or listener, such as how many people watch prime time network television, or how easily a magazine can be targeted to certain regions of the country. *Message factors*, in contrast, pertain to the advertisement itself in terms of its likely impact on the consumer. Finally, *efficiency factors* deal primarily with cost, both in terms of production and in relation to the targets reached. The remainder of the chapter will elaborate on each of these aspects. Table 6.1 also includes a summary of recent annual expenditures and sources of data for competitive advertising activity, by media category. These have already been discussed in Chapter Four and are included here for completeness.

AUDIENCE FACTORS

☐ Typical Adult Rating

Experienced media planners rely on a number of rules of thumb in the media planning and evaluation process. You too will begin to do so as familiarity with

TABLE 6-1 Strategic Aspects of Alternative Media Categories

	Television			Radio		Newspapers			Magazines			Outdoor	Direct Mail
	Network	Spot	Cable	Network	Spot	National	Local	Supplements	Consumer	Business	Farm		
Audience Factors/Data													
Typical adult rating (%)	16	16	2	2	2	14	40	25	20	20	20	60	2+
Reach (H,M,L)	H	M	L	L	L	L	H	H	H	L	L	H	M
Frequency (H,M,L)	M	H	H	H	H	M	M	L	L	L	L	H	L
Selectivity		X	X	X	X	X	X		X	X	X		X
Seasonal usage													
Controlled circulation													
Geographic flexibility		X	X		X		X	X	X	X	X	X	X
Local coverage		X	X		X		X	X	X	X	X	X	X
Ethnic appeal			X	X	X		X	X	X			X	X
Arbitron	X	X											
Nielsen	X	X											
Simmons Market Research Bureau (SMRB)	X	X	X	X		X		X	X			X	
Mediamark Research Inc. (MRI)	X	X	X	X		X		X	X			X	
Birch Radio Report					X								
Audit Bureau of Circulation (ABC)						X	X						
American Business Press										X			
Business Publications Audit of Circulation (BPA)										X			
Message Factors/Data													
Vehicle audience weight	80.0	72.5	62.5	40.0	37.5	35.0	35.0	35.0	52.5	52.5	52.5	47.5	65.0
Long message life								X	X	X	X	X	X
Simple message	X	X	X	X	X							X	
Emotional appeal	X	X	X	X	X			X	X			X	X
Immediacy				X	X	X	X						
Control ad placement	X	X	X			X	X	X	X	X	X	X	X
Editorial association	X		X			X	X	X	X	X	X		
Supporting medium			X	X	X	X	X	X	X	X	X	X	X
Good response measures								X	X	X	X	X	X
Good ad reproduction								X	X	X	X	X	X
Burke Marketing Services	X	X											
Gallup-Robinson	X	X							X				
Starch Reports									X		X		

	Television			Radio		Newspapers			Magazines			Outdoor	Direct Mail
Efficiency Factors/Data	Network	Spot	Cable	Network	Spot	National	Local	Supplements	Consumer	Business	Farm		
Typical unit cost ($000)	90	50	2	3	8	48		200	75	10+	5+	500	500+
CPM (Adults, nearest $1)	6	9	3	3	4	17	11	11	10	20+	20+	2	
Production cost (H,M,L)	H	M	L	M	L	H	L	M	M	M	M	H	H
Production-flexible			X		X		X					X	X
Discounts	X	X	X	X	X	X	X		X	X	X	X	
Standard Rate and Data Service (SRDS)	X	X		X	X	X	X	X	X	X	X		X
LNA-Buyers' Guide to Outdoor Advertising												X	
Competitor Activity													
Ad $ 1985 (millions)	8570	6570	931	423	1348	3376	23614		5317	2382	192	985	17145
Ad $ 1985 (% of total)	8.4	6.4	0.9	0.4	1.3	3.3	23.1		5.2	2.3	0.2	1.0	16.8
Ad $ 1984-5 % change	+3.4	+9.4	+21.4	+16.0	+1.0	+0.7	+8.2		+3.1	+0.63	+3.0	+4.4	+10.6
Broadcast Advertiser Report (BAR)	X	X							X				
LNA-Publishers' Information Bureau						X		X					
Media Records						X	X						
Radio Expenditures Report (RER)				X	X								
LNA (Class/Brand; Company/Brand; (Ad $ Summary)	X	X		X				X	X			X	

various media evaluation factors increases. Knowing the relative importance of media categories in terms of audience delivery is a starting point, and "typical" ratings for each one are presented in Table 6.1. Experience will also reveal that these typical ratings are very rough indeed. They vary by daypart, program, and target type; in addition, various audience measurement services will provide different ratings for comparable vehicles, due to differences in methodology. The 16 rating for network television given in the table, for example, might be the typical Nielsen prime time figure, whereas SMRB or MRI would give an average of 20. Also, daytime network television ratings are usually about half the size of those in prime time.

☐ Reach

As explained in Chapters Two and Five, broad communications effects, such as awareness or knowledge, usually require high levels of reach, suggesting a wide and varied use of media categories and vehicles. In terms of ad placement, this means selecting those media that will be used by many people to reach as many as possible of the potential target audience. In general, mass media are effective in achieving this. While network television is the main high reach platform for national advertisers, the number one outlet for advertising dollars is newspapers. Much of this is accounted for by local, especially retail advertising, but the fact that the press appeals to a wide variety of audiences means that a broad range of people are reached.

Another way to obtain wide audience attention, again on a more localized basis, is through outdoor advertising. An advertiser can buy space in many units within a small area and be assured that a large number of different people will see the ad. Unfortunately, this does not necessarily translate into high recall, as the viewing is often fleeting. Finally, magazines, which are often thought of as more specialized media, can also establish fairly high reach levels, but do so through time, gradually building up the readership of an ad as more people see the magazine.

☐ Frequency

Advertisers often consider that there is a trade-off between reach and frequency, given a fixed advertising budget. This is normally due to the high cost of using mass (high reach) media. The alternative strategy, most usefully applied when attempting to achieve higher level communications effects, such as preference, conviction and trial purchase, is to maximize frequency, buying many insertions per vehicle in fewer different vehicles.

Media which enhance the possibilities for this include radio (both network and spot), spot television, and outdoor. In all cases, they do so by allowing the same ad to be repeated often within a short period of time; although the message may be brief, the audience is still affected in a cumulative fashion, remembering a little more of the ad each time it appears.

☐ Selectivity

For many products, advertisers do not want to reach the greatest number of people possible, but instead wish to try to be more selective, targeting the ads to specific audiences. The most extreme example of this is direct mail, where the advertiser directs the message to one individual believed to be a likely prospect for the product or service. Other more specialized media are consumer, business, and farm magazines, each of which appeals to different audiences; the publications can range from the general, such as *Time* or *Cosmopolitan*, to the very specific, such as *Popular Computing, Progressive Farmer* or *Wines and Vines*. The advertising industry's own trade journal, *Advertising Age*, is another example of a targeted magazine, aimed at professionals interested and involved in advertising or marketing. The newest medium to offer specialized audiences is cable television. With more targeted programming than its broadcast counterparts, cable can reach the sports fan on ESPN, the culture buff on the Arts and Entertainment channel, and young adults on MTV: Music Television. And with the "graying" of America, more specialized media are catering to the needs of older consumers, through magazines, such as *Modern Maturity*, or direct mailings offering health insurance to those over 55. Thus companies who place their ads in any of these media can be more confident that the audiences will be more likely to be interested in what the advertiser has to offer.

☐ Seasonality

Advertisers of certain products, from sunglasses to snowmobiles, need to find media that offer seasonality. Both newspapers and television, although accepting of various messages, remain fairly similar all year round. Radio, however, experiences a considerable increase in the numbers listening to it during the summer months, due largely to the rise in the out-of-home audience. The only other medium to offer some form of seasonality is the farm magazine, although in this case it is because of the nature of its subject matter, which exhibits seasonal variation.

☐ Controlled Circulation

Controlled circulation of a print medium helps advertisers determine who and where their audiences are and how often they can be reached. It does so by giving a count of how many people are buying each issue of the publication. Accurate figures are only available from subscription counts, although newspapers and magazines also calculate overall coverage, which includes newsstand sales. Direct mail, of course, in being sent to specific individuals, also offers advertisers this feature.

☐ Geographic Flexibility

As the variety of media continues to grow, with newer electronic forms, such as cable, satellite, and videocassette recorders, or alternative media, such as shopping carts and electronic scoreboards, the established media are responding by becoming more flexible themselves. One indication of this is in a greater geographic flexibility—the ability to place different versions of an ad in several regions of the country. The growth of spot TV ad revenues, and the increase in the numbers of magazines offering regional editions, are evidence of this.

☐ Local Coverage

In 1985, local advertising was responsible for 43.7 percent of all U.S. advertising dollars. These advertisers may be as small as the neighborhood coffee shop placing an ad in the local evening paper, or as large as J.C. Penney announcing its spring sale on local television. Both TV and radio allow for such buys through spot sales, sold on a local or regional basis. In fact, for radio, it is the local station or affiliate that determines the strength of the national network.

One medium that faces problems as a result of its local nature is outdoor, where city or county regulations govern the use and placement of the ads. The long-running struggle between industry supporters and opponents seems likely to continue for many years; the advocates claim that billboards are part of our right to freedom of expression, providing a valuable, informative service to the community, while citizens' groups view them as a blight on the scenery, or an infringement on our constitutional right to privacy.

☐ Ethnic Appeal

In this "melting pot" of a country, it is often important to be able to appeal to various segments of the population either in their native (non-English) tongue, or through cultural associations. With the growth of the Hispanic segment in particular, this dimension is becoming increasingly important for advertisers. In areas with large ethnic groups one finds radio programs, billboards, TV stations, and newspapers devoted to serving that segment. There are several national equivalents too. The magazines *Ebony* and *Jet* are both directed at black audiences, while cable television offers the Black Entertainment Television channel, and Galavision. There are also plans to expand a Spanish-language newspaper, *Noticias del Mundo,* out of its Los Angeles base, making it the first national Hispanic paper.

MESSAGE FACTORS

The choice of which media to use is partly determined by what the advertiser wishes to say or convey about his product. Is it serious or funny? Simple or complex? Topical or perennial? One must also think about where within the vehicle that ad will be placed, and what effect that could have.

☐ Typical Vehicle Audience Weight

Not everyone who watches a television program or reads a newspaper pays attention to the ads present in that vehicle. Consequently, advertising audiences generally are smaller than media vehicle audiences. To account for this, many media planners discount, adjust, or weight the media vehicle audiences to give a more accurate advertising exposure distribution. This was discussed and explained in Chapter Three. One must remember that the weights shown here are only averages; considerable controversy remains over these figures, and there is wide variation in the actual numbers used in particular situations.

☐ Long Message Life

The only media that offer this advantage are magazines, due to their "pass along" nature. Once one reader finishes an issue, it is often given to a friend or colleague, or may end up in a dentist's waiting room, thereby giving other readers the chance to see the ad. This factor, then, does not imply the campaign message must remain the same over a long period of time, but rather that one ad has a longer life than is usual in this fast-moving, fast-changing business.

☐ Simple Message

Broadcast media, in using limited time frames for commercials, automatically restrict how much the advertiser can say. This means that for TV and radio, a simple message is often all that there is room for. In 15, 30, or 60 seconds, the advertiser has first to get audience attention, then offer information and persuade, and also reinforce the brand name or image; and do this while the viewers or listeners are often only paying partial attention! Thus a clear and simple message is required for these media. Billboards, too, have to follow similar guidelines, for their main audience is on the road, driving past so quickly that it is unable to take in anything other than a brief, succinct message.

☐ Emotional Appeal

By virtue of the combination of sight, sound and motion, television allows for the greatest emotional appeal of any medium. Because its ads come closest to real life, the advertiser is able to convey feelings, or perhaps evoke them in the audience. When Hallmark says to send one of their greetings cards, "When you care enough to send the very best," or when A.T. & T. remarks, "Reach out and touch someone," people can empathize with what is shown on the screen, making them also feel good about the products or services they see.

☐ Immediacy

Sometimes advertisers like to take advantage of what is happening in the world at that time as they can already rely on audience interest or awareness of the topic. The medium best suited to this kind of ad is newspapers, either national or local depending on the subject matter. Indeed, the very nature of this medium is to provide newsworthy information, thereby giving the ads a similar sense of immediacy and newness.

☐ Control Ad Placement

Rather than just buying a spot or page or billboard wherever it may be, advertisers often wish to select exactly when and where the ad will appear. This control of ad placement can be a crucial factor in the media decision process. For all broadcast media, the advertiser can buy spots in particular programs or in certain dayparts, whereas with print, the placement is left up to the editor, unless the advertiser pays more for premium positions such as the inside front cover or back page (both of which are read more). Billboards too can be bought selectively, in specific places, with the option of rotations that allow the message to be moved around a particular city or area and thus be seen by different people. Direct mail again has the most controlled ad placement, since the advertiser knows exactly to whom it is being sent.

☐ Editorial Association

The choice of where to place an ad is often closely linked to what is being seen or heard before and after it. Editorial association refers not simply to print media, in which the tone and style of the newspaper or magazine can be critical determinants in selection, but also to network and cable television. Here, the programs on either side of the commercial play an important role in deciding when to buy TV time. Does the planner, for example, want the All-Bran commercial to be seen by viewers of "World of Sports" or "World News Tonight" or "Lifestyles of the Rich and Famous"? Well it all depends on who has been chosen as the target market, and which shows they are more likely to be watching.

☐ Supporting Medium

For many advertisers, instead of placing ads only on network TV, or just in newspapers, the best strategy is to employ several media. Usually, budget constraints mean that one or more of these will act as supports. Spot TV is often used in this way, backing up a regional print campaign; newspapers can be a secondary medium too, reaching local audiences for a national campaign. Another useful addition to a media schedule is cable television, which can reach not only those households where less broadcast TV is watched (as happens in homes subscribing to cable), but also a more targeted audience than the over-the-air medium. In print, business and farm magazines perform a similarly specialized support function. Finally, radio and billboards often are used to build high frequency levels as a complement to a high reach strategy.

☐ Good Response Measures

For an industry that has been established for over 75 years, advertisers seem extremely uncertain of their ability to gauge how well it performs. The complexity of determining an ad's effectiveness, itself difficult to define, results in relatively poor measures for several media. It is worth reiterating here the objective of advertising given in Chapter Five—to communicate in order to facilitate sales or market share goals. Thus many advertisers judge advertising's effectiveness in terms of how much it helps to sell the product or service. The most efficient and reliable medium in this respect is direct mail, where response to the ad proves that it works. The magazine industry uses a "through the book" or recent reading procedure to test the recall of particular ads. Broadcast media rely on day-after-recall (DAR), theater testing scores, or diaries to see if viewers can remember or recognize commercials they have seen. The future does look brighter for this television audience measurement, however, with the introduction of the People Meter. This is a box attached directly to the TV set, accompanied by a hand-held device similar to a channel selector. Viewers push a button every time they watch TV, giving a more accurate measure of which programs (and commercials) are seen. In contrast, the best that outdoor can offer is an estimate of how many people drive past a particular billboard in a given time period. Yet while all of these measures seem somewhat crude and unreliable, they remain the only types of estimates available of advertising effectiveness, other than sales, which may be caused by numerous other factors.

EFFICIENCY FACTORS

☐ Unit Costs

With experience, planners acquire knowledge of typical ad unit costs. To help readers begin to do so, some of these have been provided in Table 6.1 for each media category, in terms of the most important unit available (e.g., 30-second prime (drive) time spots; full-page print ads; four-color magazine ads; a 100 GRP outdoor showing). Unit costs, of course, will vary widely within a particular category, depending on such factors as length, size, use of color, and audience size and characteristics. As familiarity with various media, target audiences and message characteristics increases, readers will begin to refine the numbers presented. In the preliminary stages of media planning, however, such guidelines are probably invaluable, since they will help in deciding what is feasible for the media plan, given a fixed advertising budget. With $1,000,000 to spend on prime time television, for example, one could afford approximately eleven 30-second commercials (e.g., $1,000,000/$90,000 = 11.1).

☐ Cost-per-thousand

No matter how brilliant or original an ad campaign is, the advertiser will always come down to the bottom line question—how much does it cost? When selecting which media to use, rather than simply focus on the absolute costs involved, planners should compare the alternatives in terms of cost-per-thousand impressions (CPM) against the target. Here again, it is the truly mass media that can offer favorable figures. Both network television and radio can give the advertiser more value per dollar spent; more localized media, such as spot radio and local newspapers, achieve similar cost efficiencies by virtue of their lower absolute costs. The more specialized media, such as cable TV, and business and farm magazines, are more expensive in comparison, because it is less efficient to reach their more targeted audiences.

☐ Production Costs

As noted earlier, although certain media may be cost effective, the absolute expense of producing commercials can put some media well beyond the budget of many advertisers. A 30-second commercial on prime time network television costs around $100,000, while a one-page, four-color ad in *Reader's Digest* is priced at $104,600, showing that however low the CPM may be, the costs of achieving that can be too high. Alternatively, an advertiser could have ads produced for cable TV or radio or the local newspaper at a small fraction of the cost. An ad on cable, for example, may cost only $250 to produce.

☐ Production Flexibility

Another determinant of ad efficiency to consider is how flexible the production can be. This means finding out whether last-minute changes are possible for an ad, which often applies only to local media. Spot radio and local newspapers both offer this advantage. A different aspect of flexibility is the variety that the medium allows; thus cable TV ads are not restricted to the 15-, 30-, or 60-second formats of the networks; direct mail can include almost anything the copywriter can dream up, such as test items or unusual materials.

☐ Good Ad Reproduction

The problem of ad reproduction gradually is being eliminated, as more and more of the print media turn to high quality color presses and electronic, computerized facilities. While magazines have long touted their excellent color capabilities, these are now being made available in newspapers too, led by the success and innovation of *USA Today,* which uses color graphics in every section (as opposed to just the special color supplements). Billboards too are becoming more standardized and professional, employing techniques to ensure that one ad will look the same on boards from New York to Los Angeles, rather than relying on the local printers to produce the ad to the proper specifications. Of course, if an advertiser has enough money to spend, quality reproduction is probably not a problem in any media category.

In television, there are several exciting new products in the market to improve the quality of the medium. Stereo sound is already available on many sets and programs, and a larger screen size is becoming more popular. Companies are currently testing High Definition TV, which uses 1,125 lines on the screen instead of the present 525; if successful, this would greatly enhance the picture quality. In all countries, except America and Japan, television screens currently have 625 lines, but there is increasing pressure for worldwide uniformity, as the globe is made smaller through satellite communications.

☐ Discounts

Reduced prices are available in almost every media, the only exceptions being newspaper supplements and direct mail. And even for the latter, printing costs go down with large volumes. For the rest, discounts usually are given for volume, frequency, or bulk buys. In fact, as competition among media intensifies, there appears to be a trend towards giving greater incentives for such buys; thus many magazine publishing houses now offer lower prices to advertisers who place ads in several of their publications. Spot buys for TV and radio can be made on a regional basis, while in cable, local systems are joining together to form cable interconnects that allow advertisers to place the same ad in several different systems, at a lower cost. A similar operation has recently been started in the outdoor industry with Gannett's Outdoor U.S.A. program that links 14 regional outdoor agencies together.

ADDITIONAL CONSIDERATIONS

When deciding which media to utilize in media plans, it is all too easy to focus on one or two key advantages of particular media without realizing some of the drawbacks that may result. The following is a brief summary of some of the additional problems to consider before making final selections.

☐ Television

One of the most important difficulties facing TV advertisers is escalating costs. These have been rising at an annual rate of 6-7 percent, in absolute terms, with the cost of CPMs increasing at 7-8 percent per year. With the network acceptance of 15-second spots, it is likely that this trend will continue, for while many claim that a 15-second ad will be half the price of the regular 30-second spot, it seems all too probable that before long the cost will be disproportionate to the length.

The switch to 15's was partly made to help solve another long-standing problem in TV—clutter. With only a finite amount of time allowed for commercials, advertisers have to compete not only to get audience attention between or within programs, but also somehow stand out from other commercials in that time period. This is becoming increasingly difficult as the number of alternative electronic media rises. With more channel options, the viewer is more likely to "zap" or switch between them, particularly during the commercials, to see if other networks have more appealing programs. And if shows are watched after being recorded on a VCR, there is a growing tendency to fast-forward, or "zip" the commercials during playback.

In addition, network television advertisers must also face the problem of a disparity between ratings in cable and non-cable households. In those homes with cable, network ratings are 10-15 percent lower, which forces many advertisers to allocate 5-10 percent of their network TV advertising budget to cable to offset this difference.

☐ Radio

Radio has to deal with clutter too. Indeed, the problem is worse for this medium because attention levels tend to be even lower to begin with. People usually listen to the radio while doing something else, so a commercial must work extra hard to differentiate itself from others. While this medium generally is considered appropriate for a high frequency strategy, it must be remembered that it can be expensive to achieve this. Although a 30-second network ad is priced at about $3,000 in drive time, when this is multiplied by 30, say, for a given week, it can become costly.

☐ Newspapers

The major difficulty still facing national advertisers is the issue of buying space. National advertisers are forced to pay a considerably higher rate than local ones, making it a disincentive to use this medium. So much so, in fact, that 85 percent of total newspaper ad revenue comes from local buys. Clutter exists in newspapers too; readers are not passively watching ads displayed before them, but can instead actively seek out what they want to read, so that an ad must stand out on the page to gain attention. Finally, the inherent mass nature of the medium forestalls any selectivity.

With supplements, the difficulties lie midway between those faced by newspapers and magazines. Early closing dates take away the sense of immediacy of daily publications, while the fairly small pass-along audience lowers the potential reach of this medium.

☐ Magazines

For a more selective medium, such as magazines, problems stem from other areas. Along with the early closing dates precluding highly timely ads, the magazine has to overcome the fact that it is one-dimensional. This can make it unsatisfactory for many products that wish to show a "lifelike" dimension to the audience.

☐ Outdoor

The drawbacks to using outdoor contrast completely with magazines. Billboards are nonselective, offer a short exposure time, and have extremely poor audience measurement. In addition, the absolute costs of production and printing are fairly high, leading to their use primarily as a supporting medium.

☐ Direct Mail

In spite of being the most highly targeted medium available, direct mail still has certain problems. One of the most important to consider is outdated lists. With the large number of people in this country who change their location every year, it is very hard for list houses and brokers to maintain up to date records. This can mean that the mailing, when it does occur, is no longer appropriate or relevant to the target. And reaching the desired audience is an extremely expensive task, in terms of CPM.

CONCLUSION

Although there are many media to choose from, a planner must consider carefully the strategic implications of each one to ensure that it is going to be the most cost effective method of conveying the message to the desired target audience. In addition, when selecting the medium, or media, to utilize, planners should consider some of the possible drawbacks which might accompany such buys. The following six chapters consider the various media in greater detail and show readers how to use the media planning model, ADPLAN, to facilitate the process.

ADDITIONAL READING

Leo Burnett U.S.A. 1986 Media Costs and Coverage.

Baity, Dave, "Local cable ads attract little guys," *Electronic Media*, (March 17, 1986) p. 26.

Coen, Robert J., "Juggling continues despite welcomed disinflation," *Advertising Age* (Special Report: Media Outlook, November 21, 1985) pp. 13-15.

Fitch, Ed, "Building a national Hispanic newspaper," *Advertising Age* (Special Report: Marketing to Hispanics, February 27, 1986) p. 57.

Gay, Verne, "Nielsen locks up its replacement for diaries," *Advertising Age* (October 28, 1985) p. 62.

Kaatz, Ronald B., *Cable Advertiser's Handbook* (Lincolnwood, Illinois: Crain Books, 1985).

Leckenby, John D. and Nugent Wedding, *Advertising Management* (Columbus, Ohio: Grid Publishing, Inc., 1982).

McGann, Anthony F. and J. Thomas Russell, *Advertising Media* (Homewood, Illinois: Richard D. Irwin, Inc., 1988).

Outdoor Network U.S.A., 1985.

Sissors, Jack Z. and Jim Surmanek, *Advertising Media Planning*, Second Edition (Chicago, Illinois: Crain Books, 1982).

CHAPTER SEVEN

Media Audience and Cost Data Sources

Volumes of information are available to aid in developing media schedules. The most commonly used will be discussed in this chapter. These include:

Simmons Market Research Bureau (SMRB)
Mediamark Research Inc. (MRI)
A.C. Nielsen
Arbitron
Radio All-Dimension Audience Research (RADAR)
Birch
Scarborough's National Newspaper Audience Ratings Study
Standard Rate and Data Service (SRDS)

A brief summary will be provided for each information source covered, including the type of information available and the method used to obtain it.

SIMMONS MARKET RESEARCH BUREAU (*SMRB*)

SMRB is one of the most complete sources of consumer product and media usage data and is used considerably throughout the remainder of this text. The results of this annual study are reported in two series: the media volumes (M-1 through M-12) and the product volumes (P-1 through P-30). The data are based on an annual survey of over 19,000 adults and are projectable to the population (18+) residing in the contiguous 48 states.

The media series contains audience and demographic information on nearly all media types, such as individual consumer and business magazines, daily and Sunday newspapers, Sunday supplements and comics, broadcast media, and outdoor. The data are divided into demographic categories such as adults, males, females, and female homemakers. For example, if one wanted to find out what the most popular magazines are for adults 25-34 years old, the information can be found in Volume M-5.

The product series contains all demographic and media usage data for more than 500 product categories, broken down by brand and by heavy, medium, light, and non users of the product category. Information on consumer demographics includes: age, education, employment, marital status, race, census and marketing regions, income, and number of persons in the household.

☐ SMRB Magazine Audience Data

Simmons provides four types of magazine audience data: average issue audience, two-issue rating, pair-wise reach, and duplication. Two personal interviews are conducted four weeks apart to study second-issue readership. Issue aging is taken into account and differs for weekly and monthly publications. Readership is measured in two ways: through-the-book and calibrated frequency. The through-the-book method is used for about 45 magazines with circulations over five million. Respondents are shown booklets with magazine logos and asked to pick those they recognize as having read or looked into in the previous six months. Skeletonized copies of selected magazines are used to check whether the respondent has actually done so. Calibrated frequency requires subjects to identify magazine logos seen in the last six months and to further determine if the magazine was seen in the last month. Respondents are also asked questions regarding place and frequency of reading.

Average issue audiences are based on both interviews. For calibrated frequency respondents it is an average of readers who respond that they read two of two issues plus half of those reading one of two issues. Duplication includes those reading both issues. Self-pair audience is twice the average issue audience less duplication. The beta binomial distribution is used to project readership of up to four issues.

Readership figures are also available for magazine groups and publication types as well as individual magazines.

☐ SMRB Newspaper Sunday Supplement Audience Data

SMRB provides the same audience information for newspaper supplements that it provides for magazines. Supplements include *USA Weekend, Parade, Sunday*, and the *National Supplement Package*. The package includes all three Sunday supplements in the Waiver Group and four independent newspapers, including the *Boston Herald American, Los Angeles Times, San Francisco Examiner-Chronicle*, and the Long Island *Newsday*. Respondents who read a Sunday or weekend newspaper carrying these supplements or newspapers included in the supplement package are counted as readers of the respective supplement. They are first asked what Sunday or weekend editions of newspapers they have read or looked into within the last four weeks. Newspaper logos of four newspapers are shown to aid recall including the *Chicago Tribune, New York Daily News, Los Angeles Times* and the *New York Times*. For each paper mentioned, respondents are asked to note the last time they read or looked into a Sunday or weekend paper. If a respondent notes readership last Saturday or since last Saturday he or she is counted in the Sunday/weekend edition average issue audience, and therefore the corresponding supplement.

☐ SMRB National Daily and General Newspaper Audience Data

SMRB provides average weekday newspaper audience estimates for the *Chicago Tribune, Christian Science Monitor, New York Daily News, Los Angeles*

Times, the *New York Times,* and the *Wall Street Journal.* It provides average Sunday/weekend audience estimates for all but the *Christian Science Monitor* and the *Wall Street Journal.* Also available are self- and cross-pair audience estimates and general readership of "any," "one," and "two or more" daily and Sunday/weekend newspapers. SMRB obtains daily national and general newspaper readership using the personal interview "progressive step" method which indirectly determines the newspapers read "yesterday" (or last "Friday" if the interview occurs on a weekend). The extent of reading of the entire paper or of particular sections of it is also measured and is available through tape access. A similar progressive step procedure is used for Sunday/weekend papers. The estimates are averaged across all days of the week and across both waves of the sample.

□ SMRB Network Television Audience Data

SMRB provides several measures of network television audiences, including average half-hour audience ratings and frequency, two-, three-, and four-program audiences and corresponding frequency, turnover rate, and viewing attentiveness. A two-week diary is mailed to respondents assigned to one of five survey waves. Twenty hours of recording periods for each day are further divided into 15-minute segments. Respondents are asked to note watching any television during each 15-minute period and to specify the program and channel number. Each viewer is also asked to note attentiveness in terms of whether they were out of the room, in the room paying some attention or in the room paying full attention. Estimates are averaged across all half-hour periods and across all five sample waves.

□ SMRB Network Radio Audience Data

SMRB provides average daily (Monday-Friday) cumulative audiences for numerous wired and non-wired radio networks. The estimates include the total number of different persons listening to five or more minutes of an entire daypart or quarter-hour averaged across two weekday observations. The turnover rate is based on the portion of the average weekday cumulative audience which is not reached on a second average weekday. Telephone interviews and mailed diaries are used to collect listening information. Listeners are asked to describe in half-hour increments when the radio is tuned and to what station call letters and dial location. SMRB assigns one format to each station. Station information is projected to the United States as a whole.

□ SMRB Outdoor Audience Data

Outdoor audiences include those people exposed to a particular showing size at least once per month. Showing size is determined by the percent of the population that has an opportunity for exposure to a predetermined number of billboards. SMRB provides audience information on showing sizes of 25, 50, and 100, detailed by percent and number of people reached per month, and average monthly frequency. Information from seven markets is projected to the country as a whole.

Respondents are asked to trace maps of travel in the last week, which are matched with known outdoor poster locations and facings to determine opportunities to see illuminated and non-illuminated displays.

☐ Mediamark Research Inc. (*MRI*)

MRI provides data that are similar to those provided by SMRB, including both media and product volumes, getting the information from an annual survey of 20,000 adults, which covers 250 magazines and magazine groups, radio, television and newspapers, as well as more than 450 products. First, a personal interview is conducted to collect demographic and media usage information; then, self-administered questionnaires are given out for respondents to record their product usage. The measurement technique used is known as "recent reading." Each person is asked if they have read any issue of magazine X in its most recent publication interval. He or she then sorts a deck of cards that show the magazine logos, dividing them into groups they have read, those they are not sure about, and those they have not read. For those they claim to have read, they are asked more qualitative information—where the issue was read, the number of days they spent reading it, the time spent reading it, the percent of pages looked at, their overall rating of the magazine, and their interest in the ads in that issue. MRI then estimates the page exposures, or how many times the average reader was exposed to the average page. Audience frequency of reading is used to calculate cumes and audience turnover.

For other media, similar techniques are used. Thus for newspapers, the "yesterday reading" method asks which newspapers were read "yesterday," while for radio and television, respondents are questioned on their "yesterday recall." The company also collects demographic and purchasing information on cable television viewers.

Information on product usage covers 1,900 product types and 5,700 brands. There are four types of questions: ownership and use of the item; the actual brands used; quantities and frequency of purchase; and participation in the buying decision. Then people are categorized as sole, primary, or secondary users. All of the MRI data are available through audience data systems such as IMS, Telmar, and Management Science Associates.

NIELSEN TELEVISION INDEX (*NTI*)

The NTI report provides continuous audience measurement service for network television. This is available to agencies, advertisers, networks, and producers. The information consists of a number of regularly published reports, providing continuing estimates of television viewing and national sponsored network program audiences, including national ratings 52 weeks per year. With this information, advertisers have a means of evaluating the size and demographic composition of network program audiences, and thus the commercials on each program.

The data regularly reported by NTI include person audiences and household audiences by market sections, daily ratings, fast national and multi-network area ratings, cost per thousand estimates and program and brand cumulative audiences. The *National Audience Demographics Report* provides estimates of audiences by person categories within household demographics.

☐ Nielsen National TV Ratings

This report covers a two-week period and provides several different areas of information. Television audience trends are reported for total day (current month versus a year ago) and by major dayparts (month-by-month, two previous seasons, and the current season to date). Program audience estimates by alphabetical listing give all programs and provide estimates of household audiences (average audience reported in terms of ratings and projections and audience shares) and persons audiences (viewing individuals). Program audience estimates are also provided by time periods, allowing for convenient reference to competitive and the surrounding programs.

Program type averages are reported for selected program genres, each show being weighted by its duration and frequency. Averages are provided for households (in terms of ratings) and persons (ratings and viewers per thousand viewing households) in total and by age and sex. The top program ranking is a listing of the programs having the highest average audience ratings consisting of the 15 highest-rated regular and special programs. Rankings are shown in terms of household audiences and major person audience categories.

☐ Nielsen Station Index (*NSI*)

NSI reports television program performance in more than 200 local markets. This is an excellent source of information for buying spot television advertising. The program rating reports are published for Designated Market Areas (DMAs) at regular intervals. NSI also publishes a series of supplementary reports which address special problems media planners might encounter.

☐ NSI Viewers in Profile (*VIP*) Reports

Each VIP report contains six standard sections: market data and survey details, daypart audience summary, program audience averages, time period audiences, persons shares, and a program index. The market data and survey details provide reference information on the market such as universe estimates for home, television, and demographic groups. Also included are penetration data on color television homes, multi-set homes, cable television homes, and UHF-equipped homes.

The daypart audience summary provides audience estimates for about 20 dayparts for each station. This information allows the media planner to ascertain both viewing patterns during these time periods and a station's relative strength in various dayparts. The section on program audience averages contains audience estimates for programs by total duration, rather than by quarter-hour or half-hour. The trend data included in this section allow the user to follow seasonal audience variations during the time period of a program. This section is most helpful in evaluating programs.

In the time period audiences section, audiences are estimated by the half-hour or quarter-hour, depending on the daypart. This information is used to compare stations and to see what shows compete with each other. Person shares contain data for early and late fringe time periods only. These can be used to trend and predict seasonal audience delivery for different demographic groups. The program index is simply an alphabetical index of programs to help the user locate a program, find out which station is carrying it, and see the day and time it is broadcast.

☐ **Additional Nielsen Services**

For those markets where Nielsen has electronic meters in its sample households, the company offers its Nielsen Metered Market Service, producing daily and weekly reports on viewing habits in these areas. Nielsen's Syndication Service combines data on syndicated programs with its audience reports, while its Home Video Index covers basic, pay, and local cable patterns.

ARBITRON SPOT TELEVISION AUDIENCE DATA

Arbitron provides television audience estimates detailed by age and sex and by three progressively narrower geographic coverage categories: Total Survey Area (TSA), Area of Dominant Influence (ADI), and Metro area. Ratings, shares and HUT (Households Using Television) are given for each program and quarter hour. Station break average audiences are also reported based on the average of the preceding and following quarter-hour segments.

Arbitron uses weekly diaries for recording television viewing of eligible households. This is repeated four times in each of over 200 ADIs. Respondents record length of time viewing, program, station and network, along with noting who is watching, taking into account multiple set use. Audience estimates consist of households watching television at least five minutes during a particular segment.

ARBITRON SPOT RADIO AUDIENCE DATA

Arbitron is the major producer of market by market (local) radio audience studies. Data are collected from persons age 12 and over through a radio-only seven-day diary. Arbitron lists for each market: the radio stations, power in watts for daytime and nighttime, broadcast frequency, network affiliation, and city, county, and state.

Arbitron provides quarterly data on average share trends for different segments of daytime and nighttime. Also, the average quarter hour and cume listening estimates are broken down by different demographic groups (men, women, adults, and teens).

Average quarter-hour listening includes the number of persons who listened at home and away to a station for a minimum of five minutes within a given quarter hour. The rating is simply the estimate expressed as a percentage of the universe (men, women, etc.). The cume is often referred to as the unduplicated audience or the reach; in persons it is the estimated number of different persons who listened either at home or away to a station for a minimum of five minutes within a given fifteen minute time period. The cume rating is the estimated number of cume persons expressed as a percentage of the survey area.

RADIO'S ALL-DIMENSION AUDIENCE RESEARCH (*RADAR*)

RADAR, a service provided by Statistical Research, Inc., provides estimates of national radio network audiences. The data are based on telephone interviews of 8,000 households covering seven days of radio listening. Measures are taken every spring and fall, over 8-week periods in each. More than twelve networks are included, detailed by demographic and geographic categories. Network clearance information is gathered which verifies affiliate broadcast of network program fare or commercials. RADAR provides total radio listening for all AM and FM network stations, network audiences of cleared programs, and commercial exposures. The three reports that are issued cover radio usage, in terms of average quarter-hour listening, 1-day cume, 5-day weekly, weekend, and 7-day cume; network radio audiences to all commercials; and network radio audiences to commercials within programs. Radio usage data are further listed according to age and sex of respondents, and in-home versus out-of-home listening, with the latter also noting radio listening in automobiles.

BIRCH SPOT RADIO AUDIENCE DATA

Birch provides the usual radio audience estimates in markets not adequately served by Arbitron, typically metro areas. The top 20 markets are surveyed in the first two weeks of each month while markets 21 through 35 are surveyed in weeks two and three. All other markets are analyzed the last two weeks of the month. Altogether, Birch covers 230 markets, conducting more than 70,000 interviews a year. Using telephone surveys and the yesterday recall technique, one person age 12 or over from each randomly selected household is asked to provide detailed radio listening information. This includes the location of listening, start and stop times, the day before yesterday listening (to calculate weekly cumes), and actual station heard. Five reports are issued: the Quarterly Summary, Standard Market Report, Condensed Market Report, Monthly Trend Report, and Qualitative/Product Usage Report.

SCARBOROUGH'S NATIONAL NEWSPAPER AUDIENCE RATINGS STUDY

Scarborough's report on newspaper audiences is based on a sample of over 64,000 respondents. It covers 51 ADIs and 52 Metro areas, together with eight local markets. Data for 153 daily newspapers or newspaper groups and 113 Sunday (or weekend) newspapers are included. The company utilizes a random-digit dialing telephone interview procedure and enjoys a 64.8 percent response rate after up to six callbacks. They use the aided-recall method to discover "yesterday" reading and report the average issue audience, two-, four-, and five-issue cumulative audience, and gross audience, together with demographic information such as occupation, supermarket expenditures per household, and pay television usage.

STANDARD RATE AND DATA SERVICE (*SRDS*)

Standard Rate and Data Service provides quarterly cost information on nearly all advertising sources throughout the United States. SRDS contains consumer data such as Areas of Dominant Influence (ADI) and Designated Market Area (DMA) Summary Rankings and a Market Data Summary Section.

The summary rankings array ADIs, DMAs, and MSAs in terms of several characteristics: total households, the percentage of households in the U.S., number of television households, percentage of television penetration, gross household income, total household expenditures, expenditures broken down by food store, drug store, general merchandise store, auto store, and service stations, and passenger cars. Next, all ADIs are ranked in each one of the categories.

The Consumer Market Data Summary provides the same information for the total United States, nine census divisions, and then each individual state. The various volumes are outlined below.

☐ SRDS Spot Television Rates and Data

The Spot Television book, which appears every month of the year, profiles television stations, national/regional networks, and television groups across the country. Individual profiles include basic planning and buying information, special features, commissions, programming, rates, and station representatives.

☐ SRDS Spot Radio Rates and Data

This volume profiles television stations, national/regional networks, and television groups on a monthly basis. Individual profiles include basic planning and buying information, special features, commissions, programming, rates, and station representatives.

SRDS also features a black population data section with metro and some county population estimates, leading 100 metro areas ranked by black population, and radio stations regularly scheduling Spanish language; and a Spanish Population Data section with similar listings. The majority of this volume provides station listings alphabetically by state and city. The spot announcements section is the basic rate structure for one minute, 30-second, 20-second, and 10-second spots. The section on package plans explains rates for packages or combinations of 10-second through one minute spots. And the special features section explains special rates or charges associated with feature programs, such as the news, weather, and sports.

☐ Spot Radio—Small Markets

For radio stations in markets with fewer than 25,000 population, this volume provides biannual information on buying, sales representatives, program format, facilities, network or group affiliations, and spot radio schedules.

☐ SRDS Consumer Magazines and Agri-Media Rates and Data

Here one finds a listing of more than 1,500 consumer magazines and 400 farm publications. The entry shows editorial policy, advertising rates and discounts, mechanical requirements, copy regulations, circulation, personnel, and issuance and closing dates.

The publications are listed alphabetically within an editorial classification such as general editorial, business and finance, men's and women's. Each listing contains information necessary for the media buyer: the publisher, editorial profile, personnel, representatives, commissions and cash discounts, rate cards, contract and copy regulations, mechanical requirements, issue and closing dates, and circulation. SRDS also contains advertisements from many of the publications. These ads often provide detailed profiles of the magazine readers that can be useful in targeting a particular market.

Rates for consumer magazines can be complicated. The costs may vary depending on the size of the ad (usually full or half page), whether it's black and white or color, a cover, an insert, and whether a special position is requested. SRDS provides information on any special issues a magazine may publish and the geographic and/or demographic editions it offers. Geographic editions have rates, circulation, requirements, and closing dates that pertain to only that particular edition of the magazine. Finally, SRDS provides detailed information on circulation and distribution.

☐ SRDS Business Publications Rates and Data

This issue covers more than 4,500 business, technical, and trade publications and appears monthly. Each entry includes the publisher's editorial statement, advertising rates, contract and copy regulations, mechanical requirements, issuance and closing dates, and circulation statements.

☐ SRDS Newspaper Rates and Data

The newspaper volume profiles each month 1,600 U.S. newspapers and newspaper groups. The listings show advertising rates, special features, contract and copy regulations, mechanical requirements, closing times, and the reported circulation. Each issue also contains annually updated market data estimates for population, households, income, retail and store type sales and other media and market indicators for metro areas, counties, and cities. Each edition also includes a section on national classified advertising rates and data and applicable rates and restrictions for cooperative advertising.

The newspaper industry has adopted a nationwide standard size for the measurement of advertisements. The Standard Advertisement Unit (SAU) is approximately $2^1/_4''$ wide and $1''$ deep. This makes buying advertising space easier throughout the country. Newspaper ads can also be purchased in terms of full or half pages. Newspapers have an open rate, which is usually the highest, and offer several different contract rates. SRDS provides the costs for adding color and for advertising in special feature sections.

☐ Newspaper Circulation Analysis

Appearing once a year, this edition is designed to accompany the rates and data volume. It gives information on newspapers and newspaper market rankings, showing circulation and penetration by metropolitan area, television markets, and counties.

☐ Direct Mail

Published bimonthly, the direct mail book includes more than 80,000 direct mail list selections. Each entry contains a description of the list, list selections, list source, rental rates, quantity, commission, restrictions, test arrangements, and method of addressing. In addition, the issue includes a listing of direct mail brokers, compilers, and managers.

☐ Other Services

Standard Rate and Data also provides several other more specialized services. The *Co-Op Source Directory* identifies more than 4,000 manufacturers offering cooperative advertising programs, grouped by product category and covering all advertising media. It is published twice a year. For profiles of business, consumer, farm publications, and daily newspapers, one can turn to the *Print Media Production* volume, which gives shipping instructions, the binding method and printing process used, production specifications, inserts, bleeds, special issues, and the issue and closing dates. Also available are *Print Media Editorial Calendars* and *Card Decks*. Each of the 400 Spanish-language media are listed in the *Hispanic Media and Markets* volume, while another publication offers information on *Canadian Advertising*. Finally, there is a special volume for *Community Publications* which covers the 2,000 weekly newspaper and shopping guides that appear across the country.

CHAPTER EIGHT

Print Media Evaluation

In previous chapters, a number of useful advertising media planning concepts were reviewed and the strategic implications of the various media considered. These, however, are merely a point of departure. There is more and interesting work required to extend these ideas further in order to evaluate a comprehensive advertising media plan.

In this chapter, you will be introduced to media evaluation procedures that allow you to estimate the likely impact of print media schedules on selected target audiences. These include consumer magazines, supplements, national and local newspapers, business publications, outdoor, and direct mail. Each medium is introduced by showing how to evaluate it by hand, followed by instructions on the use of the interactive media planning program, ADPLAN. Sample interactions with this program are included too.

EVALUATING MAGAZINE SCHEDULES

☐ Working with Full Information

Continuing with the bran cereal market example, it will be assumed that Kellogg's All-Bran management wishes to know the impact of a January 1988 magazine schedule designed to reach U.S. female homemakers who use cold breakfast cereals. Full-page, four-color ads will be used. The schedule under consideration follows.

☐ Obtaining the Necessary Data

First of all, it is important to understand the source of the data presented in Table 8.1. Simmons Market Research Bureau (SMRB) data on female homemakers who are users of cold breakfast cereals (Volume P-20, 1985), Column B (% down) indicates that *Reader's Digest, TV Guide* and *Good Housekeeping* are the top rated magazines against the target. This does not include national newspapers, supplements, or magazine packages. These magazines also are highly rated against female homemakers who are heavy users of the product category, an important consideration in media selection.

It is more difficult, however, to obtain estimates of self- and cross-pair audience ratings. Self-pair audience ratings can be thought of as the reach of two issues of a magazine, while cross-pair audience ratings are like the reach of a pair of magazines. Turning to SMRB, Volume M-4 (1985) one finds self- and cross-pair audience data for adults, males, females, and female homemakers but not for the target, female homemakers who use cold breakfast cereals. Self- and cross-pair audience data for narrower targets are available to those with access to SMRB data tapes, including those who subscribe to Interactive Market Systems (IMS) or Telmar, for example. But the data are generally not available in manual form since the number of volumes required to publish them would be impractical.

Cannon[1] offers a solution by showing how to use vehicle audience data for broad targets, such as female homemakers, in order to estimate audience ratings for narrower targets, such as female homemakers who are users of cold breakfast cereals. Essentially, the procedure applies the ratios that exist among the broad target ratings to the available single insertion ratings for the narrower target. Here's how Cannon's procedure is applied to obtain the self- and cross-pair data in Table 8.1.

TABLE 8.1   Magazine Advertising Schedule

Magazine	Single Insertion Rating* (%)	Self-Pair Rating* (%)	Insertions	4-Color Cost
Reader's Digest (RD)	26.6	34.1	1	$108,800
TV Guide (TVG)	25.4	32.2	4	89,300
Good Housekeeping (GH)	20.8	27.7	1	69,245

Cross Pairs	Cross-Pair Rating
RD - TVG	43.6%
RD - GH	39.6
TVG - GH	39.8

*The base for the ratings is 69,405,000 female homemakers who use cold breakfast cereals. Source is 1985 SMRB, Volume P-20.

SMRB Volume M-4 (1985) provides the following data on female home-makers who read the three magazines in this schedule (Table 8.2).

TABLE 8.2   Female Homemaker Audiences

Magazine	Audience Ratings	
	One Issue (%)	Two Issues (%)
Reader's Digest (RD)	25.9	33.2
TV Guide (TVG)	24.4	30.9
Good Housekeeping (GH)	19.6	26.1

Magazine Cross Pair	Cross-Pair (%)
RD - TVG	42.3 (34,775/82,273)
RD - GH	38.1 (31,338/82,273)
TVG - GH	38.0 (31,297/82,273)

Source is SMRB, Vol. M-4, 1985; base for the ratings is 82,273,000 U.S. female homemakers.

Now, to estimate the self-pair rating for product users, one can simply multiply the ratio of the self-pair to the one-issue audience for female homemakers, by the single issue rating for product users. Here is an example for *Reader's Digest*.

$$R_{2,RD} = (33.2\%/25.9\%)(26.6\%)$$
$$= (1.28)(26.6\%)$$
$$= 34.1\%$$

This example indicates that since the ratio of the self-pair to the one-issue rating for female homemakers who read *Reader's Digest* is 1.28, the self-pair for *Reader's Digest* against the target is estimated to be 1.28 multiplied by the one-issue rating (26.6%) against the target. If this procedure is continued for *TV Guide* and *Good Housekeeping* the following is obtained.

$$R_{2,TVG} = (30.9\%/24.4\%)(25.4\%)$$
$$= (1.27)(25.4\%)$$
$$= 32.2\%$$
$$R_{2,GH} = (26.0\%/19.6\%)(20.8\%)$$
$$= (1.33)(20.8\%)$$
$$= 27.6\%$$

Estimating cross-pair ratings is slightly more complex. In the case of cross-pair ratings, one must multiply the ratio of the cross-pair to the sum of the two one-issue audiences for the broader target by the sum of the one-issue ratings for both magazines for the narrower target. In the case of *Reader's Digest* and *TV Guide*, this means:

$$R_{RD,TVG} = (42.3\%/(25.9\% + 24.4\%))(26.6\% + 25.4\%)$$
$$= (42.3\%/50.3\%)(52\%)$$
$$= (.8409)(52\%)$$
$$= 43.6\%$$

In words, this example indicates that for the broader target of female homemakers, the ratio of the cross-pair audience for *Reader's Digest* and *TV Guide* to the sum of the one-issue audience for the pair is .8409. Therefore, the cross-pair rating for the narrower target is estimated to be 84.09 percent of the sum of the one-issue ratings for the pair of magazines against the narrower target. This procedure is repeated for the remaining pairs.

$$R_{RD,GH} = (38.1\%/(25.9\% + 19.6\%))(26.6\% + 20.8\%)$$
$$= (38.1\%/45.5\%)(47.4\%)$$
$$= (.8374)(47.4\%)$$
$$= 39.6\%$$
$$R_{TVG,GH} = (38.0\%/(24.4\% + 19.6\%))(25.4\% + 20.8\%)$$
$$= (38.0\%/44.0\%)(46.2\%)$$
$$= (.8636)(46.2\%)$$
$$= 39.8\%$$

☐ Estimating Schedule Reach with Full Information

At least two recent surveys have indicated that the beta binomial exposure distribution (BBD) model is the most heavily used in industry.[2] Several versions of this popular model will be used throughout the remainder of this text.[3] You should be aware, however, that there is a large array of additional models that have been shown to be superior to the BBD under some conditions.[4] Although space constraints prevent this text from going into each one here, the BBD model serves well for present purposes.

In presenting this model, this chapter will concentrate on the essence of the procedure in the most direct manner possible without detailing all of the mathematics. The BBD model can be thought of as a statistical procedure for calculating the likelihood of a target's exposure to a schedule a given number of times. Essentially, the model decomposes duplication so that reach and frequency can be estimated in considerable detail. At a glance, here are the steps.

1. Estimate the average audience rating of the schedule $(\bar{R}_1)$.
2. Estimate the average pair-wise audience rating of that schedule, including all possible self- and cross-pairs $(\bar{R}_2)$.
3. Use $\bar{R}_1$ and $\bar{R}_2$ to estimate exposure (A) and non-exposure (B) parameters.
4. Estimate the number of different ways target members can be exposed to the schedule 1, 2, 3 to N total insertions in the schedule (the beta distribution).
5. Estimate the average probability of exposure to the schedule 1, 2, 3 to N times (the binomial distribution).
6. Multiply the beta distribution by the binomial distribution. The product should sum to 1.00.

To proceed with the magazine example, the average single-insertion rating of a schedule is computed using Equation 8-1.

$$\bar{R}_1 = \text{GRPs}/N \tag{8-1}$$

where: GRPs = total gross rating points of the schedule,
  N   = total insertions in the schedule.

In this case, the schedule presented in Table 8.1 is analyzed:

$$\text{GRPs} = 26.6\% + 4(25.4\%) + 20.8\%$$
$$= 149$$

$$N \quad = 1 + 4 + 1$$
$$= 6$$

$$\bar{R}_1 \quad = 149/6$$
$$= 24.8\%$$

That is, the average one-insertion audience rating of the schedule is 24.8 percent. It will be more convenient in the remainder of the calculations to use .248.

Determining the average pair-wise audience rating is one of the most difficult steps of the BBD procedure. It might be useful to present this step in a more intuitive manner than is typically the case. Essentially, what is needed is the average of all possible self- and cross-pair audiences in the schedule. The difficulty usually is in determining how many pairs are possible. It turns out that for each vehicle in the schedule the number of possible self-pairs is equal to the number of pairs which can be obtained from the total number of insertions in that vehicle. In the case of this schedule one may wonder how many self-pairs are possible with one insertion in *Reader's Digest*. The answer is, of course, none. The same is true for the single insertion in *Good Housekeeping*. How many self-pairs are possible with four insertions in *TV Guide*? The answer is six. This is seen by looking at all possible pairs of the numbers 1-4.

Pair	Combination
1	1-2
2	1-3
3	1-4
4	2-3
5	2-4
6	3-4

You may recall from statistics courses that, in general, the number of possible combinations can be obtained by using formula 8-2.

$$C_{n,r} = n!/r!(n-r)! \tag{8-2}$$

Where: C = the number of combinations of n possibilities (insertions) taken r at a time,

   n = the total number of possibilities (insertions) to select from,

   r = the number of possibilities (insertions) to be combined at once,

   $!$ = factorial (i.e., $n! = (n)(n-1)...(n-n+1)$).

In the case of *TV Guide*, the six possible self-pairs would be obtained as follows:

$$\begin{aligned} C_{4,2} &= 4!/(2!)(4-2)! \\ &= 4!/(2!)(2!) \\ &= (4)(3)/(2)(1) \\ &= 12/2 \\ &= 6 \end{aligned}$$

So for this schedule the average self-pair rating is:

$$\begin{aligned} \bar{R}_{2,i} &= [(0)(34.1\%) + (6)(32.2\%) + (0)(27.7\%)]/6 \\ &= 193.2\%/6 \\ &= 32.2\% \end{aligned}$$

The next step is to compute the average cross-pair rating for the schedule. For each pair of vehicles, the total number of possible pairs is equal to the product of the number of insertions in each vehicle of the pair. So in the case of *Reader's Digest* and *TV Guide*, the total number of possible cross-pairs is equal to $(1)(4) = 4$. Thus the average cross-pair rating for the magazine schedule is:

$$\bar{R}_{i,j} = [(1)(4)(43.6\%) + (1)(1)(39.6\%) + (4)(1)(39.8\%)]/[(1)(4) + (1)(1) + (4)(1)]$$
$$= [(4)(43.6\%) + (1)(39.6\%) + (4)(39.8\%)]/(4 + 1 + 4)$$
$$= (174.4\% + 39.6\% + 159.2\%)/9$$
$$= 373.2/9$$
$$= 41.5\%$$

Now, it is not appropriate to compute the simple average of the average self- and cross-pair ratings since there are six possible self-pairs and nine possible cross-pairs. Consequently, the average of all possible self- and cross-pairs for this schedule can be obtained as follows:

$$\bar{R}_2 = [6(32.2\%) + 9(41.5\%)]/15$$
$$= 566.7\%/15$$
$$= 37.8\%$$

There is a variety of approaches that can be taken to arrive at the estimate of $\bar{R}_2$. The route chosen here has considerable intuitive appeal that may serve you better than mere memorization of formulas.

Estimating the Beta Distribution

The next two steps in the BBD procedure are to estimate the beta and the binomial distributions. The product of these two distributions is the schedule exposure distribution. The beta distribution can be understood instinctively by thinking of it as an estimate of the number of different ways target members could be exposed to all of the insertions in the schedule exactly 1, 2, 3,..., N total insertions. For example, there are exactly six ways target members could be exposed once to the example magazine schedule of six total insertions. How many ways are there to be exposed exactly twice?

$$C_{6,2} = (6)(5)/(2)(1) = 30/2 = 15$$

In this way, the beta distribution can be obtained using the combination formula for each of r insertions out of n total insertions in the schedule:

$$C_{n,r} = n!/(r!)(n-r)!$$

where n is the total number of insertions in the schedule and r is the particular insertion number. In the example:

$$C_{6,0} = 6!/(0!)(6-0)! = 1$$
$$C_{6,1} = 6!/(1!)(6-1)! = 6$$
$$C_{6,2} = 6!/(2!)(6-2)! = 15$$
$$C_{6,3} = 6!/(3!)(6-3)! = 20$$
$$C_{6,4} = 6!/(4!)(6-4)! = 15$$
$$C_{6,5} = 6!/(5!)(6-5)! = 6$$
$$C_{6,6} = 6!/(6!)(6-6)! = 1$$

It is left to you to demonstrate that the number of combinations computed for each exposure level is, in fact, correct. In addition, it should be noticed that the beta distribution is symmetrical and that, after the midpoint, the number of combinations will mirror those for lower exposure levels.

Generating the binomial distribution

The beta distribution provides an estimate of the *number of ways* target members can be exposed to a schedule a particular number of times. The binomial distribution estimates the *average probability* of exposure to a schedule a particular number of times. For example, there is only one way not to be exposed to this magazine schedule and that is to miss all six vehicles in the schedule. The probability of this occurring throughout the given target audience is 1.0 minus the reach of the schedule, or the probability of not being exposed to the schedule. To estimate this, the estimates of $\bar{R}_1$ and $\bar{R}_2$ are needed to compute an exposure parameter and a non-exposure parameter.

The exposure parameter can be calculated as follows.

$$A = (\bar{R}_1(\bar{R}_2-\bar{R}_1))/(2(\bar{R}_1)-\bar{R}_2-\bar{R}_1^2) \tag{8-3}$$

One may recall that in the magazine schedule $\bar{R}_1 = 24.8\%$ and $\bar{R}_2 = 37.8\%$. Therefore this gives:

$$A = (.248(.378-.248))/(2(.248)-.378-.248^2)$$
$$= .032/.0565$$
$$= .57$$

The non-exposure parameter is given by:

$$B = A(1 - \bar{R}_1)/\bar{R}_1 \tag{8-4}$$
$$= .57(1 - .248)/.248$$
$$= 1.728$$

Now, if A and B are added, the result is called "D."

$$D = A + B$$
$$D = .57 + 1.73$$
$$D = 2.3$$

Given this definition, one will notice that A/D is always equal to $\bar{R}_1$ and B/D is always equal to $1-\bar{R}_1$. Although these ratios remain constant for all schedules, the sizes of A, B, and D increase steadily with the reach of the schedule. An interesting research project might be to examine the functional relationship between A, B, and D and various schedule characteristics, such as reach. This knowledge could be used to solve more quickly a variety of other versions of the BBD procedure.

It turns out that the probability of not being exposed to this schedule is equal to:

$$P(0) = \frac{(B)(B+1)(B+2)(B+3)(B+4)(B+5)}{(D)(D+1)(D+2)(D+3)(D+4)(D+5)}$$

Thus there are always an equal number of terms in the numerator and the denominator and the number of terms is equal to the total number of insertions in the schedule. You can also notice that one is added to each parameter after the first. In this example, to compute P(0), rounding B and D for the sake of convenience would give the following:

$$P(0) = \frac{(1.73)(2.73)(3.73)(4.73)(5.73)(6.73)}{(2.3)(3.3)(4.3)(5.3)(6.3)(7.3)}$$
$$= 3213/7993$$
$$= .4020$$

P(0) = .402 is the probability of not being exposed to this magazine schedule. That is, it is the probability of *not* being exposed to any of the six insertions in the campaign. This is true because the number of ways not to be exposed (that is, the number of combinations of six insertions taken zero times) is equal to 1.0 and (1)(.402) = .402.

In continuing for other exposure levels, the denominator at each exposure level remains unchanged. The number of exposure parameters (A's) in the numerator for each exposure level is equal to the number of exposures at that level. You should note too that there are always N (six in this case) total terms in both the numerator and the denominator and that the second, third, etc. exposure and non-exposure parameter are increased by one, two, etc., respectively.

$$P(1) = [(A)(B)(B+1)(B+2)(B+3)(B+4)]/7993$$
$$= [(.57)(1.73)(2.73)(3.73)(4.73)(5.73)]/7993$$
$$= 272.15/7993$$
$$= .0341$$

$$P(2) = [(A)(A+1)(B)(B+1)(B+2)(B+3)]/7993$$
$$= [(.57)(1.57)(1.73)(2.73)(3.73)(4.73)]/7993$$
$$= 74.57/7993$$
$$= .0094$$

$$P(3) = [(A)(A+1)(A+2)(B)(B+1)(B+2)]/7993$$
$$= [(.57)(1.57)(2.57)(1.73)(2.73)(3.73)]/7993$$

$$= 40.52/7993$$
$$= .0051$$
$$P(4) = [(A)(A+1)(A+2)(A+3)(B)(B+1)]/7993$$
$$= [(.57)(1.57)(2.57)(3.57)(1.73)(2.73)]/7993$$
$$= 38.78/7993$$
$$= .0049$$
$$P(5) = [(A)(A+1)(A+2)(A+3)(A+4)(B)]/7993$$
$$= [(.57)(1.57)(2.57)(3.57)(4.57)(1.73)]/7993$$
$$= 64.91/7993$$
$$= .0081$$
$$P(6) = [(A)(A+1)(A+2)(A+3)(A+4)(A+5)]/7993$$
$$= [(.57)(1.57)(2.57)(3.57)(4.57)(5.57)]/7993$$
$$= 209/7993$$
$$= .0261$$

To estimate the entire exposure distribution, one must now multiply the beta distribution by the binomial distribution.

Exposure Distribution		=	Beta Distribution	x	Binomial Distribution
f	%				
0	.402	=	1	×	.402
1	.205	=	6	×	.0341
2	.141	=	15	×	.0094
3	.102	=	20	×	.0051
4	.074	=	15	×	.0049
5	.049	=	6	×	.0081
6	.027	=	1	×	.0261
Sum =	1.000				

If all of the computations have been done correctly, the sum of the exposure distribution percentages should add to 1.00, or close to it, depending on the rounding error.

Armed with this information, it is now possible to evaluate fully the magazine schedule.

$$\text{Reach} = 1 - .402$$
$$= .598$$
$$= 59.8\%$$

You will recall that GRPs = 149. Therefore:

$$\text{Average Frequency} = 149/59.8$$
$$= 2.5$$
$$\text{Reach (3+)} = .102 + .074 + .049 + .027$$
$$= .252$$
$$= 25.2\%$$

Gross Impressions = (149/100)(69,405,000)
          = 103,413,450

Total Schedule Cost = $108,800 + (4)($89,300) + $69,245
          = $535,245

CPM/Gross Impressions = $535,245/103,413.450
          = $5.18

Cost-per-rating point = $535,245/149
          = $3,592.25

The media evaluation factors presented here normally are not useful in themselves. Rather, they are intended to be of help in comparison to brand objectives and to other schedules designed to contribute to those objectives. The goal at this point, however, is to acquaint you with the procedures used to evaluate media schedules to understand what is required to improve the schedule. For example, one might consider the following questions. How would this schedule be modified to increase Reach (3 +) given the $535,245 total schedule cost ceiling? This could perhaps be achieved by replacing *Reader's Digest*, which has the highest CPM in the schedule ($5.89), with lower rated, but more efficient vehicles. It might be possible to purchase two full-page, four-color ads in *Women's Day* ($65,100, R_i = 19.4), and *People* ($56,425, R_i = 15.2). Although the sum of the costs and ratings of these two magazines ($121,525, GRPs = 34.6) is more than *Reader's Digest*, it is clear that the addition of two publications will increase the duplication between vehicles and therefore increase average frequency and effective reach (3 +). Also, together these two publications have a CPM of $5.06 compared to $5.89 for *Reader's Digest*. This assumes, of course, that the editorial environments provided by *Women's Day* and *People* are suitable for brand objectives.

☐ Estimating Schedule Reach Given Limited Information

There are situations in which the media planner may not have full information when evaluating a magazine schedule. Also, in the case of large schedules, the work required to obtain self- and cross-pair data may not be justified by the small improvement in accuracy. In such an instance, there are alternate procedures available that use single insertion ratings only. Such methods provide reasonably accurate results under specified conditions.[5] The approach actually is simple.

First, an estimate of schedule reach is obtained based on the schedule GRPs and total insertions (N). Then a value of the exposure parameter (A) is chosen along with the corresponding value of the nonexposure parameter (B). As shown earlier, this is sufficient information to obtain a complete exposure distribution. The reach based on the exposure distribution of this first "iteration" ($Reach_i$) is then compared to the reach ($Reach_E$) estimated on the basis of GRPs and N. The difference is then added to, or subtracted from, the exposure parameter A and the process is repeated until the two estimates of reach are approximately equal. An example will clarify this.

It is assumed that planners want to assess the magazine schedule used in the example above but have only single insertion ratings and do not have self- and cross-pair ratings. The available information follows.

Magazine	Insertions (N)	Single Insertion Rating (R_i)* (%)	GRPs	Four-Color Page Cost
Reader's Digest	1	26.6%	26.6	$108,800
TV Guide	4	25.4	101.6	$ 89,300
Good Housekeeping	1	20.8	20.8	$ 69,245
Total	6		149.0	

*Base is female homemakers who use cold breakfast cereal.
Source is SMRB, 1985, Volume P-20.

This information is sufficient to evaluate the schedule fully.

The work of Rice and Leckenby[6] has shown that the following power equation, selected here for its simplicity, provides an accurate estimate of reach based on GRPs and N for an adult target and with SMRB magazine audience ratings. Using it here for a target comprised of female homemakers introduces some error, but probably not enough to be of particular concern, as will become evident. Rice and Leckenby's power equation can be expressed as follows:

$$\text{Reach}_E = (1.1335)(\text{GRPs})^{.8939}(N)^{-.1567} \qquad (8\text{-}5)$$

where: Reach_E = schedule reach estimated on the basis of the power function,
   GRPs = schedule gross rating points,
   N = total insertions in the schedule.

Substituting the values for GRPs and N from the magazine schedule yields the following estimate of reach.

$$
\begin{aligned}
\text{Reach}_E &= (1.1335)(149)^{.8939}(6)^{-.1567} \\
&= (1.1335)(87.6216)(.7552) \\
&= .7504 \\
&= 75.04\%
\end{aligned}
$$

You can prove that the ratio of the exposure parameter (A) to the denominator (D) of the BBD model is always equal to the average single insertion rating of the schedule ($\bar{R}_1$ or GRPs/N). Indeed, $\bar{R}_1$ is the lower limit of the exposure parameter. As the size of the schedule increases, the sizes of A and D both increase but the ratio of A to D remains constant and equal to $\bar{R}_1$. Consequently, it makes sense to use $\bar{R}_1$ as the initial estimate of A when evaluating a schedule. One can recall that $\bar{R}_1$ = GRPs/N = 149/6 = 24.8 percent. A, then, will be set equal to 24.8 percent. To estimate B, the following formula is used.

$$B = (A(N - \text{GRPs}/100))/(\text{GRPs}/100) \qquad (8\text{-}6)$$

In the example:

$$B = (.248(6 - 149/100))/(149/100)$$
$$= (.248(6 - 1.49))/1.49$$
$$= (.248(4.51))/1.49$$
$$= .752$$

And since $D = A + B$, then $D = .248 + .752 = 1.00$. For the first iteration, $B = 1 - A$, but subsequent iterations require Equation 8-6 since D generally is greater than 1.00.

Once A and B have been found, the initial or iterative estimate of reach ($Reach_I$) will be obtained by evaluating $1 - P(0)$ as it is using the BBD full information (BBD-F) model.

$$Reach_I = 1 - P(0)$$
$$= 1 - \frac{[(.752)(1.752)(2.752)(3.752)(4.752)(5.752)]}{(1)(2)(3)(4)(5)(6)}$$
$$= 1 - 371.84/720$$
$$= 1 - .5164$$
$$= .4835 = 48.35\%$$

As stated earlier, $Reach_E = 75.04\%$. Therefore, $Reach_I = 48.35\%$ is too low and $Reach_I$ should be estimated again using a higher value of A. Since there are diminishing returns in reach due to increases in A, it makes sense to add at least $Reach_E - Reach_I$ to A. In this way the resulting estimate of $Reach_I$ will not exceed $Reach_E$. Following this procedure:

$$A = A + (Reach_E - Reach_I) \tag{8-7}$$
$$= 24.8\% + (75.04\% - 48.35\%)$$
$$= 24.8\% + 26.69\%$$
$$= 51.5\%$$

Using Equation (8-6):

$$B = (.515(6 - 149/100))/(149/100)$$
$$= (.515(6 - 1.49))/(1.49)$$
$$= (.515)(4.51)/1.49$$
$$= 1.56$$

Now, $D = A + B = .515 + 1.56 = 2.075$. This is sufficient to re-estimate $1 - P(0) = Reach_I$ and to continue the iterative process.

Unfortunately, for schedules such as this, the iterative process will take considerable time. In the magazine schedule above, for example, numerous iterations are required so that $Reach_I$ is within two percent of $Reach_E$. This would not be practical to do by hand, of course. Fortunately, there is the power and speed of the computer to rely on for this chore. A personal computer, for example, can complete the necessary iterations in seconds.

Using the computer model ADPLAN, described later on, it turns out that the last iteration yields the following BBD parameters.

$$A = 3.379$$
$$B = 10.228$$
$$Reach_1 = 76.15\%$$

This information easily could be used to expand the BBD model and to generate the usual media evaluation factors. Although it would take too much space to do that here, it is instructive to compare the media evaluation factors generated by the BBD-F model with those generated by the BBD limited information (BBD-L) model. These are displayed in Table 8.3.

The BBD-L will tend to overstate reach (3+) compared to the BBD-F. It is thought this problem occurs, in part, because Rice and Leckenby[7] developed Equation 8-5 using schedules with a maximum of two insertions per vehicle. That shown in Table 8.3 has either one or four insertions per vehicle. Still, the BBD-L saves much time and effort in gathering self- and cross-pair data, which may even be un-

TABLE 8.3 Magazine Advertising Media Plan Evaluation Using Full (BBD-F) and Limited (BBD-L) Information

Brand = Kellogg's All-Bran
Target = Female Homemakers Who Use Cold Breakfast Cereals
Target Size = 69,405,000

	Exposure Distributions	
Frequency	**BBD-L (%)**	**BBD-F (%)**
0	23.85	40.59
1	31.75	20.35
2	24.43	13.93
3	13.25	10.13
4	5.18	7.32
5	1.36	4.96
6	0.19	2.71

BBD-L Parameters: $\bar{R}_1 = .248$ $Reach_E = .748$ $A = 3.379$ $B = 10.228$
BBD-F Parameters: $\bar{R}_1 = .248$ $\bar{R}_2 = .378$ $A = .57$ $B = 1.73$

Overall Evaluation	**BBD-L**	**BBD-F**
Reach (1+):	76.15%	59.41%
Effective Reach (3+):	19.98%	25.13%
Average Frequency:	1.96	2.51
Gross Rating Points:	149.00	149.00
Gross Impressions (000):	103,413.45	103,413.45
CPM/Gross Impressions:	$5.18	$5.18
Cost Per Rating Point:	$3,592.25	$3,592.25

Vehicles	Rating	CUME (BBD-F)	Ad Cost	CPM	Number of Ads	Total Cost
RD	26.6	34.1	$108,800	$5.90	1	$108,800
TVG	25.4	32.2	$ 89,300	$5.07	4	$357,200
GH	20.8	27.6	$ 69,245	$4.80	1	$ 69,245
Total				$5.18	6	$535,245

available in many situations. Furthermore, as Chapter Three indicated, substantial adjustments to audience ratings can be made to account for advertising exposure, which render the errors associated with model choice of secondary importance.

INTRODUCTION TO *ADPLAN*

ADPLAN is designed to provide users with operational state-of-the-art theories and concepts that are available on a routine basis. Although such tools have been used by practitioners for nearly 20 years, there have been too few equivalent procedures for those with limited objectives.[8] Many face financial constraints which often place costly industry procedures out of reach.[9] Time constraints limit the scope of material that can be analyzed as well. Consequently, the most sophisticated techniques are often by-passed for sheer expediency and the lack of practical tools needed to implement them.

The system described here greatly reduces obstacles to bringing the best available theories and techniques to those eager to learn them. It does this by combining a number of elements, including syndicated advertising media audience, message, and cost data through computer-based interactive advertising media exposure distribution models. All of the system's procedures are demonstrated in this and the following three chapters with simple examples that can be worked by hand.

By using the data, techniques, and interactive computer program described in this chapter, you should be able to develop estimates of reach, gross rating points, gross impressions, average frequency, total schedule cost, cost-per-thousand impressions, frequency distributions, and effective reach, among others, for a variety of major print and broadcast media categories, and target audiences. The model is first introduced in general terms and then explained in greater detail for each of the print media.

CAPABILITIES

ADPLAN will evaluate national, regional, and local advertising media schedules for a dozen media categories:

1. Local newspapers
2. National newspapers
3. Newspaper supplements
4. Consumer magazines
5. Business publications
6. Network television
7. Spot television
8. Cable television
9. Network radio
10. Spot radio
11. Direct mail
12. Outdoor

In addition, the program can evaluate the combined impact of media schedules, involving two or more media categories, on the same target audience. The weight of a national campaign in a regional or local market can also be assessed by ADPLAN and combined with other regional or local media schedules.

INPUT REQUIREMENTS

ADPLAN is designed to use audience data from Simmons Market Research Bureau (SMRB), Mediamark Research Inc. (MRI), A. C. Nielsen Co., Arbitron, the Birch Report, and Scarborough, among others.

For each separate media category, the following data are required.

1. National, regional, or local target audience description and size.
2. For each vehicle in the schedule:
   a. single-insertion audience rating,
   b. ad cost for a single insertion,
   c. number of insertions.

For consumer magazines, national and local newspapers and newspaper supplements, ADPLAN will also use the following additional data for each vehicle in a schedule, if it is available.

3. Self-pair audience rating.
4. Cross-pair audience rating.

The network and spot radio subroutines have been adapted to the cumulative audience ratings provided by SMRB, but they can also handle the average quarter-hour data published by Arbitron or Birch, for example. In the case of outdoor advertising schedules, the program requires the one-day gross audience rating for a selected showing, and the 30-day reach of the showing, and assumes 30 insertions per month.

In order to estimate advertising exposures or other desired communication effects delivered by a particular schedule, ADPLAN allows the user to input weights to adjust vehicle audience ratings. These can be obtained from Starch Inra Hooper, Burke Marketing Research, Gallup and Robinson, Simmons Market Research Bureau (SMRB), and Mediamark Research (MRI), among others.[10]

ADPLAN retains in memory all inputs and estimated evaluation factors for up to ten individual media schedules, which can then be combined in order to examine the weight of multiple media category schedules against the target audience. When this is done, there is the option of accounting for levels of duplication between media categories.

EVALUATING MEDIA CATEGORIES

ADPLAN evaluates separate advertising media category schedules based on the beta binomial exposure distribution model (BBD). For each vehicle in a schedule, the BBD model requires single-insertion plus self- and cross-pair audience ratings. It should be noted that ADPLAN allows the user to input all three types of data for magazines, national newspapers, and newspaper supplements.

However, ADPLAN will compute self- and cross-pair audience ratings, or use iterative procedures, for all remaining media categories other than direct mail. It does this by using the "random combination" method[11] in conjunction with unique correction factors and/or equations for each media category, which are used to estimate within- and between-vehicle duplication and self- and/or cross-pair reach.

The random combination method, as applied in ADPLAN, can be expressed as follows.

$$R_{2i} = 2(R_i) - (k_{wm})(R_i)^2, \qquad (8\text{-}8)$$
$$R_{ij} = R_i + R_j - (k_{bm})(R_i)(R_j), \qquad (8\text{-}9)$$

where:

R_{2i} = self-pair audience rating for vehicle i,
R_{ij} = cross-pair audience rating for vehicles i and j,
R_i = single insertion audience rating for vehicle i,
R_j = single insertion audience rating for vehicle j,
k_{wm} = correction factor for within-vehicle duplication in media category m,
k_{bm} = correction factor for between-vehicle duplication in media category m,
i = 1, ..., n-1 total vehicles in a schedule,
j = 2, ..., n total vehicles in a schedule,
m = any media category for which R_{2i} and R_{ij} are required but not available.

The specific within- and between-vehicle duplication correction factors and self- and cross-pair rating estimating equations used for several media categories are listed below. Space constraints do not allow a discussion of the derivation of each of the equations. However, it has been shown that they lead to reasonable estimates of reach and frequency when compared with those provided by Interactive Market Systems, Inc. (IMS), a popular media software house,[12] or when compared to available self- and cross-pair audience data (see Chapter Fourteen).

1. Local newspapers:
$$R_{2i} = -.0037 + 1.3616(R_i) - .3506(R_i)^2 \qquad (8\text{-}10)$$
$$R_{ij} = -.0092 + 1.057(R_i + R_j) - 1.2259(R_i)(R_j) \qquad (8\text{-}11)$$

2. Network, spot and cable (intercepts = 0)[13] television:
$$R_{2i} = -.00651 + 1.7946(R_i) - 1.3308(R_i)^2 \qquad (8\text{-}12)$$
$$R_{ij} = -.00149 + 1.0095(R_i + R_j) - 1.5012(R_i)(R_j) \qquad (8\text{-}13)$$

3. Network and spot radio:
$$R_i = R_i \text{ for average-quarter-hour ratings provided by Arbitron}$$
$$\text{and Birch, for example} \qquad (8\text{-}14)$$
$$R_i = .17(R_i) \text{ for SMRB and MRI cumulative audience ratings} \qquad (8\text{-}15)$$
$$k_w = 14.12 + 1480.99(R_i) + .00046(1/R_i^2) - 91648.66(R_i^2) \qquad (8\text{-}16)$$
$$R_{ij} = R_i + R_j - (R_i)(R_j) \qquad (8\text{-}17)$$

ADPLAN uses procedures similar to those described by Rice and Leckenby[14] to estimate exposure distributions for magazines, national newspapers, and supplements when self- and cross-pair ratings are not available or when their use would be impractical in the case of schedules with a large number of vehicles. After the single insertion-ratings are entered, ADPLAN uses the following equation to estimate schedule reach.

$$\text{Reach} = 1.1335(\text{GRPs})^{.893951}(\text{N})^{-.156725} \tag{8-18}$$

where: GRPs = total schedule gross rating points
N = total schedule insertions

ADPLAN then chooses a BBD exposure parameter (A), starting at the value predicted by Equation 8-19.

$$A = e^{-2.1401}N^{-.00527}(\text{GRP}/100)^{1.8024}((\text{GRP}/100)^3)^{.21274} \tag{8-19}$$

The non-exposure parameter (B) is defined as:

$$B = (\text{N-GRPs}/100)/(\text{GRPs}/100) \tag{8-20}$$

The BBD procedure uses A and B to estimate reach which is then compared to that estimated by Equation 8-18. If the difference between the two estimates is greater or less than two percent of the reach estimated by Equation 8-18, then an iterative procedure is used whereby A is gradually increased or decreased until the iterative reach is within that interval.

For outdoor advertising, the user must input both the one-day gross audience rating (R_1) and the 30-day net reach (R_{30}) of a 25, 50 or 100 showing, as provided by SMRB for selected targets. ADPLAN then follows an iterative procedure, similar to that for magazines in a limited information situation, until an iterative reach is obtained that is within two percent of R_{30}. The A parameter initially is predicted using Equation 8-21.

$$A = e^{.91012}\text{GRP}^{-.29084} \tag{8-21}$$

The objectives of this process are to calculate an outdoor exposure distribution that can be weighted and combined with other media schedules and to estimate effective reach (3+).

For direct mail and all other schedules involving one insertion in one vehicle, the BBD subroutine is bypassed, with the reach set equal to the user-input single-insertion rating.

☐ Weighting Media Categories

ADPLAN computes a number of important media evaluation factors. These are output for all schedules on both a *weighted* basis, to account for advertising exposures or other desired communication effects, and on an *unweighted* basis, providing estimates based on user-input media vehicle audiences. A recent survey of media directors has shown that almost one third of the top agencies surveyed use weights.[15] ADPLAN uses the unweighted exposure distribution to compute one that is weighted (see Chapter Three), which also serves as the basis for computing the remaining weighted media evaluation factors.

☐ Combining Media Categories

ADPLAN estimates the effects of schedules involving pairs of media categories by using principles of matrix algebra to obtain the product of the two separate exposure distributions. Such joint exposure distributions might then be combined with yet another to estimate the likely impact of three media categories to be used simultaneously, and so on. Media evaluation factors for combined schedules are provided in both weighted and unweighted form.

This procedure assumes that duplication between pairs of media categories is random, which is an appropriate assumption in certain circumstances, but not in others. To determine whether random duplication between two categories is valid, one can compute the ratio of "random dual" to "actual dual" using the quintile/tercile and media imperative data available from SMRB. The random dual can be found by summing the product of the upper quintiles or terciles constituting the dual for a particular pair of media categories. The SMRB Technical Appendix (Volume T-1) identifies which quintiles or terciles constitute the dual for each pair of media categories. The actual dual can be taken directly from SMRB reports.

If the ratio of random dual to actual dual is close to one, the duplication between media categories is assumed to be random, otherwise the duplication is greater or less than would be expected on the basis of chance. This ratio is then used by ADPLAN to increase or decrease the duplication at all exposure levels for each pair of media categories. The weighted average ratio for all possible pairs of media categories can be used when combining more than two media categories. More is said on this in Chapter Eleven.

☐ Evaluating the Regional or Local Weight of a National Schedule

ADPLAN will evaluate the regional or local weight of a national schedule. To do so, the user must provide the regional or local and U.S. target audience sizes. Absolute values of the regional or local schedule (e.g., gross impressions, vehicle costs) are assumed to be proportional to the percent of the U.S. target audience that resides in the region or locale. All factors based on percentages (e.g., reach, average frequency, GRPs) are taken as the same for the national and regional or local markets, although the base is lower for the smaller markets.

☐ Output

ADPLAN output includes a number of weighted and unweighted media evaluation factors, which are listed below.

1. Exposure distributions, both cumulative and non-cumulative
2. BBD parameters
3. Reach (1+)
4. Effective reach (3+)
5. Gross rating points
6. Gross impressions
7. Average frequency
8. Cost-per-thousand for the entire schedule based on gross impressions
9. Cost-per-rating point
10. Total insertions
11. Total cost

In addition, ADPLAN summarizes all of the input data and some computed variables including: target market size(s), the vehicle weight and its basis, vehicle names, one-insertion ratings, self- and cross-pair ratings or predicted reach (1+) when appropriate, cost-per-insertion, cost-per-thousand based on weighted gross impressions, the number of insertions, and the total cost per vehicle. All of this information can also be printed and saved in table and raw data disk files.

☐ Accuracy

ADPLAN accuracy depends upon the number of estimated equations. No doubt these can be improved. Also, other models are available for some media categories.[16] However, the purpose of using ADPLAN is to give users experience designing and evaluating media plans and to allow them to observe the various reach/frequency tradeoffs under various budget constraints. If the program provides reasonable estimates, it should be satisfactory yet not mislead as to the likely impact of alternatives.

The model estimates have been compared with those of IMS for a variety of schedules to insure that the results are reasonable. In addition, actual audience data were used in estimating equations that predict self- and cross-pair audience ratings. In most cases, the equations fit the observations quite well with $R^2 = .99$.

EVALUATING MAGAZINES (FULL INFORMATION) USING *ADPLAN*

This section gives examples of the interactions with the ADPLAN program for magazines. You are reminded that all data used here come from SMRB 1985 on female homemakers who are users of ready-to-eat breakfast cereals. The chosen vehicles that are used in the examples and their corresponding audience and cost data are the same as those used earlier in the text.

A full-information magazine evaluation requires that the user provide the program with three types of audience ratings. The example here uses: *Reader's Digest*, *TV Guide*, and *Good Housekeeping*. In order to evaluate such a schedule, one needs: single-insertion ratings, self-pair ratings, cost-per-insertion, and the number of insertions. It is also necessary to have the cross-pair ratings for each possible combination of two vehicles.

```
Describe the geographic coverage of your schedule

   1 = National schedule
   2 = National schedule evaluated in a particular region
   3 = Regional schedule

Your choice? 1

Describe your target (e.g., Female Homemakers)   ? Female Homemakers

Type target size (e.g., 67502000)                ? 69405000

Select the media category you want to use.

   1=Consumer Magazines      5=Local Newspapers    9=Network Radio
   2=Business Publications    6=Network TV         10=Spot Radio
   3=National Newspapers      7=Spot TV            11=Outdoor
   4=Newspaper Supplements    8=Cable TV           12=Direct Mail

Your choice? 1

Available audience data:

   1 = Single insertion ratings only
   2 = Single insertion ratings plus all self- and cross-pairs

Your choice? 2
```

In addition, one must decide whether to weight the exposure distribution, and what communication effect is being used. Here, the typical factor of 0.525 will be used, based on "Recall." What follows is a complete evaluation of this schedule, including all prompts, inputs, and results.

```
Input vehicle audience weight to account for advertising
exposures or other communication effects.  For example:

   1.000 = Unweighted (vehicle exposures = ad exposures)
    .525 = Typical weight for CONSUMER MAGAZINES

Enter weight? .525

Describe basis of weight (e.g., awareness, recall, knowledge)

Communication effect? Recall

How many vehicles in your CONSUMER MAGAZINES schedule? 3

For each CONSUMER MAGAZINES vehicle, enter:
```

Vehicle Number/Name	Ad Cost	Ads(#)	Rating	Self-pair	1=OK 2=no
1? Reader's Digest	? 108800	? 1	? .266	? .341	? 1
2? TV Guide	? 89300	? 4	? .254	? .322	? 1
3? Good Housekeeping	? 69245	? 1	? .208	? .277	? 1

For each vehicle pair, enter cross-pair rating.

Cross-pair Numbers/Names	Rating	(1=OK, 2=no)
1- 2 Reader's Digest-TV Guide	? .436	? 1
1- 3 Reader's Digest-Good Housekeeping	? .396	? 1
2- 3 TV Guide-Good Housekeeping	? .398	? 1

View estimated cross-pair ratings (1=yes, 2=no)? 1

Cross-pair Numbers/Names	Rating
1- 2 Reader's Digest-TV Guide	.4360
1- 3 Reader's Digest-Good Housekeeping	.3960
2- 3 TV Guide-Good Housekeeping	.3980

Change cross-pair rating (1=yes, 2=no)? 2

ADPLAN RESULTS: CONSUMER MAGAZINES

Name = Kent Lancaster   Target ID = Female Homemakers
Brand = Kellogg's All-Bran   Target Size = 69,405,000
Period = January 1988

Frequency (f) Distribution	Unweighted		Weighted	
f	% f	% f+	% f	% f+
0	40.59%	100.00%	68.81%	100.00%
1	20.35%	59.41%	10.68%	31.19%
2	13.93%	39.07%	7.32%	20.51%
3	10.13%	25.13%	5.32%	13.19%
4	7.32%	15.00%	3.85%	7.87%
5	4.96%	7.68%	2.60%	4.03%
6	2.71%	2.71%	1.43%	1.43%

BBD Factors: R1 = .248, R2 = .378, A = .5592815876, B = 1.692859053
Weight (recall) = 52.5%

Summary Evaluation	Unweighted	Weighted
Reach (1+)	59.41%	31.19%
Effective Reach (3+)	25.13%	13.19%
Average Frequency	2.51	2.51
Gross Rating Points	149.00	78.22
Gross Impressions (000)	103,413.45	54,292.06
CPM/Gross Impressions	$5.18	$9.86
Cost Per Rating Point	$3,592.25	$6,842.38

Vehicle List	Rating	Cume	Ad Cost	CPM	Ads	Total Cost
Reader's Diges	26.60	34.10	$108,800	$11.23	1	$108,800
TV Guide	25.40	32.20	$89,300	$9.65	4	$357,200
Good Housekeep	20.80	27.70	$69,245	$9.14	1	$69,245
			Totals:	$9.86	6	$535,245

EVALUATING MAGAZINES (LIMITED INFORMATION) USING *ADPLAN*

The procedures described here allow one to evaluate a magazine schedule when the only audience information available is the single insertion rating for each vehicle in the schedule. The three vehicles considered in the Magazine (Full Information) evaluation will again be used: *Reader's Digest, TV Guide, Good Housekeeping*. For each vehicle in the schedule the following data are needed: single-insertion rating, cost-per-insertion, and the number of insertions.

ADPLAN will calculate the exposure distribution using an iterative method which will mean that these results will differ from those obtained from the full information procedures. This should not be a disincentive to using the limited information version because it can save a great deal of time in the planning process in situations when accuracy may not be of critical importance.

Again, one decides whether to discount or weight the exposure distribution, and what communication effect to use as the basis for that weight. This schedule uses 0.525, once more based on "Recall." Here are the results obtained by using ADPLAN on such a schedule.

```
Describe the geographic coverage of your schedule

   1 = National schedule
   2 = National schedule evaluated in a particular region
   3 = Regional schedule

Your choice? 1

Describe your target (e.g., Female Homemakers)    ? Female Homemakers

Type target size (e.g., 67502000)                 ? 69405000

Select the media category you want to use.

   1=Consumer Magazines      5=Local Newspapers    9=Network Radio
   2=Business Publications    6=Network TV         10=Spot Radio
   3=National Newspapers      7=Spot TV            11=Outdoor
   4=Newspaper Supplements    8=Cable TV           12=Direct Mail

Your choice? 1

Available audience data:

   1 = Single insertion ratings only
   2 = Single insertion ratings plus all self- and cross-pairs

Your choice? 1

Input vehicle audience weight to account for advertising
exposures or other communication effects.  For example:

   1.000 = Unweighted (vehicle exposures = ad exposures)
    .525 = Typical weight for CONSUMER MAGAZINES

Enter weight? .525

Describe basis of weight (e.g., awareness, recall, knowledge)
```

Communication effect? Recall

How many vehicles in your CONSUMER MAGAZINES schedule? 3

For each CONSUMER MAGAZINES vehicle, enter:

Vehicle Number/Name	Ad Cost	Ads(#)	Rating	1=OK 2=no
1? Reader's Digest	? 108800	? 1	? .266	? 1
2? TV Guide	? 89300	? 4	? .254	? 1
3? Good Housekeeping	? 69425	? 1	? .208	? 1

ADPLAN RESULTS: CONSUMER MAGAZINES

Name = Kent Lancaster   Target ID = Female Homemakers
Brand = All-Bran   Target Size = 69,405,000
Period = June 1988

Frequency (f) Distribution	Unweighted		Weighted	
f	% f	% f+	% f	% f+
0	23.85%	100.00%	60.02%	100.00%
1	31.75%	76.15%	16.67%	39.98%
2	24.43%	44.41%	12.83%	23.31%
3	13.25%	19.98%	6.95%	10.49%
4	5.18%	6.73%	2.72%	3.53%
5	1.36%	1.55%	0.72%	0.81%
6	0.19%	0.19%	0.10%	0.10%

BBD Factors: R1 = .248, RE = .748, A = 3.378990888, B = 10.22768402
Weight (Recall) = 52.5%

Summary Evaluation	Unweighted	Weighted
Reach (1+)	76.15%	39.98%
Effective Reach (3+)	19.98%	10.49%
Average Frequency	1.96	1.96
Gross Rating Points	149.00	78.22
Gross Impressions (000)	103,413.45	54,292.06
CPM/Gross Impressions	$5.18	$9.86
Cost Per Rating Point	$3,592.25	$6,842.38

Vehicle List	Rating	Cume	Ad Cost	CPM	Ads	Total Cost
Reader's Diges	26.60	N/A	$108,800	$11.23	1	$108,800
TV Guide	25.40	N/A	$89,300	$9.65	4	$357,200
Good Housekeep	20.80	N/A	$69,245	$9.14	1	$69,245
			Totals:	$9.86	6	$535,245

In order to see the effect of using fewer vehicles, one can modify the schedule by selecting option ''2'' after the run. An example of this follows.

```
 1 = Review LAST schedule
 2 = Modify LAST schedule
 3 = Create NEW schedule using parts of LAST schedule
 4 = Create NEW schedule from scratch
 5 = Combine two or more schedules
 6 = Save raw data on disk file
 7 = Get raw data on disk file
 8 = Save table on disk file
 9 = Print table
10 = Select Optimum Schedule
11 = Return to DOS
12 = Stop, return to DOS

Your choice? 2

The LAST schedule is summarized below.
Change which line number?

     1.  No changes, evaluate schedule
     2.  Your name                      Kent Lancaster
     3.  Brand name                     All-Bran
     4.  Campaign period                June 1988
     5.  Geographic coverage            National
     6.  National target description    Female Homemakers
     7.  National target size           69405000
     8.  Regional target description
     9.  Regional target size
    10.  Media category                 CONSUMER MAGAZINES
    11.  Vehicle weight (Recall)        0.525
    12.  Number of vehicles             3
    13.  Number of insertions           6
    14.  Review/change vehicles

Your choice? 12


Add(+)/delete(-) how many vehicles (e.g., -1, 0, 2)? -1

The following vehicles are in the LAST schedule
```

Vehicle #/Name	Ad Cost	Ads	Ri	Vehicle #/Name	Ad Cost	Ads	Ri
1 Reader's Dig	108800	1	.266	2 TV Guide	89300	4	.254
3 Good Houseke	69425	1	.208				

```
    Delete vehicle #? 3

The LAST schedule is summarized below.
Change which line number?

     1.  No changes, evaluate schedule
     2.  Your name                      Kent Lancaster
     3.  Brand name                     All-Bran
```

```
        4.  Campaign period              June 1988
        5.  Geographic coverage          National
        6.  National target description  Female Homemakers
        7.  National target size         69405000
        8.  Regional target description
        9.  Regional target size
       10.  Media category               CONSUMER MAGAZINES
       11.  Vehicle weight (Recall)       0.525
       12.  Number of vehicles           3
       13.  Number of insertions         6
       14.  Review/change vehicles
```

Your choice? 1

ADPLAN RESULTS: CONSUMER MAGAZINES

Name = Kent Lancaster   Target ID = Female Homemakers
Brand = All-Bran   Target Size = 69,405,000
Period = June 1988

Frequency (f) Distribution	Unweighted		Weighted	
f	% f	% f+	% f	% f+
0	31.65%	100.00%	64.12%	100.00%
1	30.96%	68.35%	16.25%	35.88%
2	21.09%	37.39%	11.07%	19.63%
3	11.09%	16.30%	5.82%	8.56%
4	4.27%	5.21%	2.24%	2.74%
5	0.95%	0.95%	0.50%	0.50%

BBD Factors: R1 = .256, RE = .673, A = 1.808431148, B = 5.244731903
Weight (Recall) = 52.5%

Summary Evaluation	Unweighted	Weighted
Reach (1+)	68.35%	35.88%
Effective Reach (3+)	16.30%	8.56%
Average Frequency	1.88	1.88
Gross Rating Points	128.20	67.30
Gross Impressions (000)	88,977.22	46,713.04
CPM/Gross Impressions	$5.24	$9.98
Cost Per Rating Point	$3,634.95	$6,923.71

Vehicle List	Rating	Cume	Ad Cost	CPM	Ads	Total Cost
Reader's Diges	26.60	N/A	$108,800	$11.23	1	$108,800
TV Guide	25.40	N/A	$89,300	$9.65	4	$357,200
			Totals:	$9.98	5	$466,000

When ready to move on to another medium, the user selects option 3 and alters line 10.

EVALUATING REGIONAL MAGAZINES USING *ADPLAN*

As many national magazines also have regional editions, you should also be able to evaluate a national magazine schedule on a regional basis. One can do this simply with the ADPLAN program, which allows users to take their national schedule and scale it down to a regional size. If one begins this evaluation on the computer after several others, it is important to modify the last one, altering line number 5, the geographic coverage, to ensure that it reflects a national budget scaled to regional size.

As an example, the same magazines used to demonstrate an evaluation of a national schedule will be included, in addition to information on the regional target and its size. For the sake of convenience, the schedule impact is evaluated in the top 50 U.S. markets. As a practical matter, contiguous regions would be a better basis for this evaluation, but the procedure would be similar. The three vehicles are: *Reader's Digest*, *TV Guide*, and *Good Housekeeping*. The following information is needed for each vehicle for the limited information magazine evaluation procedures: single-insertion rating, cost-per-insertion, and the number of insertions.

If the full-information magazine evaluation procedure is used, one must also provide all self- and cross-pair audience ratings. The previous consumer magazine weighting factor of 0.525, based on "Recall," can again be used. Below is an example of much of an interaction using the limited information magazine subroutine.

```
The LAST schedule is summarized below.
Change which line number?

      1.   No changes, evaluate schedule
      2.   Your name                       Kent Lancaster
      3.   Brand name                      All-Bran
      4.   Campaign period                 June 1988
      5.   Geographic coverage             National
      6.   National target description     Female Homemakers
      7.   National target size            69405000
      8.   Regional target description     Top 50 Markets
      9.   Regional target size            28023940
     10.   Media category                  CONSUMER MAGAZINES
     11.   Vehicle weight (Recall)         0.525
     12.   Number of vehicles              3
     13.   Number of insertions            6
     14.   Review/change vehicles

Your choice? 5

Describe the geographic coverage of your schedule

     1 = National schedule
     2 = National schedule evaluated in a particular region
     3 = Regional schedule
```

```
Your choice? 2

Describe your target (e.g., Female Homemakers)    ? Female Homemakers

Type national target size (e.g., 67502000)        ? 69405000

Type regional target size (e.g., 22000000)        ? 28023940

Describe regional target (e.g., Top 10 ADIs)      ? Top 50 Markets

The LAST schedule is summarized below.
Change which line number?

     1.  No changes, evaluate schedule
     2.  Your name                        Kent Lancaster
     3.  Brand name                       All-Bran
     4.  Campaign period                  June 1988
     5.  Geographic coverage              National
     6.  National target description      Female Homemakers
     7.  National target size             69405000
     8.  Regional target description      Top 50 Markets
     9.  Regional target size             28023940
    10.  Media category                   CONSUMER MAGAZINES
    11.  Vehicle weight (Recall)          0.525
    12.  Number of vehicles               3
    13.  Number of insertions             6
    14.  Review/change vehicles

Your choice? 1
---------------------------------------------------------------------
ADPLAN RESULTS:

Name = Kent Lancaster          National Target ID = Female Homemakers
Brand = Kellogg's All-Bran         Size =  69,405,000
Period = January 1988          Regional Target ID = Top 50 Markets
                                   Size =  28,023,940
```

Frequency (f) Distribution	Unweighted		Weighted	
f	% f	% f+	% f	% f+
0	23.85%	100.00%	60.02%	100.00%
1	31.75%	76.15%	16.67%	39.98%
2	24.43%	44.41%	12.83%	23.31%
3	13.25%	19.98%	6.95%	10.49%
4	5.18%	6.73%	2.72%	3.53%
5	1.36%	1.55%	0.72%	0.81%
6	0.19%	0.19%	0.10%	0.10%

```
BBD Factors:  R1 = .248, RE = .748, A = 3.378990888, B = 10.22768402
Weight (recall) = 52.5%
```

Summary Evaluation	Unweighted	Weighted
Reach (1+)	76.15%	39.98%
Effective Reach (3+)	19.98%	10.49%
Average Frequency	1.96	1.96
Gross Rating Points	149.00	78.22
Gross Impressions (000)	41,755.67	21,921.73
CPM/Gross Impressions	$5.18	$9.86
Cost Per Rating Point	$1,450.46	$2,762.77

Vehicle List	Rating	Cume	Ad Cost	CPM	Ads	Total Cost
Reader's Diges	26.60	N/A	$43,931	$11.23	1	$43,931
TV Guide	25.40	N/A	$36,057	$9.65	4	$144,228
Good Housekeep	20.80	N/A	$27,959	$9.14	1	$27,959
			Totals:	$9.86	6	$216,118

EVALUATING SCHEDULES USING NATIONAL NEWSPAPERS AND SUPPLEMENTS

SMRB and MRI provide audience data for several national newspapers and newspaper supplements. In the case of SMRB, the available data also include self- and cross-pair ratings. As a result, in evaluating a national magazine schedule using SMRB data and full information, it would be most advisable also to include any national newspapers and supplements, because SMRB provides cross-pair ratings among all magazines, national newspapers, and supplements that it evaluates. The entire schedule can then be evaluated in the usual manner using the full-information version of the BBD.

When self- and cross-pair audience information is not available or their use is not practical, the iterative BBD procedure, which was described earlier for magazines, would be appropriate.

Examining SMRB data for female homemakers who use cold breakfast cereals (Vol. P-20, 1985), one finds the following national newspapers and supplements and their corresponding single-issue ratings.

National Newspapers	Single Issue Rating	Cost/Page 4-color
National Enquirer	11.5%	$34,270
The N.Y. Times Daily Edition	1.3	34,650*
The Wall Street Journal	1.8	75,356*
USA Today	1.4	44,739
Supplements		
USA Weekend	12.5	140,815
Parade Magazine	34.3	284,560
Sunday	28.1	238,307

*Black and white rate.

Since the procedures for schedule evaluation used for national newspapers and supplements are identical to magazines, a sample ADPLAN interaction will not be shown. Even without this it is apparent that it would probably not be a sound media strategy to attempt to reach the target using *The Wall Street Journal*, *The New York Times Daily Edition*, or *USA Today*. The CPM is far too high. Nevertheless, if a schedule were evaluated which included the *National Enquirer* one could proceed through the BBD model in the usual fashion, having available estimates of self- and cross-pair audience ratings.

LOCAL NEWSPAPERS

There are a number of techniques that can be used to evaluate the likely impact of a local newspaper schedule. The method demonstrated here is probably the simplest.

If one were to evaluate a local newspaper schedule that will run in the top 50 U.S. markets in order to cover at least 50 percent of each market, one turns first to a media guide that shows that to purchase enough daily newspapers in each of the top 50 markets, their combined metro circulation would be 23,250,000 copies at an open line rate of $332.88.

Now one must estimate target rating points. If one knows that there are 1.14 adult female readers of the average daily paper, since there are 69,405,000 target members in the U.S. out of 90,744,000 adult females, then 76.5 percent of all adult females are in the target. Therefore, there would be .872 target readers per average daily newspaper copy (.765 x 1.14 = .872).

With a circulation of 23,250,000 copies in the top 50 U.S. markets, one would estimate a readership of .872 target readers per copy for a total of 20,274,000 target readers. Since there are estimated to be 27,900,810 target members in the top 50 metro markets, this schedule would deliver 72.6 GRPs against the target per day. (20,274,000/27,900,810 = .726).

From SMRB (1985, Volume P-20, p. 27) it is seen that 7.7 percent of the target reads two or more daily papers. To account for this overlap, it would be useful to assume that at least two papers in each market will be required to obtain the estimated 72.6 GRPs or 36.3 rating points per paper, on average (72.6/2 = 36.3). In fact, an average of two papers is needed to reach at least 50 percent penetration in the top ten markets.

To summarize, it is recommended that a local newspaper schedule in the top 50 U.S. markets is evaluated using the following data.

Newspapers	Daily Rating
Newspaper A	36.3%
Newspaper B	36.3

Now, one can assume further that one black and white advertisement is run per week in each paper, for four total insertions per month in each paper. Each ad will be 50 Standard Advertising Units (SAUs) which will run about 700 agate lines (there are 14 agate lines per SAU). Since the line cost for all papers combined in the top 50 U.S. markets is $332.88, the line cost per paper is $166.44 ($332.88/2 = $166.44). The cost per advertisement, then, is $116,508 (700 x $166.44 = $116,508).

The schedule to be evaluated is as follows, assuming 27,900,810 target members in the top 50 U.S. markets.

Newspaper	Daily Rating	Cost	Insertions
Newspaper A	36.8%	$116,508	4
Newspaper B	36.8	116,508	4

To evaluate fully this schedule using the BBD model also requires estimates of self- and cross-pair ratings. Equations that will serve this purpose were presented previously in this chapter in the section on national newspapers. You may wish to test your command of this material by estimating the self- and cross-pair ratings using the appropriate equations. With this information, one can then evaluate the likely impact of the local newspaper schedule.

This process will probably seem complex and subject to some error. Both criticisms are accepted. Nevertheless, one should compare this procedure with a more realistic one where a media planner evaluates each of the top 50 markets on a market-by-market basis. Data across markets are likely to be highly variable, particularly with respect to the selected target. Furthermore, the conclusion is not likely to be substantially different from the one using the fairly crude steps described above. In fact, for the top 10 U.S. markets it was found that the results using the procedures given here came out very close to those obtained by conducting a market-by-market analysis. As a practical matter, by the time readers finish this text, they will probably be able to do a local newspaper analysis of the type described here in less than five minutes.

EVALUATING LOCAL NEWSPAPERS USING *ADPLAN*

As an example, a newspaper schedule in the top 50 markets was chosen. Two newspapers in each of the top 50 markets were used, called Newspaper A and Newspaper B. For each of these vehicles one must estimate: daily rating (single-insertion rating), cost-per-insertion, and the number of insertions.

A typical weighting factor for this media category is 0.375. It is included here and is based on ''Recall.'' What follows is a sample interaction on ADPLAN.

```
Describe the geographic coverage of your schedule

    1 = National schedule
    2 = National schedule evaluated in a particular region
    3 = Regional schedule


Your choice? 3

Describe your target (e.g., Female Homemakers)   ? Female Homemakers

Type target size (e.g., 67502000)               ? 27900810


Select the media category you want to use.

    1=Consumer Magazines      5=Local Newspapers     9=Network Radio
    2=Business Publications    6=Network TV          10=Spot Radio
    3=National Newspapers      7=Spot TV             11=Outdoor
    4=Newspaper Supplements    8=Cable TV            12=Direct Mail


Your choice? 5

Available audience data:

    1 = Single insertion ratings only
    2 = Single insertion ratings plus all self- and cross-pairs
```

Your choice? 1

Input vehicle audience weight to account for advertising exposures or other communication effects. For example:

   1.000 = Unweighted (vehicle exposures = ad exposures)
    .350 = Typical weight for LOCAL NEWSPAPERS

Enter weight? .350

Describe basis of weight (e.g., awareness, recall, knowledge)

Communication effect? Recall

How many vehicles in your LOCAL NEWSPAPERS schedule? 2

For each LOCAL NEWSPAPERS vehicle, enter:

				1=OK
Vehicle Number/Name	Ad Cost	Ads(#)	Rating	2=no
-------------------	-------	------	------	----
1? Newspaper A	? 116508	? 4	? .368	? 1
2? Newspaper B	? 116508	? 4	? .368	? 1

View estimated cross-pair ratings (1=yes, 2=no)? 1

Cross-pair Numbers/Names	Rating
1- 2 Newspaper A-Newspaper B	.6027

                    Press any key to continue

ADPLAN RESULTS: LOCAL NEWSPAPERS

Name = Kent Lancaster   Target ID = Female Homemakers
Brand = All-Bran   Target Size = 27,900,810
Period = June 1988

Frequency (f) Distribution.	Unweighted		Weighted	
f	% f	% f+	% f	% f+
------------	------	------	------	------
0	17.88%	100.00%	71.26%	100.00%
1	16.19%	82.12%	5.67%	28.74%
2	14.62%	65.93%	5.12%	23.07%
3	13.04%	51.31%	4.56%	17.96%
4	11.41%	38.28%	3.99%	13.40%

5	9.70%	26.86%	3.40%	9.40%
6	7.87%	17.16%	2.75%	6.01%
7	5.84%	9.29%	2.04%	3.25%
8	3.45%	3.45%	1.21%	1.21%

BBD Factors: R1 = .368, R2 = .537, A = .9831190705, B = 1.688400149
Weight (Recall) = 35.0%

Summary Evaluation	Unweighted	Weighted
Reach (1+)	82.12%	28.74%
Effective Reach (3+)	51.31%	17.96%
Average Frequency	3.59	3.59
Gross Rating Points	294.40	103.04
Gross Impressions (000)	82,139.98	28,749.00
CPM/Gross Impressions	$11.35	$32.42
Cost Per Rating Point	$3,165.98	$9,045.65

Vehicle List	Rating	Cume	Ad Cost	CPM	Ads	Total Cost
Newspaper A	36.80	44.99	$116,508	$32.42	4	$466,032
Newspaper B	36.80	44.99	$116,508	$32.42	4	$466,032
			Totals:	$32.42	8	$932,064

OUTDOOR

SMRB provides audience data for various outdoor advertising showing sizes including 100, 50, and 25 showings. For each one, 30-day average frequency and reach are given. For the target of female homemakers who use cold breakfast cereals, for example, SMRB (1985, Volume P-20, p. 39) provides the following information.

Outdoor Showing Size	30-Day Frequency	Reach	Daily Rating (Gross) (Frequency $\times$ Reach/30)
100	28.22	86.9%	81.7%
50	14.89	82.4	40.9
25	8.08	76.1	20.5

You will notice that this data situation is similar to that of magazines in the case of limited information. SMRB provides an estimate of 30-day reach. The problem, then, is to estimate an exposure distribution with that reach. As in the case of the limited information magazine procedure, one would simply choose a starting point for the exposure parameter, A, then estimate B based on A. Next, the exposure distribution can be calculated based on A and B, and the iterative reach checked to see how it compares to the 30-day net obtained from SMRB. If the percent difference between estimated and actual reach is greater than 2.5 percent of the latter, A would then be adjusted up or down and the exposure distribution re-estimated. This iterative process is continued until an acceptable estimate of reach is obtained. An appropriate starting point for A is the daily rating. This can be estimated by dividing monthly GRPs (30-day frequency multiplied by reach) by 30.

To evaluate fully an outdoor schedule, some additional assumptions must be made. One is that the total number of ''insertions'' in a 30-day period is equal to 30—essentially one per day for each day of the month. A second is that the gross and net audiences, as a percentage of the base, delivered on a national basis would be approximately the same in each market or group of markets evaluated. That is, if a 50 showing in the top ten U.S. markets were purchased, one would assume that in a 30-day period 82.4 percent of the target members who reside in each of the top ten U.S. markets would be reached. Likewise, if a 50 showing in the top 20 U.S. markets were bought, one would assume that it would reach 82.4 percent of the target per month in each of the top 20 U.S. markets. Only the base is assumed to change from one market to the next.

If one wanted to evaluate a 50 showing in the top 50 U.S. markets in terms of its likely impact on the target audience, the following information would be needed.

Daily Rating (Gross)	40.9%
30-day net	82.4%
National target size	69,405,000
Percent of target in top 50 ADIs	67.0%
Target size, top 50 markets	46,501,350
Monthly cost	$1,138,719
Monthly insertions	30
Average daily cost	$37,957

The daily rating, 30-day reach and national target audience figures come from SMRB (1985, Volume P-20, p. 39). The percentage of the target in the top 50 ADIs is obtained from a media guide. To estimate the target size in the top 50 markets, one can simply multiply the U.S. target size (69,405,000) by the percent of the target in the top 50 U.S. ADIs (.67) to obtain 46,501,350 target members in the top 50 U.S. ADIs.

The monthly schedule cost for the top 50 U.S. markets can also be found in an agency media guide. Dividing the monthly cost of $1,138,719 by 30 gives an average daily cost of $37,957.

This information, in conjunction with the BBD iterative procedure described above, can give an overall evaluation of the outdoor schedule.

EVALUATING OUTDOOR SCHEDULES USING *ADPLAN*

The evaluation of outdoor schedules on ADPLAN is unique. As billboards are geographically limited to particular regions, one must assume only one vehicle or plant per region although there are many separate illuminated and nonilluminated billboards in each. The planner's interest is in the target coverage of the poster showing in a region, regardless of the number of posters involved. This schedule has one vehicle. It could be called "Billboards." For the showing or GRP size (e.g., 25, 50, or 100), the user must also provide: one-day gross rating (similar to single-insertion rating, for example, .58), ad cost (daily cost = monthly cost/30), and the number of insertions (30). Then the program will ask for the 30-day net reach of the showing (entered as rating, e.g., .869).

In addition, the user must decide whether to discount the exposure distribution and what communication effect is used as the basis. The typical factor, used here, is 0.475, based on "Recall." The outdoor interaction with ADPLAN for the top 50 U.S. markets follows.

```
Select the media category you want to use.

    1=Consumer Magazines      5=Local Newspapers      9=Network Radio
    2=Business Publications   6=Network TV           10=Spot Radio
    3=National Newspapers     7=Spot TV              11=Outdoor
    4=Newspaper Supplements   8=Cable TV             12=Direct Mail

Your choice? 11


Input vehicle audience weight to account for advertising
exposures or other communication effects.  For example:

    1.000 = Unweighted (vehicle exposures = ad exposures)
     .475 = Typical weight for OUTDOOR

Enter weight? .475

Describe basis of weight (e.g., awareness, recall, knowledge)

Communication effect? Recall

How many vehicles in your OUTDOOR schedule? 1

For each OUTDOOR vehicle, enter:
```

| | | | | 1=OK
2=no |
Vehicle Number/Name	Ad Cost	Ads(#)	Rating	
1? Billboards	? 37957	? 30	? .409	? 1

```
Enter OUTDOOR showing 30-day reach (e.g., .845) ? .824
```

```
-------------------------------------------------------------------
ADPLAN RESULTS:  OUTDOOR

Name = Kent Lancaster          Target ID = Female Homemakers
Brand = All-Bran               Target Size =  46,501,000
Period = June 1988
```

Frequency (f) Distribution	Unweighted		Weighted	
f	% f	% f+	% f	% f+
0	18.50%	100.00%	61.29%	100.00%
1	6.83%	81.50%	3.24%	38.71%
2	4.73%	74.68%	2.25%	35.47%
3	3.79%	69.94%	1.80%	33.22%
4	3.25%	66.15%	1.54%	31.42%
5	2.88%	62.91%	1.37%	29.88%
6	2.63%	60.02%	1.25%	28.51%
7	2.44%	57.39%	1.16%	27.26%
8	2.29%	54.96%	1.09%	26.10%
9	2.18%	52.67%	1.03%	25.02%
10	2.08%	50.49%	0.99%	23.98%
11+	48.41%	48.41%	22.99%	22.99%

```
BBD Factors:  R1 = .409, RE = .824, A = .3632703423, B = .5249211788
Weight (Recall) = 47.5%
```

Summary Evaluation	Unweighted	Weighted
Reach (1+)	81.50%	38.71%
Effective Reach (3+)	69.94%	33.22%
Average Frequency	15.05	15.05
Gross Rating Points	1,227.00	582.82
Gross Impressions (000)	570,567.30	271,019.46
CPM/Gross Impressions	$2.00	$4.20
Cost Per Rating Point	$928.04	$1,953.78

Vehicle List	Rating	Cume	Ad Cost	CPM	Ads	Total Cost
Billboards	40.90	N/A	$37,957	$4.20	30	$1,138,710
			Totals:	$4.20	30	$1,138,710

ENDNOTES

1. Hugh M. Cannon, "Reach and Frequency Estimates for Specialized Target Markets," *Journal of Advertising Research*, 23 (June/July 1983), pp. 45-50.

2. John D. Leckenby and Marsha Boyd, "How Media Directors View Reach/Frequency Model Evaluation Standards," *Journal of Advertising Research*, 24 (October/November 1984), pp. 43-52; John D. Leckenby and Shizue Kishi, "How Media Directors View Reach/Frequency Estimation," *Journal of Advertising Research*, 22 (1980) pp. 64-69.

3. John D. Leckenby and Nugent Wedding. *Advertising Management: Criteria, Analysis, and Decision-Making* (Columbus: Grid Publishing, Inc., 1982); Anthony F. McGann and J. Thomas Russell, *Advertising Media* (Homewood: Richard D. Irwin, Inc., 1988).

4. Rust, Roland T. *Advertising Media Models: A Practical Guide* (Massachusetts: Lexington Books, 1986).

5. Marshall D. Rice and John D. Leckenby. "Estimating the Exposure Distribution of Magazine Schedules in Limited Data Situations," *Proceedings*, American Academy of Advertising, March 1985.

6. Ibid.

7. Ibid.

8. Kent M. Lancaster, John D. Leckenby and Judith A. Stern, "Teaching Advertising Media Planning Using Interactive Media Models," *Journal of Marketing Education*, 7 (1985), pp. 22-28.

9. David R. Gusse and Kent M. Lancaster, "Using on-line data services makes course more realistic," *Journalism Educator*, 38 (1983), pp. 6-10, 38.

10. Peggy J. Kreshel, Kent M. Lancaster and Margaret A. Toomey, "How Leading Advertising Agencies Perceive Effective Reach and Frequency," *Journal of Advertising*, 14 (3, 1985), pp. 32-51.

11. Arnold M. Barban, Donald W. Jugenheimer, Lee F. Young, and Peter B. Turk, *Advertising Media Sourcebook and Workbook* (Columbus: Grid Publishing, 1981).

12. David R. Gusse and Kent M. Lancaster, op. cit.

13. Intercepts of zero are assumed in Equations 8-12 and 8-13 for cable television since those presented here are the size of many cable network ratings and lead to negative self- and cross-pair audience estimates.

14. Marshall D. Rice and John D. Leckenby, op. cit.

15. Kent M. Lancaster, Peggy J. Kreshel and Joya R. Harris, "Estimating the Impact of Advertising Media Plans: Media Executives Describe Weighting and Timing Factors," *Journal of Advertising*, 15:3 (September 1986), pp. 21-29, 45.

16. Robert S. Headen, Jay E. Klompmaker and Roland T. Rust, "The Duplication of Viewing Law and Television Media Schedule Evaluation," *Journal of Marketing Research*, 16 (1979), pp. 333-340; Robert S. Headen, Jay E. Klompmaker and Jesse E. Teel, Jr. "Increasing the Informational Content of Reach and Frequency Estimates," *Journal of Advertising*, 5 (1976a), pp. 18-22, 27; Robert S. Headen, Jay E. Klompmaker and Jesse E. Teel, Jr. "TV Audience Exposure," *Journal of Advertising Research*, 16 (1976b), pp. 49-52; Robert S. Headen, Jay E. Klompmaker and Jesse E. Teel, Jr., "Predicting Audience Exposure to Spot TV Advertising Schedules," *Journal of Marketing Research*, 14 (1977),

pp. 1-9; John D. Leckenby and Marsha Boyd, ''An Improved Beta Binomial Reach/Frequency Model for Magazines,'' *Current Issues and Research in Advertising*, (1984), pp. 1-24; John D. Leckenby and Shizue Kishi, ''The Dirichlet Multinomial Distribution as a Magazine Exposure Model,'' *Journal of Marketing Research*, 21 (1984), pp. 100-106; John D. Leckenby and Marshall D. Rice, ''A Beta Binomial Network TV Exposure Model Using Limited Data,'' *Journal of Advertising*, 3 (1985), pp. 25-31; Roland T. Rust, *Advertising Media Models: A Practical Guide*, op. cit.; Roland T. Rust and Robert T. Leone, ''The Mixed-Media Dirichlet Multinomial Distribution: A Model for Evaluating Television-Magazine Schedules,'' *Journal of Marketing Research* 21 (1984), pp. 89-99.

ADDITIONAL READING

Lancaster, Kent M., Jung-Sook Lee and Helen Katz, ''Evaluating Daily and Sunday Newspaper Advertising Schedules,'' *Proceedings of the American Academy of Advertising*, 1988 Annual Conference, Chicago, Illinois, April 1988.

CHAPTER NINE

Broadcast Media Evaluation

As Chapter Eight indicated, in many instances a media planner may wish or need to use broadcast media instead of, or in addition to, print vehicles. The methods for evaluating such schedules are basically similar, and in the absence of complete data the limited information model (BBD-L) is used to estimate the impact of a broadcast schedule on the target audience.

The media to be covered in this chapter include network and spot television, and radio. Each evaluation is first shown mathematically through examples, and then reiterated using the interactive computer program ADPLAN.

EVALUATING TELEVISION SCHEDULES

The BBD model can be easily applied to television schedules using SMRB, MRI, A.C. Nielsen, and Arbitron data. For convenience, this text will continue to focus on SMRB data in the examples that follow. In the case of television programs, SMRB provides self-pair audience ratings for some targets, but does not provide cross-pair ratings, at least in published SMRB manuals. Although there are alternative procedures for evaluating television schedules using SMRB data, the procedures described here are relatively straightforward and accurate in the case of broad targets.

Here it will be assumed that the Kellogg's All-Bran media planner wishes to evaluate the following television schedule for the month of January 1988.

Program	Insertions	Rating*
Young and Restless (YR)	2	8.8%
All My Children (AC)	2	8.4%
Dallas (DS)	2	23.8%
Bill Cosby Show (BC)	2	21.7%
	8	

*Base is 69,405,000 female homemakers who use cold breakfast cereals.
Source is 1985 SMRB, Volume P-20.

To evaluate this schedule using the BBD model, procedures are needed to estimate self- and cross-pair audience ratings. This can be done using the logic behind the "random combination method."

☐ The Random Combination Method Revisited

You will remember that in the previous chapter a procedure for estimating self- and cross-pair audience ratings was demonstrated in order to construct an exposure distribution model with the beta binomial method in situations where audience data are limited. To remind you of the formulas for this random combination method, they are reproduced as Equations 9-1 and 9-2.

One should notice that this method is nothing more than GRPs for a pair of ratings minus duplication. The specific within- and between-vehicle duplication correction factors and self- and cross-pair rating estimating equations that are used for television are listed below. Space constraints do not allow a discussion here of the derivation of each of them. However, it will be shown in Chapter Fourteen that the correction factors lead to reasonable estimates of reach and frequency when compared to estimates provided by Interactive Market Systems, Inc. (IMS), a popular media software house, or when compared to available self- and cross-pair audience data.

$$R_{2i} = 2(R_i) - (k_{wm})(R_i)^2, \tag{9-1}$$
$$R_{ij} = R_i + R_j - (k_{bm})(R_i)(R_j), \tag{9-2}$$

where:

R_{2i} = self-pair audience rating for vehicle i,

R_{ij} = cross-pair audience rating for vehicles i and j.

R_i = single insertion audience rating for vehicle i,

R_j = single insertion audience rating for vehicle j,

k_{wm} = correction factor for within-vehicle duplication in media category m,

k_{bm} = correction factor for between-vehicle duplication in media category m,

i = 1, ..., n, or n-1, total vehicles in a schedule,

j = 2, ..., n total vehicles in a schedule,

m = any media category for which R_{2i} and R_{ij} are required but not available.

☐ Estimating Television Self- and Cross-Pair Audience Ratings

After analyzing a variety of SMRB self- and cross-pair television audience ratings, the authors were able to use the random combination method to fit the following curves to the ratings.

$$R_{2i} = -.0065 + 1.7946(R_i) - 1.3308(R_i)^2 \ N=72 \ R^2=.985 \tag{9-3}$$
$$R_{ij} = -.00149 + 1.0095(R_i + R_j) - 1.5012(R_i)(R_j) \ N=400 \ R^2=.995 \tag{9-4}$$

The convenient aspect of these equations is that they do not require daypart information since they were estimated from a data set that pooled programs and dayparts. Although other television models are available, these should be sufficient for the purposes here.

To estimate self- and cross-pair audiences, one can simply substitute program ratings as appropriate. For example, the self-pair rating for "Young and Restless" (YR) is computed as follows:

$$R_{2.YR} = -.0065 + 1.7946(.088) - 1.3308(.088)^2$$
$$= -.0065 + .1579 - .0103$$
$$= .1411$$
$$= 14.1\%$$

Likewise, the cross-pair audience for "Young and Restless" and "All My Children" (AC) is estimated as follows:

$$R_{YR.AC} = -.00149 + 1.0095(.088 + .084) - 1.5012(.088)(.084)$$
$$= -.00149 + .1736 - .0111$$
$$= .161$$
$$= 16.1\%$$

You might try a few others on your own. Fortunately, computer programs take the drudgery out of this procedure. It is important, nevertheless, to understand the methods that are used. If the process is continued, here is what should result.

Program/Pair	Insertions	Single Insertion Rating (%)	Self/Cross-Pair Rating (%)
Young and Restless (YR)	2	8.8	14.1
All My Children (AC)	2	8.4	13.5
Dallas (DS)	2	23.8	34.5
Bill Cosby (BC)	2	21.7	32.0
YR-AC			16.1
YR-DS			29.6
YR-BC			27.8
AC-DS			29.4
AC-BC			27.5
DS-BC			38.0

With this information, readers should be able to evaluate the entire schedule using the BBD model. Readers might try it at least to the point of estimating reach (that is, 1 - P(0); see Chapter Eight).

Estimating television costs can be a difficult task. Here, a simple procedure is recommended, but others may be developed that are just as useful. One can find average quarterly cost estimates in media cost guides, usually given for the major television dayparts. The upper limit of the cost estimate should be used and adjusted up or down depending on the size of the SMRB program's target audience.

For example, the hypothetical television schedule described above is to run in January 1988, so the Winter quarter cost should be used. "Young and Restless" and "All My Children" are daytime programs. For such programs, then, one can assume the average cost will be $22,000. The average SMRB rating against the target for these two programs is 8.6 percent ((8.8% + 8.4%)/2 = 8.6%). Dividing $22,000 by 8.6 gives a daytime CPP against the target of $2,558. Since "Young and Restless" has a rating of 8.8 percent, the program is estimated to cost an advertiser $22,510 (that is, $22,510 = 8.8($2,558)).

The same procedure is employed for the prime time television programs or programs in other dayparts. The more programs included to derive the average daypart rating, the more realistic cost estimates will be. One should note that this method matches the highest costs with the highest rated programs. Here are the cost estimates and procedures for all four programs.

Program	Estimated Cost		Procedure
Young and Restless	$22,510	=	(8.8)($22,000/8.6)
All My Children	21,487	=	(8.4)($22,000/8.6)
Dallas	107,528	=	(23.8)($103,000/22.8)
Bill Cosby Show	98,040	=	(21.7)($103,000/22.8)

This information will make it possible to evaluate the proposed network television schedule, estimating all of the usual media evaluation factors.

NETWORK TELEVISION ON *ADPLAN*

Evaluating a network television schedule on ADPLAN is a similar process to that of print media. Once again a "limited information" form of the BBD model is used. For this schedule there are four different vehicles: "Young and Restless," "All My Children," "Dallas," and the "Bill Cosby Show." For each of these one must have: single-insertion rating, cost-per-insertion, and the number of insertions.

Again, one needs to decide on the discount factor and its source. Here, 0.73, based on "Recall," is used, which is a GRP-weighted average of the typical prime time and daytime network television weights. The GRP-weighted average weight of .73 was obtained by multiplying the typical network television weight of .80 by the percent of the total schedule of GRPs (125.4) that are devoted to that daypart (72.6%). To this is added the product of the typical daytime network television weight (.547) and the percent of the total schedule GRPs devoted to that daypart (27.4%) (that is, $.73 = ((2(23.8) + 2(21.7))/125.4)(.8) + ((2(8.8) + 2(8.4))/125.4)(.547))$. The ADPLAN results follow.

```
Select the media category you want to use.

    1=Consumer Magazines      5=Local Newspapers    9=Network Radio
    2=Business Publications   6=Network TV         10=Spot Radio
    3=National Newspapers     7=Spot TV            11=Outdoor
    4=Newspaper Supplements   8=Cable TV           12=Direct Mail

Your choice? 6

Input vehicle audience weight to account for advertising
exposures or other communication effects.  For example:

    1.000 = Unweighted (vehicle exposures = ad exposures)
     .800 = Typical weight for NETWORK TV

Enter weight? .73
```

Describe basis of weight (e.g., awareness, recall, knowledge)
Communication effect? Recall

How many vehicles in your NETWORK TV schedule? 4

For each NETWORK TV vehicle

Vehicle Number/Name	Ad Cost	Ads(#)	Rating	1=OK 2=no
1? Young and Restless	? 22510	? 2	? .088	? 1
2? All My Children	? 21487	? 2	? .084	? 1
3? Dallas	? 107528	? 2	? .238	? 1
4? Bill Cosby Show	? 98040	? 2	? .217	? 1

View estimated cross-pair ratings (1=yes, 2=no)? 1

Cross-pair Numbers/Names	Rating
1- 2 Young and Restless-All My Children	.1610
1- 3 Young and Restless-Dallas	.2962
1- 4 Young and Restless-Bill Cosby Show	.2778
2- 3 All My Children-Dallas	.2936
2- 4 All My Children-Bill Cosby Show	.2750
3- 4 Dallas-Bill Cosby Show	.3804

ADPLAN RESULTS: NETWORK TV

Name = Kent Lancaster   Target ID = Female Homemakers
Brand = All-Bran   Target Size = 69,405,000
Period = June 1988

Frequency (f) Distribution	Unweighted		Weighted	
f	% f	% f+	% f	% f+
0	38.00%	100.00%	54.74%	100.00%
1	27.68%	62.00%	20.21%	45.26%
2	17.13%	34.32%	12.50%	25.05%
3	9.50%	17.19%	6.93%	12.55%
4	4.71%	7.69%	3.44%	5.62%
5	2.03%	2.99%	1.48%	2.18%
6	0.73%	0.95%	0.53%	0.70%
7	0.20%	0.23%	0.14%	0.16%
8	0.03%	0.03%	0.02%	0.02%

BBD Factors: R1 = .157, R2 = .274, A = 1.249175190, B = 6.720045089
Weight (Recall) = 73.0%

Summary Evaluation	Unweighted	Weighted
Reach (1+)	62.00%	45.26%
Effective Reach (3+)	17.19%	12.55%
Average Frequency	2.02	2.02
Gross Rating Points	125.40	91.54
Gross Impressions (000)	87,033.86	63,534.72
CPM/Gross Impressions	$5.73	$7.86
Cost Per Rating Point	$3,980.30	$5,452.47

Vehicle List	Rating	Cume	Ad Cost	CPM	Ads	Total Cost
Young and Rest	8.80	14.12	$22,510	$5.05	2	$45,020
All My Childre	8.40	13.49	$21,487	$5.05	2	$42,974
Dallas	23.80	34.53	$107,528	$8.92	2	$215,056
Bill Cosby Sho	21.70	32.03	$98,040	$8.92	2	$196,080
			Totals:	$7.86	8	$499,130

NETWORK RADIO

SMRB, MRI, and Arbitron, for example, provide data on target listenership of radio dayparts, formats, and networks. With SMRB or MRI the network radio audience data are the only kind that can be used to evaluate particular schedules since daypart and format audiences are aggregated across stations, networks and dayparts. A network radio schedule can be evaluated using the wired network radio audience data provided by SMRB and MRI. For the target of female homemakers who use cold breakfast cereals, the following audience and cost data are obtained from SMRB.

Radio Network	Average Daily M-F Cume 6 a.m.-mdnt (%)	Estimated AQH Rating (%)	Cost/:30
ABC Contemporary	4.7	.80	$2,800
ABC Direction	3.4	.58	2,000
ABC Entertainment	5.6	.95	2,700
ABC FM	3.2	.54	2,400
ABC Information	7.1	1.21	2,500
ABC Rock	2.2	.37	2,400
CBS	5.1	.87	2,000
Mutual	6.5	1.11	2,300
NBC	6.5	1.11	3,000
Radio Radio	3.0	.51	1,500
The Source	2.2	.37	3,200
US One	3.9	.66	3,000
US Two	4.0	.68	1,300

The average daily Monday through Friday cumulative audience ratings were obtained directly from SMRB (1985, Volume P-20, p. 40). They represent average cumulative half-hour ratings and therefore overstate the audience size for, say, typical quarter hour, five minute, and one minute segments. The usual procedure employed by media software houses, such as IMS, is to assume that the average quarter hour rating (AQH) for a given network is approximately 17 percent of the SMRB or MRI average daily cume. That is:

$$R_{i,radio} = .17 \text{ (SMRB or MRI cumulative audience rating)} \qquad (9\text{-}5)$$

The second column of AQH ratings presented above, then, is based on Equation 9-5.

SMRB does not provide self- and cross-pair audience data for radio networks. These must be estimated using the random combination method in conjunction with unique correction factors for network radio. It turns out that the duplication within and between networks can be expressed by Equations 9-6 and 9-7.

$$k_{w,radio} = 14.12 + 1480.99(R_i) + .00046(1/R_i^2) - 91648.66(R_i^2) \qquad (9\text{-}6)$$
$$R_{ij,radio} = (R_i + R_j)\ (R_i)(R_j) \qquad (9\text{-}7)$$

Using them leads to estimates of self- and cross-pair audiences which can then be used in the BBD model to estimate the exposure distribution for a given network radio schedule. For example, the self-pair AQH rating for the ABC Information (ABCI) network is estimated as follows.

$$
\begin{aligned}
R_{2,ABCI} &= 2(R_{ABCI}) - (14.12 + 1480.99(R_{ABCI}) + .00046(1/\ (R_{ABCI})^2 - \\
&\quad 91648.66(R_{ABCI})^2)(R_{ABCI})^2 \\
&= 2(.0121) - (14.12 + 1480.99(.0121) + .00046(1/(.0121)^2 - \\
&\quad 91648.66(.0121)^2)(.0121)^2 \\
&= .0242 - (14.12 + 17.92 + 3.14 - 13.42)(.0001464) \\
&= .0242 - .0032 \\
&= .021 \\
&= 2.1\%
\end{aligned}
$$

The same procedure for the NBC radio network results in a self-pair rating of 1.88%. The cross-pair rating for these two networks is computed below.

$$
\begin{aligned}
R_{ABCI,NBC} &= (R_{ABCI} + R_{NBC}) - (R_{ABCI})(R_{NBC}) \\
&= .0121 + .0111 - (.0121)(.0111) \\
&= .0232 - .0001343 \\
&= .023 \\
&= 2.3\%
\end{aligned}
$$

Using the estimates of AQH along with the self- and cross-pair audience data, the BBD procedure is straightforward.

NETWORK RADIO ON *ADPLAN*

The network radio schedule procedure on ADPLAN is similar to evaluating a network television schedule. Although radio stations are local, this is a national schedule since network radio refers to a group of radio stations. The example uses two wired networks: ABC Information, and NBC.

For each of these vehicles one must have: single-insertion rating, cost-per-insertion, and the number of insertions.

The discount factor should be chosen along with the communication effect to use as the basis for the discount. This schedule uses the typical factor of 0.40, based on "Recall."

In addition, one needs to know the source of the radio ratings, to be able to select whether they are based on an average daily cume (for example, SMRB, MRI) or an average quarter hour (for example, Arbitron, Birch). ADPLAN will prompt users for this information. Users should enter the unscaled SMRB or MRI ratings when asked for this information, but calculate program costs with the scaled down numbers.

Here are the ADPLAN results of an evaluation of such a schedule.

```
Select the media category you want to use.

    1=Consumer Magazines      5=Local Newspapers    9=Network Radio
    2=Business Publications    6=Network TV          10=Spot Radio
    3=National Newspapers      7=Spot TV             11=Outdoor
    4=Newspaper Supplements    8=Cable TV            12=Direct Mail


Your choice? 9

What kind of radio ratings will you be using?

    1 = Average Daily Cume (e.g., source is SMRB, MRI)
    2 = Average Quarter Hour (e.g., source is ARBITRON, BIRCH)


Your choice? 1

Input vehicle audience weight to account for advertising
exposures or other communication effects.  For example:

    1.000 = Unweighted (vehicle exposures = ad exposures)
     .400 = Typical weight for NETWORK RADIO

Enter weight? .4


Describe basis of weight (e.g., awareness, recall, knowledge)
Communication effect? Recall

How many vehicles in your NETWORK RADIO schedule? 2

For each NETWORK RADIO vehicle
```

				1=OK
Vehicle Number/Name	Ad Cost	Ads(#)	Rating	2=no
------------------	-------	------	------	----
1? ABC-Information	? 2500	? 28	? .071	? 1
2? NBC	? 3000	? 28	? .065	? 1

View estimated cross-pair ratings (1=yes, 2=no)? 1

Cross-pair Numbers/Names	Rating
1- 2 ABC-Information-NBC	.0224

ADPLAN RESULTS: NETWORK RADIO

Name = Kent Lancaster   Target ID = Female Homemakers
Brand = All-Bran   Target Size = 69,405,000
Period = June 1988

Frequency (f) Distribution	Unweighted		Weighted	
f	% f	% f+	% f	% f+
0	83.39%	100.00%	93.36%	100.00%
1	6.10%	16.61%	2.44%	6.64%
2	2.96%	10.51%	1.19%	4.20%
3	1.85%	7.55%	0.74%	3.02%
4	1.28%	5.70%	0.51%	2.28%
5	0.93%	4.42%	0.37%	1.77%
6	0.70%	3.49%	0.28%	1.40%
7	0.54%	2.79%	0.22%	1.12%
8	0.43%	2.24%	0.17%	0.90%
9	0.34%	1.82%	0.14%	0.73%
10	0.27%	1.47%	0.11%	0.59%
11+	1.20%	1.20%	0.48%	0.48%

BBD Factors: R1 = .011, R2 = .021, A = 8.111098408, B = 7.131318569
Weight (Recall) = 40.0%

Summary Evaluation	Unweighted	Weighted
Reach (1+)	16.61%	6.64%
Effective Reach (3+)	7.55%	3.02%
Average Frequency	3.79	3.79
Gross Rating Points	62.98	25.19
Gross Impressions (000)	43,709.60	17,483.84
CPM/Gross Impressions	$3.52	$8.81
Cost Per Rating Point	$2,445.31	$6,113.28

Vehicle List	Rating	Cume	Ad Cost	CPM	Ads	Total Cost
ABC-Informatio	1.18	2.04	$2,500	$7.66	28	$70,000
NBC	1.07	1.88	$3,000	$10.06	28	$84,000
			Totals:	$8.81	56	$154,000

SPOT TELEVISION

You will recall that one method for evaluating a national network television schedule already has been presented. How does a planner handle a situation when an advertiser, such as Kellogg's All-Bran, chooses to focus on a particular region instead of, or in addition to, its network television advertising schedule? There are a number of methods that can be used in such a situation, but the focus here will be on one that is simple.

With spot television an advertiser buys commercial time on a market-by-market basis. Since each one is unique, when a number of them are involved, accurate evaluation of schedules can become a monumental task. Fortunately there are techniques available that provide media planners with an overview of the likely weight of a spot television schedule without burying them under unwieldy detail. One method is to assemble a schedule of programs in the same manner as for network television. Then it is assumed that the spot television programs will achieve the same ratings, on average, in each market of interest. After estimating the cost-per-rating point in the selected region, it is applied to each program rating to estimate the cost of the programs as well as the entire schedule.

As an example, the network television schedule evaluated earlier will be evaluated in the top 50 U.S. markets. You will recall that this was the chosen schedule.

Program	Insertions	Single Insertion Rating
Young and Restless (YR)	2	8.8%
All My Children (AC)	2	8.4
Dallas (DS)	2	23.8
Bill Cosby Show (BC)	2	21.7

As a practical matter, a planner may not be able to achieve such a schedule in many of the top 50 markets. Nevertheless, it may come close if this schedule is used as a guide. An alternative procedure might be to assume that one will obtain two average daytime programs and two average prime time programs. This was not done here because it adds additional and unnecessary complexity to the process. An understanding of the overall reasoning process is more important at the moment than is realism. To avoid confusion, however, it is suggested that arbitrary station call letters are substituted for each of the specific programs to show that one may not get a particular program in each of the 50 markets, but may achieve similar ratings (e.g., WAAA = YR, WBBB = AC, and so on).

To proceed with this evaluation, one can assume that the schedule will achieve similar ratings in each market in the lineup. Now, to continue, the total "station" costs must be estimated for the top 50 U.S. markets as well as the number and percent of the target audience members who reside in the top 50 markets.

Estimating total "station" costs in the top 50 markets is a simple matter. A media cost guide shows spot television costs per rating point (CPP) by daypart for groups of ten of the top 100 U.S. markets. Since the rating point for each "station" is already known, total cost across all 50 markets equals the rating multiplied by the CPP. For the top 50 U.S. markets, the prime time CPP is $6,831 while the daytime CPP is $2,134. The cost of each "station" in the top 50 U.S. markets is computed as follows:

Top 50 U.S. Markets				
Station	R_i	× CPP	=	Total Cost
WAAA	8.8%	$2,134		$18,779
WBBB	8.4	2,134		17,926
WCCC	23.8	6,831		162,578
WDDD	21.7	6,831		148,233

The next step is to estimate the percent of the target that resides in the top 50 U.S. markets. Estimates show that in 1986 the top 50 U.S. markets accounted for 67 percent of U.S. TV households which therefore includes 46,501,350 target members.

Having this information, you should be able to estimate self- and cross-pair audiences and the exposure distribution in the manner described for network television.

SPOT TELEVISION ON *ADPLAN*

The spot television schedule evaluation is similar to that for network television. This regional schedule will use, for this example, the top 50 U.S. markets.

One can assume that available programs in each market will be similar to those of the network television schedule evaluated earlier. Since the buys are on a market-by-market basis, however, one in fact buys through stations, not networks and programs. Thus call letters have been used in place of program names, although the information entered is based on the latter. Four "stations" are used in each market, called WAAA, WBBB, WCCC, and WDDD.

Each of the four stations needs: single-insertion rating (same as in network television), cost-per-insertion (scaled to the region used), and the number of insertions.

Since this is a regional schedule, you should check that the regional target size of 46,501,350 has been entered. The discount factor and its source are then chosen. For this schedule, the typical GRP-weighted adjustment of 0.66 is used, based on "Recall." Here is the ADPLAN output derived from evaluating such a schedule.

```
Select the media category you want to use.

    1=Consumer Magazines      5=Local Newspapers    9=Network Radio
    2=Business Publications   6=Network TV         10=Spot Radio
    3=National Newspapers     7=Spot TV            11=Outdoor
    4=Newspaper Supplements   8=Cable TV           12=Direct Mail

Your choice? 7

Input vehicle audience weight to account for advertising
exposures or other communication effects.  For example:

    1.000 = Unweighted (vehicle exposures = ad exposures)
     .725 = Typical weight for SPOT TV
```

Enter weight? .658

Describe basis of weight (e.g., awareness, recall, knowledge)
Communication effect? Recall

How many vehicles in your SPOT TV schedule? 4

For each SPOT TV vehicle

Vehicle Number/Name	Ad Cost	Ads(#)	Rating	1=OK 2=no
1? WAAA	? 18779	? 2	? .088	? 1
2? WBBB	? 17926	? 2	? .084	? 1
3? WCCC	? 162578	? 2	? .238	? 1
4? WDDD	? 148233	? 2	? .217	? 1

View estimated cross-pair ratings (1=yes, 2=no)? 2

ADPLAN RESULTS: SPOT TV

Name = Kent Lancaster   Target ID = Female Homemakers
Brand = All-Bran   Target Size = 46,501,352
Period = June 1988

Frequency (f) Distribution	Unweighted		Weighted	
f	% f	% f+	% f	% f+
0	38.00%	100.00%	59.20%	100.00%
1	27.68%	62.00%	18.21%	40.80%
2	17.13%	34.32%	11.27%	22.58%
3	9.50%	17.19%	6.25%	11.31%
4	4.71%	7.69%	3.10%	5.06%
5	2.03%	2.99%	1.34%	1.97%
6	0.73%	0.95%	0.48%	0.63%
7	0.20%	0.23%	0.13%	0.15%
8	0.03%	0.03%	0.02%	0.02%

BBD Factors: R1 = .157, R2 = .274, A = 1.249175190, B = 6.720045089
Weight (Recall) = 65.8%

Summary Evaluation	Unweighted	Weighted
Reach (1+)	62.00%	40.80%
Effective Reach (3+)	17.19%	11.31%
Average Frequency	2.02	2.02
Gross Rating Points	125.40	82.51
Gross Impressions (000)	58,312.69	38,369.75
CPM/Gross Impressions	$11.92	$18.11
Cost Per Rating Point	$5,542.52	$8,423.28

Vehicle List	Rating	Cume	Ad Cost	CPM	Ads	Total Cost
WAAA	8.80	14.12	$18,779	$6.97	2	$37,558
WBBB	8.40	13.49	$17,926	$6.97	2	$35,852
WCCC	23.80	34.53	$162,578	$22.33	2	$325,156
WDDD	21.70	32.03	$148,233	$22.33	2	$296,466
			Totals:	$18.11	8	$695,032

SPOT RADIO

As you might expect, the reasoning behind a spot radio media evaluation is similar to that of a spot television analysis. One can simply put together a schedule of network radio programs and assume that the ratings achieved in each market in the region will, on average, be about the same, particularly with respect to the number of different stations and the number of spots per station. Once a schedule is worked out that is reasonable, one can estimate the cost by multiplying the "network radio" rating by the cost-per-rating point associated with the chosen region. That will give a rough estimate of schedule cost in the group of markets selected. Of course, one must not forget to estimate the percent and number of target persons in the region.

As an example, the network radio schedule compiled previously will be evaluated in terms of its likely weight in the top 50 U.S. markets, but use hypothetical "station" call letters instead of the corresponding network name.

Radio "Station"	R_i	×	CPP	=	Total Cost
WAAA	1.21%		$3,249		$3,931
WBBB	1.11		3,249		3,606

The CPP for the top 50 U.S. markets was obtained from a media cost guide, where the CPPs were broken down by age and sex, so those for women 18+ were selected as being most closely associated with female homemakers. Multiplying the rating by the CPP gives the total cost column.

SPOT RADIO ON *ADPLAN*

The spot radio schedule procedure on ADPLAN resembles the one for spot television. Once again, the slots purchased will be according to stations and not networks, although the audience data are assumed to be similar to that of the network radio example. Thus one may assume that the local audience ratings in the top 50 markets are similar to those achieved by ABC Information and NBC. But here, imaginary call letters are included: WAAA, and WBBB. Once again, each will need: single-insertion rating (same as network radio), cost-per-insertion (scaled to the region), and the number of insertions. The typical discount factor is 0.375, based on "Recall." Here is a sample ADPLAN interaction for Spot Radio.

```
Select the media category you want to use.

    1=Consumer Magazines      5=Local Newspapers    9=Network Radio
    2=Business Publications   6=Network TV          10=Spot Radio
    3=National Newspapers     7=Spot TV             11=Outdoor
    4=Newspaper Supplements   8=Cable TV            12=Direct Mail

Your choice? 10

What kind of radio ratings will you be using?

    1 = Average Daily Cume (e.g., source is SMRB, MRI)
    2 = Average Quarter Hour (e.g., source is ARBITRON, BIRCH)
```

Your choice? 1

Input vehicle audience weight to account for advertising
exposures or other communication effects. For example:

1.000 = Unweighted (vehicle exposures = ad exposures)
.375 = Typical weight for SPOT RADIO

Enter weight? .375

Describe basis of weight (e.g., awareness, recall, knowledge)

Communication effect? Recall

How many vehicles in your SPOT RADIO schedule? 2

For each SPOT RADIO vehicle

Vehicle Number/Name	Ad Cost	Ads(#)	Rating	1=OK 2=no
1? WAAA	? 3931	? 28	? .071	? 1
2? WBBB	? 3606	? 28	? .065	? 1

View estimated cross-pair ratings (1=yes, 2=no)? 2

ADPLAN RESULTS: SPOT RADIO

Name = Kent Lancaster   Target ID = Female Homemakers
Brand = All-Bran   Target Size = 46,501,352
Period = June 1988

Frequency (f) Distribution	Unweighted		Weighted	
f	% f	% f+	% f	% f+
0	83.39%	100.00%	93.77%	100.00%
1	6.10%	16.61%	2.29%	6.23%
2	2.96%	10.51%	1.11%	3.94%
3	1.85%	7.55%	0.69%	2.83%
4	1.28%	5.70%	0.48%	2.14%
5	0.93%	4.42%	0.35%	1.66%
6	0.70%	3.49%	0.26%	1.31%
7	0.54%	2.79%	0.20%	1.05%
8	0.43%	2.24%	0.16%	0.84%
9	0.34%	1.82%	0.13%	0.68%
10	0.27%	1.47%	0.10%	0.55%
11+	1.20%	1.20%	0.45%	0.45%

BBD Factors: R1 = .011, R2 = .021, A = 8.111098408, B = 7.131318569
Weight (Recall) = 37.5%

```
Summary Evaluation          Unweighted        Weighted
------------------          ----------        --------
Reach (1+)                    16.61%            6.23%
Effective Reach (3+)           7.55%            2.83%
Average Frequency              3.79             3.79
Gross Rating Points           62.98            23.62
Gross Impressions (000)   29,285.44        10,982.04
CPM/Gross Impressions         $7.21           $19.22
Cost Per Rating Point      $3,350.97        $8,935.92
```

Vehicle List	Rating	Cume	Ad Cost	CPM	Ads	Total Cost
WAAA	1.18	2.04	$3,931	$19.18	28	$110,068
WBBB	1.07	1.88	$3,606	$19.26	28	$100,968
			Totals:	$19.22	56	$211,036

The examples provided in this chapter are merely a point of departure. From now on, you should be able to apply the programs to a variety of media planning situations. One just has to think the problem through in relation to the capabilities of ADPLAN and will then be able to come up with a satisfactory method. You should not be afraid to experiment, testing the limits of the program and of your knowledge.

CHAPTER TEN

Cable and New Media Planning and Evaluation

As the development and consumer use of new mass media technologies become increasingly important, affecting not only accepted broadcast and print media, but advertisers, agencies and consumers too, it is vital that these diverse forms are understood, utilized, and evaluated in the media planning process. This chapter provides a broad overview of the current status of each one.

One of the biggest challenges facing advertisers, agencies, and media alike is how to deal with the panoply of new media technology available. The concern of the television networks in losing audience share to cable and pay cable services; the growing interest of advertisers in these and other more specialized media, and the growing attention being paid by agencies to these alternatives are significant happenings that media planners cannot ignore. In addition, and perhaps most importantly, there has been a substantial increase in the use of these media by consumers.

The material presented here attempts to give a brief history and development of cable television, reflecting its use by advertisers, and showing its effects on the other media. This is followed by an explanation and example of how the computer program, ADPLAN, can be used to evaluate an advertising schedule for cable television. The chapter then looks at other new technologies.

TABLE 10.1 Overview of Evolving Media Technologies

Technology	Number of HH subscribing (000)	U.S. HH Penetration (Base = 85,407,000)	
Basic Cable			
Superstations			
WTBS	41,952	49.1%	*
WGN	22,481	26.3	*
WPIX	12,470	26.3	*
WOR	9,464	11.1	*
Sports			
ESPN	43,700	51.2	*
News			
CNN	41,642	48.8	*
C-SPAN	31,000	36.3	
The Weather Channel	31,053	36.4	
Headline News	28,352	33.2	*
FNN	26,700	31.3	*
C-SPAN II	11,600	13.6	

Reuters	3,250	3.8	*
Dow Jones Cable News	600	0.7	
Ethnic			
BET	17,000	19.9	*
Galavision	900	1.1	
Entertainment, Information and Education			
USA Network	39,178	45.9	*
CBN	36,708	43.0	*
The Nashville Network	35,000	41.0	*
Lifetime	34,000	39.8	*
A & E	27,000	31.6	*
Discovery	24,848	29.1	*
Home Shopping Network	15,200	17.8	*
Tempo Television	12,500	14.6	
The Learning Channel	10,340	12.1	
The Silent Network	9,500	11.1	
The Nostalgia Channel	1,400	1.6	
Religion			
PTL	14,000	16.4	
Trinity	7,037	8.2	
National Jewish TV Net.	6,800	8.0	
Eternal Word TV Network	6,800	8.0	
ACTS	6,000	7.0	
Music			
MTV	37,100	43.4	*
Video Hits One	22,900	26.8	*
Country Music TV	6,750	7.9	
Youth			
Nickelodeon	35,800	41.9	*
Pay Cable			
Home Box Office	15,000	17.6	
American Movie Classics	7,000	8.2	
Showtime	5,400	6.2	
Cinemax	4,100	4.8	
The Movie Channel	3,250	3.8	
The Disney Channel	3,175	3.7	
The Playboy Channel	550	0.6	
Bravo	500	0.6	
Videocassette Recorders		44.0	
Pay-per-view		9.3	
Multipoint Distribution Services (MDS)	273	2.7	
Television Receive-Only (TVRO)		1.5	
Satellite Master Antenna Television (SMATV)		1.2	
Electronic Banking		0.5	
Subscription Television (STV)	187	0.2	
Low Power Television (LPTV)			
Direct Broadcasting by Satellite (DBS)			*
Teletext			
Videotex			

*Indicates advertiser-supported medium

Sources: This table was compiled from diverse sources to reflect the most up-to-date information available (see Endnotes and Additional Reading). When using cable in media planning, you should be sure to use the latest available audience data possible.

All the media to be covered here are displayed, for clarity, in Table 10.1. Although each of the services presented will be discussed in this chapter, it will be enormously helpful to have a clear picture of the various categories, the total number of subscribers currently using each one, and the percentage of all U.S. households (HH) each potentially can reach. It is also important to know which ones are advertiser-supported.

Due to the rapidly changing nature of these new communications technologies, the data presented must be considered tentative. The number and popularity of services change sharply from year to year; the information offered here is based on the best available published data at the time of printing. You may want to update the table as you come across new information in the months ahead.

What follows, therefore, is an amplification of the nature and scope of the services listed in Table 10.1.

DEVELOPMENT OF CABLE TELEVISION

In contrast to the popular conception of cable as a fairly recent extra TV service, something that costs $10-30 a month to receive, it began in 1948, as community antenna television (CATV). The name explains its purpose; the earliest systems were set up in remote parts of Pennsylvania and Oregon to improve TV reception to distant communities. Antennas placed on towers could pick up the nearest TV stations' signals and relay them by coaxial cables strung on poles, often those carrying telephone wires.[1]

The development of microwave relays in the 1950s, each carrying multiple signals, encouraged channel diversification. Yet cable television was still a rarity, with cable penetration at about six percent of all TV households in the 1960s. In contrast, Nielsen reports a figure for October 1987 of 50 percent.

One of the restrictions on cable's growth during these early years was the heavy government regulation, through the Federal Communications Commission, which viewed cable as a threat to broadcast services. But through legal challenges in the courts and the changing deregulatory climate in communications in the 1980s, culminating in the 1984 *Cable Communications Policy Act*, cable finally took off. At the same time as deregulation was occurring, major technological developments were also taking place. In 1974, the first communications satellite, Satcom 1, was launched into geosynchronous orbit, 22,300 miles above the earth. By this, programs could be beamed up from one city to Satcom 1 then down again to a distant city's earth receiving station, and broadcast to cable subscribers in that area.[2] These satellites are also used for the superstations, such as WTBS, WOR, and WGN, regular broadcast stations which relay their television signals to distant markets, thereby increasing their out-of-market audiences.[3]

Since the 1970s cable TV's growth has been phenomenal. Table 10.2 provides a brief overview. From 16 percent of all TV households subscribing to basic cable in 1975, the forecast for 1990 now stands at 54 percent. Already 74.7 percent of TV households are passed by cable.[4] Pay cable services are being used by about 25 percent of all TV households, and of all homes that subscribe to basic cable, about

TABLE 10.2   Cable Barometer

Users of Cable	Number
Television households	86,304,000
Homes passed by cable	64,571,000
Basic cable subscribers	36,120,000
Pay cable subscribers	21,672,000
	Percentage (%)
TVHH passed by cable	74.7
TVHH with basic cable	41.8
Homes passed with basic cable	56.0
TVHH with pay cable	25.1
Homes passed with pay cable	33.6
Basic subscribers with pay cable	60.0

Source: *CableVision*, February 10, 1986.

60 percent pay extra to receive networks such as Home Box Office (HBO), Cinemax, or the Playboy Channel. The fact that people are now willing, in effect, to pay not to see commercials, is worth bearing in mind in considering the impact of cable TV on media planning.

The large array of cable network options given in Table 10.1 are amplified in Table 10.3 to provide an overview of the content of each service. This kind of information is important in the media planning process in order to place advertising insertions in vehicles that are of particular interest to the target audience.

Despite the extent of the information given in Tables 10.1 and 10.3, they are nonetheless incomplete. You may wish to consult the latest edition of *Broadcasting Cablecasting Yearbook* for additional information.

TABLE 10.3   Guide to Cable Networks

Basic Cable

Superstation WTBS.   The original superstation featuring a blend of action oriented family entertainment, sitcoms, and movies. Plus the complete Atlanta Braves baseball schedule, a special package of NBA games, and selected SEC college football.

Superstation WGN.   Twenty-four hour programming featuring sports, family movies, entertainment, and comedy series.

Superstation WOR.   Sports coverage of the Mets, Knicks, Nets, Rangers, Islanders, and N.J. Devils; movies and first-run morning programming.

Superstation WPIX.   New York's other superstation, featuring a variety of sports and entertainment programs.

ESPN (Entertainment and Sports Programing Network).   Twenty-four hour schedule featuring professional, collegiate, and amateur sports along with sports news, interviews, and features.

CNN (Cable News Network).   Twenty-four hour in-depth coverage of international and national events, business, finance, fashion, health, and human interest.

CNN-Headline News.   Designed for viewers too busy to wait for the evening news. Shows major news stories every half hour.

C-SPAN (Cable Satellite Public Affairs Network). A non-profit organization created and funded by the cable industry, C-SPAN transmits public affairs programming twenty-four hours a day, including live coverage of Congressional proceedings.

C-SPAN II. Live coverage of the U.S. Senate proceedings, congressional hearings, and public affairs programming.

Dow Jones Cable News. Full time business, financial and economic news service, with information from ''The Wall Street Journal,'' ''Barron's,'' and the Dow Jones News Service.

FNN (Financial News Network). Live financial and business news including up-to-the-minute reports on all major stock, commodity and open exchanges. Includes both AMEX and NYSE reports. Thirteen and a half hours each weekday.

Reuters. News retrieval service. NEWS VIEW, a two-channel alphanumeric news service, carries general, financial and sports news, with the New York stock ticker.

The Weather Channel. Twenty-four hour live national, regional, and local weather customized for each cable system. Localization of commercial text material provided.

BET (Black Entertainment Television). Twenty-four hours of black college sports, news, classic movies, music videos, and family entertainment.

Galavision. Spanish language programs.

A & E (Arts and Entertainment Network). Committed to excellence and innovation in television. Presenting distinctive, high quality programming in a mix of comedy, drama, movies, dance, opera, and documentaries from around the world.

CBN Cable Network. Twenty-four hours of family entertainment, including westerns, classic comedies, children's programs, game shows, a live daily TV magazine program, news updates, informative women's programs, Christian inspirational programs, and movies.

The Discovery Channel. Programs focus on scientific and educational material for all ages.

The Learning Channel. Informational, educational, public affairs, and ''how-to'' programming.

Lifetime. Entertainment and information concerning important issues such as careers, money, parenting, health, and fitness. Includes several interactive shows.

The Nashville Network. Country programming including music, comedies, game and variety shows, and sporting events.

Tempo Television. International programs of classic movies, regional sports, and home shopping.

The Silent Network. Features classic movies predating the advent of sound in motion pictures.

USA Network. A 24-hour broad-based entertainment network.

ACTS. Twenty-four hour family-oriented programs for entertainment, information and inspiration, including live counseling shows, dramas, documentaries, and specials.

ETWN (Eternal Word Television Network). Religious and entertainment programming service aimed at the Catholic audience.

National Jewish Television. Programming about Israel and other topics of interest to the national Jewish community.

PTL-The Inspirational Network. Nationwide religious network; 160 hours a week of Christian theme programs.

Trinity Broadcasting Network. Christian religious programming 24 hours a day.

Country Music Television. Country music focus 24 hours a day.

MTV: Music Television. Video music channel in stereo, offering music 24 hours a day, every day. Exclusive sneak previews, music news, exclusive interviews, Saturday concerts, and specials. Targeted to viewers ages 12-34.

Video Hits One. Similar to MTV. Video music 24 hours a day, targeted to viewers ages 25-54. Popular contemporary, soft rock, rhythm and blues, and country hits.

Nickelodeon. The first and only all-day network exclusively for children. Offers 17 hours a day of programming targeted to ages 2-17.

Pay Cable

HBO (Home Box Office). Nationwide programmer offering a package of theatrical movies, sports, and HBO-produced entertainment specials to both cable and MDS affiliates.

Cinemax. A fully-programmed pay-cable service designed to complement HBO.

Showtime. Twenty-four hour variety programming including movies, series, concerts and family entertainment.

The Movie Channel. Movies and movie-related material, as a complement to Showtime.

The Nostalgia Channel. Vintage programming of movies, cartoons, sports, and documentaries.

The Playboy Channel. Adult entertainment and films.

The Disney Channel. Family entertainment from Disney studios.

American Movie Classics. Hollywood classics from the 1930s to the 1970s.

Bravo. Performing arts programming including films, opera and symphony performances and specials.

Buena Vista Channel. Bi-lingual programming for Spanish-speaking subscribers.

Sources: *Cable TV Facts*, 1985; *Broadcasting Cablecasting Yearbook*, 1985; *Channels 1987 Field Guide to the Electronic Media.*

ADVERTISING ON CABLE

In 1986, the cable networks took in a total of $735 million from advertising revenue, up from about $60 million in 1980, while local ads brought in another $213 million. Nearly all of the major ad-supported networks predict large increases in their 1988 ad revenue. Table 10.4 provides an overview of the principal characteristics of the major advertiser-supported media vehicles, as a media planner might use them, in terms of audience size in relation to cost per insertion. Overall popularity can be assessed by looking at the percentage of U.S. households reached on a national coverage (Column 1 of Table 10.4). The importance of a vehicle is partly shown by how much advertisers choose to invest in it (Column 2). Most notably, however, media planners are interested in audience size as a percentage of their target audience. Organizations such as A.C. Nielsen and Mediamark Research Inc. (MRI) provide such information as a basis for a variety of targets and, in the case of Nielsen, dayparts. Average quarter-hour (AQH) audiences come closest to the audience size associated with a particular ad insertion. The upper limits, or highest ratings currently obtainable from any of the listed services, aside from specials, are displayed in Column 3 of the table, in terms of their national coverage (network base) and, in Column 4, for all U.S. households. At the present time, A. C. Nielsen reports AQH audiences for about a dozen advertiser-supported networks. MRI, however, provides cumulative audiences (viewing in the last seven days) for several of the others.

TABLE 10.4 Cable Network Audience and Cost Data

Network	National Coverage	$Ad 1985	Nielsen Rating		MRI Rating		Target AQH	High Cost Per :30
			Network Base	U.S. Base	Adults	Target		
Sports Programing (ESPN)	42%	$89.6mm	1.6%	0.672%	13.3%	9.3%	0.469%	$ 578
WTBS (Atlanta)	42	180.3	3.1	1.302	12.4	11.0	1.155	3,233
Cable Network News	40	71.0	1.3	0.520	5.6	4.8	0.445	584
CBN Cable Network	35	43.1	1.1	0.385	4.0	4.5	0.433	1,318
MTV: Music Television	33	97.2	1.4	0.462	6.6	5.7	0.373	1,385
Nickelodeon (NICK)	30	15.9	1.2	0.360			0.360	
The Nashville Network	29	44.0	1.2	0.348	3.1	3.1	0.348	1,075
The Weather Channel (TWC)	23	20.0	0.3	0.069	6.7	6.7	0.069	500
Financial News Network (FNN)	20	17.6	1.2	0.240			0.240	1,050
Lifetime	28	30.4	0.7	0.196	2.3	2.7	0.230	500
Arts & Entertainment (A & E)	15	8.0			0.8	0.6	0.141	450
Satellite Program Network	13	6.7			1.0	0.9	0.161	
Black Entertainment (BET)	8	5.0						850
USA Network	37	48.0	1.1	0.407	5.1	3.4	0.271	
WGN-TV (Chicago)	18	13.0			6.8	6.1	0.511	
WOR-TV (New York)	6				4.0	4.0	0.370	86

Sources: Mediamark Research Inc., *Multimedia Audiences*, Spring 1986, Volume M-3, and *Breakfast Cereals (Cold)*, Spring 1984, Volume P-20; Leo Burnett U.S.A., *Research Newsletter*, March 1986, Vol. 6, No. 2, p. 4; *Broadcast Advertisers Reports, Inc.*, January 1985; Foote, Cone and Belding, *Broadcast Update* September 1984; *Marketing & Media Decisions*, February 1986.

Method: Nielsen Rating U.S. Base = National Coverage X Nielsen Rating Network Base. Target = 67,502,000 female homemakers who use cold breakfast cereals as defined by MRI, Spring 1984, Volume P-20. Target AQH Rating Estimate = (1) (Nielsen Rating U.S. Base / MRI Rating Target, or (2) Nielsen Rating U.S. Base, or (3) 0.10041 + 0.067276 X MRI Target Rating.

The advertising industry, with its typical caution, has been slow to take full advantage of cable TV. Despite the more specialized audiences, programming environment, chance for sponsorship, flexible message lengths and formats, product exclusivity in programs, and ability to offset broadcast network erosion, it is really only in the past few years that many of the country's major advertisers (and indeed agencies) have ventured into the world of cable. Young & Rubicam leads the agencies in its cable spending, with $50.3 million, a mere drop in the ocean compared to its broadcast spending of $2.25 billion, but nonetheless almost double its 1984 billings.[5] Indeed, in 1985 only 1.2 percent of the total $35.5 billion placed by the top 500 advertising agencies went to cable, compared to the 26.6 percent spent on network television.[6] Not surprisingly, perhaps, the major advertisers on cable are those who spend generously on broadcast television too. Procter & Gamble heads the list of companies utilizing cable, spending $31,404,000 (2.0 percent of their total ad expenditures in 1985) on the newer medium.[7] One reason for their reluctance could be the agencies' belief that a 30 percent penetration is the critical mass for a medium to have enough broad-based appeal for advertisers. Such was the case with the growth of advertising on TV, away from radio, in the 1950s, or the move to color commercials in the 1960s.[8] Since it has now surpassed this, many expect the late 1980s to see a considerable increase in advertisers' use of the medium.

☐ Advertising–Related Problems for New Technology

The most serious difficulty for new media is the lack of definitive data. The four main sources of cable audience measurement are *Nielsen Cable Status Reports*, giving quarterly penetration rates and audience viewing trends based on metered samples; the *Nielsen Home Video Index*, tracking basic cable networks; the *National Audience Demographic Report*, which shows monthly cable/noncable breakouts for network programs and various time periods; and Arbitron's *Cable Audience Measurement Profile* (CAMP), studies of local cable systems based on the telephone recall method. In all four reports, the question arises as to what is the viewing area being measured. Traditional broadcast definitions—such as Nielsen's Designated Market Area (DMA), Arbitron's Area of Dominant Influence (ADI), or the Standard Metropolitan Statistical Area (SMSA)—do not fit the wider areas reached by cable, especially since the big cities, where the population concentration is highest, are the last to be fully wired. Table 10.5 shows a comparison of cable penetration in the top five DMAs, against the top five cable cities, which makes this clear. While places in Texas or California have three-quarters of the TV homes wired, the nation's biggest cities are not yet up to 50 percent cable penetration.

There is also a problem in estimating cable penetration, due to the high turnover rate among subscribers (up to three percent each month). Piracy is another concern among the networks; in 1983 up to $300 million were estimated to be lost from this cause alone. For continued growth in cable the industry needs to attract new subscribers and offer additional services to its current ones. Only now is the

TABLE 10.5 Comparison of Cable Penetration (%) in Top Five DMAs with Top Five Cabled Cities

Top Five DMAs		Top Five Cable Cities	
New York NY	39.3	Palm Springs CA	83.5
Los Angeles CA	37.9	Santa Barbara CA	82.7
Chicago IL	31.3	San Angelo TX	80.6
Philadelphia PA	47.4	Laredo TX	78.8
San Francisco CA	49.5	Yuma AZ/El Centro CA	75.7

Sources: *Nielsen Newscast* (Number 2, 1985); *Entertainment Merchandising* October 1987.

industry really starting to promote itself. In spring 1985 the Council for Cable Information launched a $6 million campaign, aimed at three non-user groups: 1) traditional families, 2) young professionals, and 3) "empty nesters," those whose children have grown up and left home. In addition, April has now been designated by the National Cable Television Association as National Cable Month, in which the cable networks and operators run special promotions and features.

EFFECTS ON OTHER MEDIA

☐ Cable Television

It is true that cable audiences are smaller than those of broadcast TV. But as cable continues to cut into the networks' shares, the cost of reaching a truly mass audience will rise. At the same time, the audience watching a particular cable show is more likely to be homogeneous and interested in that show than the varied millions who might tune in to "The Cosby Show" or "Miami Vice."

☐ Magazines

In fact, the more specialized, defined target audience in cable is part of a general trend in most media to greater selectivity and fragmentation. Magazines are catering to more and more special interests. Cable TV has perhaps developed the strongest media links with magazines, just as broadcast television did in the early days of that medium. And similarly, this has been through its ability to offer program sponsorship. Young mothers can not only read advice or information in *American Baby,* they can also see and hear it on CBN's "The American Baby Show." It is not simply a matter of literally translating print to screen.[9] Each medium can maintain its individual identity and format, while at the same time promoting its "partner" in advertisements. This helps maximize reach, increasing the potential combined magazine and television audience.

The effect of reaching an interested audience could have a crucial effect on sales. In a study conducted by Television Audience Assessment, Inc., viewers who are more "involved" with a program (as the interested audience of a cable show are assumed to be) are more likely to: 1) remember the main message points of a commercial; 2) like the ads and believe the product claim; and 3) prefer to buy the advertised product.[10]

☐ Newspapers

Newspapers across the country are in search of their audience. From holding an 11 percent share of all national advertising in 1960, they now have only seven percent. Circulation figures mirror demographic trends; as city papers struggle for survival the suburban dailies are flourishing. New technology offers a solution for improving newspapers at both the national and local level with the AdSat project. Through this scheme, which involves four major New York agencies and 10 newspapers, a single ad is prepared and delivered simultaneously to subscribing newspapers in all major markets, at a cost to each paper of $7,500 per year plus $23 for each advertisement received.[11] The idea originally was discussed when the first communications satellite went up but was previously considered too costly and impractical, despite the fact that typical newspapers were estimated to be losing up to $30,000 a year from lost or delayed ads. The advertisement travels from one to the other in four and a half minutes, making newspapers a viable national advertising medium, especially for national or corporate chains.[12] It is estimated that this project will soon involve all of the top 50 advertising agencies and reach the top 100 markets.[13]

☐ Radio

Cable's effect on radio is only starting to be felt. Star Ship Stereo, in West Virginia, offers cable audio, the radio equivalent of pay cable TV. For a $4 subscription fee, and $7.88 a month, one can receive ten extra radio stations, transmitted by satellite.[14] And many other cable systems already offer radio stations on unused channels. Like cable, radio advertising has low costs and a high frequency of exposure, but the new medium's frequency accumulates over time.

☐ Broadcast Television

The greatest impact of cable TV, and the one most often talked about, is on network television. The combined network shares fell from 91, in 1976, to 71, in 1986. In that same period, cable's share tripled from 16 to 48. A ten-year forecast for cable's effect on the networks predicts that by 1990 the 3-network share will be 61, with an average program rating of 13, both down from their 1984 levels of 74 and 15, respectively.[15]

Unlike the broadcast medium, however, cable channels do not rely wholly on ratings. With more flexible dayparts, cumulative audiences, and the potential to effectively reach the target audience with fewer than three exposures, a cable program may be evaluated on a number of criteria, such as the cable operators' opinions of it. They are the ones responsible for selling local advertising, a task facilitated through the use of interconnects that link several systems together for this purpose. With a "hard" interconnect, the systems themselves are linked by cable on microwave relay to ensure simultaneous transmission of the ads, while the "soft" interconnect allows the operator to insert ads on videotape into the local avails in that system.

These methods can be profitable for the operators. The Bay Area Interconnect, which links 32 systems and about 500,000 subscribers, enjoyed revenues of $3,000,000 for 1985. The typical rate charged for placing an advertisement in each cable system is $150 for a 30-second spot.[16] At the present time, however, only 1,300 out of the 7,000 systems sell local advertising time.[17] It is hoped that a new scheme known as CableOne, which will allow one-stop buying of ads on seventeen basic cable networks, will provide more competition to spot television and enhance local cable advertising revenues.[18]

It appears that two distinct television universes, cable and non-cable, are developing. One of the beneficial effects of this has been to force the networks to upgrade the quality of their programming to compete with cable's more upscale audience.[19] Additional news coverage appeared soon after CNN was available and proved popular. More intelligent entertainment shows, such as "L.A. Law" and "Family Ties," are now also produced by the networks.

The cable household is, in general, younger and more affluent than its broadcast equivalent. The viewer tends to be more active, selecting his or her programs from a wider choice. There is greater flexibility of daypart, with shows repeated at different times to fit in with more varied lifestyles, as well as less seasonal variation in people's viewing habits. People who subscribe to basic cable tend to do so to improve reception and add program diversity. Perhaps not surprisingly, only a small increase has been noted in the total amount of TV viewed. The additional hours that are watched on cable come out of the networks' prime time and daytime shows.

Subscribers to pay cable, however, do watch significantly more television. They live in larger households, are wealthier, more adventurous in product purchases, and use cable TV to seek qualitatively varied programs. Time flexibility is even more noticeable, with a big increase in late-night viewing. Yet pay cable is far from being the perfect medium. The major problem, and one reason why people drop their pay cable subscription, is the heavy duplication of programs, especially movies. In one study of evening television on pay cable in September 1983, the four main movie channels (HBO, Cinemax, Showtime, and The Movie Channel) showed the same five movies a total of 57 times. In order to rectify this, the pay cable channels are trying to include more original programs, or are making deals with the film studios to buy exclusive film rights to a movie before it is made.[20]

CABLE TELEVISION ON *ADPLAN*

Cable television, one of the most recent mass media to gain advertiser acceptance, can also be evaluated on ADPLAN. SMRB, MRI, and A. C. Nielsen provide audience data for a variety of cable television networks. Some of those data are summarized in Table 10.4, and cost data are also presented there. Self- and cross-pair audience data are not readily available for cable television networks, and published cable television network reach and frequency models are still in the development stage.[21] Consequently, the network television self- and cross-pair estimating procedures (Equations 9-3 and 9-4) have been adapted for cable television networks. The assumption required to do this, of course, is that audience accumulation rates within and between cable television networks are similar to those of their broadcast counterparts. While that still remains to be seen, in the meantime, the belief seems reasonable.

Equations 9-3 and 9-4 must first be modified in order to use them here. The reason for this is that the equations' intercepts (-.0065 and -.0049, respectively) are negative, and about the same size or larger than some cable network ratings. This would lead to negative values for some self- and cross-pair audience ratings. Equation intercepts affect the height of the equation (or magnitude) of all estimated self- and cross-pair ratings equally, but do not affect audience accumulation rates (slope). Therefore, the intercepts are dropped from Equations 9-3 and 9-4, yielding the following cable television network self- and cross-pair estimating equations.

$$R_{2i} = 1.7946(R_i) - 1.3308(R_i)^2 \qquad (10\text{-}1)$$
$$R_{ij} = 1.0095(R_i + R_j) - 1.5012(R_i)(R_j) \qquad (10\text{-}2)$$

Equations 10-1 and 10-2 allow one to estimate self- and cross-pair audiences using average quarter hour (AQH) audience estimates. Cumulative audience estimates, such as those published by MRI, must first be converted to AQH ratings in the manner of Table 10.4.

When developing and evaluating cable television network schedules, it is recommended that you use the high costs and ratings presented in Table 10.4, in the absence of better and more current information. That way, you will have some idea of the relative merits of cable television in relation to other options under consideration, keeping in mind the limitations of the data and procedures.

As an example, a schedule is evaluated using eight cable networks.

Entertainment and Sports Programming Network (ESPN),
Cable News Network (CNN),
Christian Broadcasting Network (CBN),
MTV: Music Television (MTV),
The Nashville Network (TNN),
Lifetime (LIFE),
Arts and Entertainment (A & E),
USA Cable Network (USA).

For each one, the user will need the single-insertion rating, cost-per-insertion, and the number of insertions. Also, the appropriate message weight must be selected. The typical figure is 0.625, which is based on "Recall," and will be used here. The example schedule evaluation assuming 30 insertions per network appears in Figure 10.1.

FIGURE 10.1   Cable Television Sample ADPLAN Output

Select the media category you want to use.

1=Consumer Magazines	5=Local Newspapers	9=Network Radio
2=Business Publications	6=Network TV	10=Spot Radio
3=National Newspapers	7=Spot TV	11=Outdoor
4=Newspaper Supplements	8=Cable TV	12=Direct Mail

Your choice? 8

Input vehicle audience weight to account for advertising exposures or other communication effects. For example:

   1.000 = Unweighted (vehicle exposures = ad exposures)
    .625 = Typical weight for CABLE TV

Enter weight? .625

Describe basis of weight (e.g., awareness, recall, knowledge)
Communication effect? Recall

How many vehicles in your CABLE TV schedule? 8

For each CABLE TV vehicle

Vehicle Number/Name	Ad Cost	Ads(#)	Rating	1=OK 2=no
1? ESPN	? 578	? 30	? .00469	? 1
2? CNN	? 584	? 30	? .00445	? 1
3? CBN	? 1318	? 30	? .00433	? 1
4? MTV	? 1385	? 30	? .00373	? 1
5? TNN	? 1075	? 30	? .00348	? 1
6? LIFE	? 500	? 30	? .0023	? 1
7? A & E	? 450	? 30	? .00141	? 1
8? USA	? 86	? 30	? .00329	? 1

View estimated cross-pair ratings (1=yes, 2=no)? 2

ADPLAN RESULTS: CABLE TV

Name = Kent Lancaster   Target ID = Female Homemakers
Brand = All-Bran   Target Size = 69,405,000
Period = June 1988

Frequency (f) Distribution	Unweighted		Weighted	
f	% f	% f+	% f	% f+
0	65.33%	100.00%	78.33%	100.00%
1	16.06%	34.67%	10.04%	21.67%
2	7.65%	18.61%	4.78%	11.63%
3	4.23%	10.96%	2.64%	6.85%
4	2.49%	6.73%	1.56%	4.21%
5	1.53%	4.24%	0.95%	2.65%
6	0.96%	2.71%	0.60%	1.69%
7	0.61%	1.75%	0.38%	1.10%
8	0.39%	1.14%	0.25%	0.71%
9	0.26%	0.75%	0.16%	0.47%
10	0.17%	0.49%	0.10%	0.31%
11+	0.33%	0.33%	0.20%	0.20%

BBD Factors: R1 = .003, R2 = .007, A = .3472942709, B = 100.0267791
Weight (Recall) = 62.5%

Summary Evaluation	Unweighted	Weighted
Reach (1+)	34.67%	21.67%
Effective Reach (3+)	10.96%	6.85%
Average Frequency	2.40	2.40
Gross Rating Points	83.04	51.90
Gross Impressions (000)	57,633.91	36,021.19
CPM/Gross Impressions	$3.11	$4.98
Cost Per Rating Point	$2,158.96	$3,454.34

Vehicle List	Rating	Cume	Ad Cost	CPM	Ads	Total Cost
ESPN	0.47	0.84	$578	$2.84	30	$17,340
CNN	0.44	0.80	$584	$3.03	30	$17,520
CBN	0.43	0.77	$1,318	$7.02	30	$39,540
MTV	0.37	0.67	$1,385	$8.56	30	$41,550
TNN	0.35	0.62	$1,075	$7.12	30	$32,250
LIFE	0.23	0.41	$500	$5.01	30	$15,000
A & E	0.14	0.25	$450	$7.36	30	$13,500
USA	0.33	0.59	$86	$0.60	30	$2,580
Totals:				$4.98	240	$179,280

OTHER NEW TECHNOLOGIES

☐ **Subscription Television (STV)**

In the 1950s and '60s subscription television was hailed as a marvelous alternative form of pay television for those without access to cable. A scrambled signal is transmitted electronically over the air to subscribers, on the UHF band.[22] The operators lease time from conventional stations, although the 50-mile range of the systems limits the channel capacity to about 25 stations.[23]

Despite a loosening of restrictions on this newer technology in the 1980s to encourage its growth, STV never really became commercially viable or popular because it could only offer a limited number of channels. Today, there are only six services in ten markets, mostly in large cities such as Los Angeles or Chicago.

☐ **Multipoint Distribution Services (MDS)**

Another alternative to pay cable TV that proved similarly disappointing was multipoint distribution service, or MDS, which offered one channel by closed-circuit microwave within a 25-mile range of the subscriber.[24] Again, it was expected to be a success in non-cabled areas, but as these continue to dwindle, prospects look bleak.

A more successful version of this may be multichannel system, or MMDS (also known as "wireless cable"). After inordinate delay, the FCC finally held lotteries in 1985 to hand out permits to companies wishing to offer this service. By this time, however, cable was fairly well established and even the prospect of more channels, perhaps as many as 29 of them, distributed via microwave, is unlikely to be enough of an incentive.[25]

☐ Satellite Master Antenna Television (SMATV)

Like MDS, Satellite Master Antenna Television (SMATV) also is aimed primarily at apartment buildings. It resembles a mini-cable system, with each household hooked up to a private satellite antenna located on the roof of the building, or adjacent to it, in order to receive multichannel programs.[26] The signals are picked up from the satellite, amplified, and sent through the cable wires. Its initial success was due to the delay in wiring big cities where most multiple dwelling units are found, but now that urban franchises have been allocated and, in many cities completed, its future is more uncertain. There currently are estimated to be about 500,000 subscribers, concentrated in metropolitan areas.[27]

☐ Low Power Television (LPTV)

While cable services first flourished in rural areas, they still have not gained 100 percent penetration. One option for these uncabled rural communities is low power television (LPTV). Since the FCC first permitted the service to begin in 1980, 383 stations have begun operations, 225 in Alaska alone. In the fall of 1986 1,500 construction permits were also granted for additional low power operators.[28] This medium amplifies and rebroadcasts signals of distant full-power stations in a range of five to 40 miles. The operator chooses the programs, and whether to use UHF or VHF signals. The service is advertiser-supported, with extremely low rates. The national costs of a 30-second spot range between $4 and $50, with full program sponsorship costing between $45 and $500 per hour.[29]

☐ Television Receive Only (TVRO)

As people grow more accustomed to having a wide range of TV forms to choose from, the logical extension is to set up one's own earth dish in the back yard. This technology, TV Receive Only (TVRO), is becoming increasingly popular. There are estimated to be over 1.5 million of these dishes in use. By aiming their dish in the right direction, the owners receive cable or satellite programs at no charge.

This free television was legitimized by the 1984 *Cable Communications Policy Act.* So in order not to lose money from subscription fees, the cable and satellite companies started in 1986 to scramble their signals, supplying decoder boxes, thereby forcing TVRO owners to negotiate with the cable networks via cable operators for paid access to these devices.[30]

☐ Direct Broadcasting by Satellite (DBS)

One of the most volatile areas in new media technology is a form that is not yet fully operational. Direct Broadcasting by Satellite (DBS) is really an expansion of TVRO. Signals from the cable or broadcast network are transmitted up to a communications satellite, scrambled, and sent back down to homes of individual subscribers, each of whom is supplied with a two-foot wide rooftop dish antenna and a decoder box.[31]

The industry has had problems in attracting subscribers, although since fifteen million homes will probably never be cabled, it still represents a sizable potential.[32]

Primary users will be households in rural areas with poor broadcast reception and no cable service. Also, subscribers to older cable systems with a limited channel capacity might be attracted to the wider viewing options of the satellite medium.

INTERACTIVE SERVICES

As viewers take more and more control of their media, choosing whether to watch one of 30 cable networks or to buy their own satellite dish, the era of interactivity is fast approaching, with consumers not only receiving these services into their homes, but also sending digital information back to the cable company. As far as the advertising industry is concerned, there are four main components to a fully interactive system:

1. addressability—locating the right home for messages;
2. a two-way communications link, by phone or cable;
3. a keyboard or pad for viewer requests; and
4. a data base for the information. [33]

One of the newest forms to become popular and successful is home shopping. One television network, Home Shopping Network, already reaches 13 million homes across the nation, with 24-hour broadcasts of its "Home Shopping Club." That network, together with seventeen other operating or planned national or regional versions, expected to sell over $200 million in goods in 1986, compared to the $24.5 million sold in 1984. Programs are live, in contrast to the mixed success of computerized home shopping ventures such as the Comp-u-card service or Cableshop. Following HSN's success, it has started another channel, already reaching 2.3 million, selling to more affluent consumers, and featuring more upscale, brand-name goods such as stereos and cameras. The implications for advertising are noteworthy; this is, in effect, a pure advertising medium, and is proving popular with consumers. It is also profitable for the cable operator who receives up to five percent of the total sales in his franchise area. Indeed, there are now seventeen similar networks either in operation or planned, with major retail chains and information services anxious to be involved. [34]

☐ Videocassette Recorders

Videocassette recorders (VCRs) first became popular in the late-1970s. Currently, penetration stands at 44 percent, with forecasts for 1990 as high as 70 percent. [35] While cassette rental of movies and old TV shows, for about $2 each, is presently a boom industry, experts predict the sales end of the market is where the real profits will come. In 1986, this business was worth $2.1 billion. Predictions for 1990 are as high as $4 billion, mostly due to the entrance of nonspecialty dealers, such as Seven Eleven, into the market. Indeed, consumers now spend almost as much on purchasing video software as they do on renting it—38 percent of the $5.5 billion total spent in 1986. [36]

As VCR prices fall rapidly, they are becoming as common in the home as the stereo. Users still tend to be the affluent and well educated, similar to subscribers to cable. In fact, in homes with VCRs, cable penetration is 48 percent,[37] while 25 percent of homes subscribing to cable also own VCRs.[38] Although it is not primarily an ad-supported medium, there is strong potential for advertiser involvement. Some companies are already marketing or sponsoring videos. Stouffer Foods, for example, the makers of Lean Cuisine, has developed the ''Living Lean Kit,'' a home video weight reduction package, for $130. One company already offers sponsorships in pre-recorded cassettes that include an opening company identification and a 30-, 60- or 120-second commercial at the end of the tape.[39] And with the 1987 collaboration of Pepsi and Warner Home Video in the marketing of the movie ''Top Gun'' on cassette, there may well be greater use of commercials if they serve to reduce the retail price.

The VCR, often called a time-shift medium, is changing the nature of television, encouraging two tendencies among viewers: ''zipping'' (fast-forwarding the tape to avoid the ads), and ''zapping'' (channel switching), which has the same effect. As the viewer now has control over programming schedules and dayparts, media planners do not know when the shows will be seen.[40] Interestingly, it seems that soap operas are the most frequently recorded programs, suggesting that advertisers need to reconsider daytime audience estimates.[41] Of all that is recorded on a VCR, about 80 percent is played back, but at this time, over 50 percent of the ads are skipped.[42] In one study, 75 percent of VCR users fast-forwarded the tape during the commercials, despite the fact that 66 percent of them claimed to find television ads entertaining.[43]

Remote control sets also increase commercial avoidance. Of all TV viewers, 24 percent are considered ''hyperactive,'' changing channels an average of nine to ten times an hour. During prime time it is believed that up to 40 percent of the audience leaves the room when the commercials appear.[44] Taking both forms of zapping together, research indicates that men are more likely to zap than women, and younger adults more prone than older ones, having grown up with the idea of greater channel choice. The way people watch television is probably changing as a result. Zappers tend to plan their viewing less, switching channels before deciding what to watch. They also flip the switch between and during shows (frequently during the commercials), suggesting that future users may watch two or more channels simultaneously. Television is thus becoming much more of a background medium, similar to the way people now listen to the radio.[45]

☐ Teletext and Videotex

The simplest level of interactivity involves data transmission services such as teletext and videotex. Each sends information through the vertical blanking interval (VBI, or unused picture linage) of the television.[46] While the teletext subscriber sits passively in front of the information he or she has called up onto the screen, videotex allows the viewer to respond to it. Subscribers can access the information using phone lines or the faster, more efficient two-way cable systems.

However, two main videotex tests undertaken by major publishers, Knight-Ridder's Viewtron service in Miami, and Times Mirror's Gateway system in Orange County, California, proved unsuccessful. For $19.95 a month, Gateway offered three dozen news sources, home shopping, restaurant guides, a calendar of events, TV program guides and electronic mail (at 20 cents a message). Advertising was accepted in logos on index pages, infomercials, or classified or full page ads.[47] Yet both services were cancelled in 1986 due to lack of response.[48] Nevertheless, an estimated one million users, many of them in businesses, now subscribe to videotex services. Today, the most popular form of the system is in transactional services, such as the Covidea project from AT & T, Chemical Bank, the Bank of America and Time, Incorporated, that provides 45,000 subscribers with electronic banking, news and information, and brokerage services. In 1988, Sears and IBM intend to offer their similar Trintex system under the Prodigy name.[49] And the success of teletext services across Europe provides further incentive to companies in the U.S. to continue experimenting with the concept.

Yet one of the main hopes for the continued growth of teletext and videotex services is their ability to be accessed through the personal computer, forecast to be in 50 percent of all U.S. households by the year 2000.[50] The Teletext-5 service, in Salt Lake City, Utah, enables readers to call up the required information and program their computer to store it in memory to be viewed at leisure. The user profile for this service matches that of computer owners, tending to be well-educated males, more than half of whom are between the ages of 20 and 40.[51] The potential for linking interactive services to the computer suggests that viewers may soon be able to see ads in their own time and at their own pace, perhaps further altering the concept of effective reach.

The first two-way interactive service, QUBE, was set up in Columbus, Ohio, by Warner Cable Communications, Inc. (WACCI), employing both TV and computers. Viewers respond to messages on their television screens using a keypad, perhaps voting on how a program should end, or responding to a viewer poll; as their answers automatically are computed the outcome becomes an integral part of the program. The potential for viewer polling and research is limited by the unreliability and lack of representativeness in the small sample.[52]

☐ Electronic Banking

Several elements offered by WACCI are being tested on their own. Electronic banking is now used by 44,000 consumers and small businesses across the states. By phone lines and computers, subscribers can perform most banking activities. There are already more than 25 separate electronic banking systems, from over 65 different banks, savings and loan institutions or credit unions; the two major services are Chemical Bank's Pronto service and Bank of America's Homebanking.[53]

☐ Pay-per-View

Another promising interactive service, pay-per-view (PPV), lets subscribers purchase individual programs when they wish. This eliminates one of the major complaints about regular cable services—being forced to pay for programs one neither watches nor wants. Cox Cable in San Diego features sports events in this way. For $120 the subscriber can see 40 baseball games, or purchase them on an individual basis at a slightly higher fee. The system estimates 25,000 viewers have so far tuned in to the PPV showings.[54]

The major pay cable services, such as HBO and Showtime, are acquiring PPV rights to their original programs and feature films, realizing that this could become a major segment of the new media industry.[55] There are now six general-interest satellite-fed PPV services which show movies and sports events, the former at about the same time they're available on videocassettes (four and a half months after the theater release), suggesting PPV could become a major competitor to the VCR. The two main PPV networks are Request TV and Viewer's Choice, each with one million subscribers. Furthermore, about 50 of the 110 cable systems offering PPV do so on a stand-alone basis, deciding themselves what to show. Although eight million homes already have PPV capability, only three million of these use it for the PPV service. Prices for events range from $2.50 to $20, depending both on the network and the feature, but problems remain with finding the best way to offer customers shows, and how to bill them afterwards.[56]

CONCLUSION

Only now is cable television becoming a feasible alternative medium both for viewers and advertisers, but its progress has been extremely slow. For while it is a distinctive new technology, offering numerous benefits for advertisers such as flexible message length, targeted audiences, lower CPMs, and favorable program environment, the lack of sufficient audience data and the comparatively low ratings have hindered cable's development. Today, although alternative technologies such as STV or MDS appear to present a minimal threat to cable, individual cable networks are now vying for consumer and commercial dollars both among themselves and against an increasing array of other electronic options, such as PPV or videotex. For media planners, it is increasingly important to consider cable television in any media schedule, and the ADPLAN program has been designed to allow users to do so. Perhaps all that can be said with certainty regarding new technologies is that their future looks as exciting and challenging for advertisers and the viewing public as their past has been!

ENDNOTES

1. Leo Burnett, *Media, Superstations and Satellites* (Report from Media Research, 1979).

2. J. Walter Thompson, *New Communications Opportunities in a Changing Consumer Environment* (March, 1984).

3. Leo Burnett, op. cit.

4. "Cable Stats," *CableVision* (January 21, 1985), p. 44.

5. *Advertising Age*, March 1986.

6. Judann Dagnoli, "Cable tests hot-wired to consumer preferences," *Advertising Age* (Special Report on Cable Television, December 1, 1986), p. S10-11.

7. Leading National Advertisers, *Class/Brand YTD$*, January-December, 1986.

8. Robert M. Reed, *The American Telecommunications Market*, (The National Video Clearinghouse, Inc. 1982).

9. Betsy Gilbert, "Translating print into programming," *Advertising Age* (Special Report on Cable, May 31, 1984), p. 44.

10. Cecilia Capuzzi, "Attention-grabbing programming gives punch to advertiser's dollar," *CableVision* (November 5, 1984), p. 25.

11. Fred Pfaff, "Clear Signals For Ad/Sat," *Marketing and Media Decisions*, February 1987, pp. 35-36.

12. Ilene V. Smith, "All the ads that are fit to print," *Satellite Communications* (April, 1985), pp. 42-43.

13. Fred Pfaff, op. cit.

14. Simon Applebaum, "SSS stands by Star Ship Stereo, moves forward with SPN plans," *CableVision* (March 4, 1985), p. 25.

15. Ronald B. Kaatz, *Cable: An Advertiser's Guide to the New Electronic Media* (Chicago: Crain Books, 1982).

16. Edmond M. Rosenthal, "Ad interconnects take new forms, add new markets," *Cable Age* (January 21, 1985), pp. C8-12.

17. Rich Zahradnik, "On The Loose," *Marketing and Media Decisions*, February 1987, pp.52-54.

18. Richard Tedesco, "Cable pact will offer 1-stop buy," *Electronic Media*, February 23, 1987, p. 2.

19. John Saeman, "The Marketplace - Now and Through the '80's," *Cable 83 - Proceedings of the International Conference on Satellite and Cable Television* (Northwood UK: Online Publications 1983), 95-105.

20. Timothy Hollins, *Beyond Broadcasting: Into the Cable Age* (London: BFI Publishing, 1984).

21. Roland T. Rust, *Advertising Media Models: A Practical Guide* (Massachusetts: Lexington Books, 1986), p. 140.

22. Leo Burnett, *Subscription Television (STV)* (Report from Media Research, 1982).

23. Robert M. Reed, op. cit.

24. Ronald B. Kaatz, op. cit.

25. Richard Barbieri, "The Quick Fix That Came Late," *Channels* (Field Guide to the Electronic Media 1987), p. 57.

26. Ronald B. Kaatz, op. cit.

27. Hugh M. Belville Jr., "The Audience Potential of the New Technologies: 1985:1990," *Journal of Advertising Research* (April 1985), pp. RC3-10.

28. Michael Couzens, "They Jes' Keep a-Growin'," *Channels* (Field Guide to the Electronic Media 1987), p. 54.

29. John Reilly, "LPTV Update," *Videography* (April 1985), pp. 65-72.

30. David Bollier, "There's Life after Scrambling," *Channels* (Field Guide to the Electronic Media 1987), p. 66.

31. Robert M. Reed, op. cit.

32. Guy M. Stephens, "Will DBS Bridge Its Troubled Waters?" *Satellite Communications* (February 1985), pp. 34-35.

33. Jayne Zenaty, "Media Outlook: Year 2000," *American Advertising* (April 1985), p. 7.

34. John Motavalli, "Home Is Where the Mart Is," *Channels* (Field Guide to the Electronic Media 1987), p. 77.

35. David Lachenbruch, "The Makers' Lament: Not-So-Fast-Forward," *Channels* (Field Guide to the Electronic Media 1987), pp. 88-89.

36. Ira Mayer and Paul Sweeting, "Beyond Rentals: The Next Push for Growth," *Channels* (Field Guide to the Electronic Media 1987), p. 92.

37. Stephen Advokat, "Zapping becomes a Madison Ave. nightmare," *CableVision*, (February 18, 1985), p. 21.

38. *CableVision*, February 1985.

39. J. Walter Thompson, *Media Report* Volume 8, Number 1 (Jan/Feb 1986), p. 8.

40. Jayne Zenaty, op. cit.

41. "Nielsen Releases New VCR Study," *Nielsen Newscast* (Number 2, 1984).

42. Barry M. Kaplan, "Zapping—The Real Issue Is Communication," *Journal of Advertising Research* (April 1985), pp. 9-14.

43. *Cable Age*, "Commercial avoidance study," July 8, 1985, p. 26.

44. Stephen Advokat, op. cit.

45. Carrie Heeter and Bradley S. Greenberg, "Profiling the Zappers," *Journal of Advertising Research* (April 1985), pp. 15-19.

46. Leo Burnett, *Interactive Cable* (Report from Media Research, 1983).

47. Sally Russell, "Study claims MMDS no threat," *Communications and Engineering Design* (June 1985), pp. 30-31.

48. Lee Goldberg, "Videotex fortunes," *Electronic Media* (March 24, 1986), p. 3.

49. Gary Arlen, "High Rollers with High Hopes," *Channels* (Field Guide to the Electronic Media 1987) pp. 86-87.

50. Jayne Zenaty, op. cit.

51. David Webb, "Teletext-5: Giving the people what they want," *Television/Broadcast Communications* (April 1985), pp. 91-92.

52. Leo Burnett, 1983, op. cit.

53. John Wolfe, "Home Banking: Does the fast track lead to cable?" *CableVision* (February 4, 1985), pp. 34-35.

54. Cecilia Capuzzi, "PPV possesses potential for popularity," *CableVision* (December 12, 1984), pp. 55-56.

55. Eric Taub, "Home Movies—Will PPV cure the VCR blues?" *CableVision* (October 22, 1984), pp. 32-36.

56. Mark Frankel, "Forcing Open a New Window," *Channels* (Field Guide to the Electronic Media 1987), p. 82.

ADDITIONAL READING

Ahrold, Robbin, "Pay TV and Cable Promotion," *Strategies in Broadcast and Cable Promotion*, eds. Susan Tyler Eastman and Robert A. Klein (Belmont, California: Wadsworth Publishing Company).

Brown, Kevin, "Spot cable hopes to connect with interconnects," *Advertising Age* (Special Report on Cable, December 5, 1985), pp. 20-21.

Broadcasting/Cable Yearbook 1986.

"Cable networks' outlook for 1985," *Marketing and Media Decisions* (February 1985), pp. 74-82.

"Churn may still be the chink in SMATV's armor," *Cablenews* (January 7, 1985), p. 8.

Halliday, David Graham, "Home dish sales burst spawns heady growth predictions," *Cable Age* (April 29, 1985), pp. 43-45.

Howard, Herbert M. and Sidney S. Carroll, *SMATV: Strategic Opportunities in Private Cable*, (Report for The National Association of Broadcasters, 1982).

Lancaster, Kent M. and Helen E. Katz, "Evaluating Cable Television Network Advertising Schedules," *Proceedings of the American Academy of Advertising,* Las Vegas, Nevada, March 1987, pp. R44-R49.

McCloskey, Paul, "FCC set to award MMDS blocks early next year," *CableVision* (December 10, 1984), p. 14.

Motavalli, John, "Getting friendly with VCRs," *CableVision* (October 28, 1985), pp. 40-47.

Russell, Sally, "Videotex service scheduled for Los Angeles suburb," *CableVision* (December 10, 1984), p. 74.

TV and Cable Factbook (No. 53, 1985).

Veraska, Don and Len Strazewski, "Industry works to improve fuzzy image," *Advertising Age* (Special Report on Cable, December 5, 1985), pp. 15-16.

CHAPTER ELEVEN

Mixed Media Evaluation

MULTIPLE MEDIA EXPOSURE DISTRIBUTIONS[1]

Advertising campaigns for most major consumer goods brands involve more than one media category. This presents a challenge to media planners who wish to evaluate the overall media weight of an entire campaign in addition to individual media categories. This chapter explores a simple method used to evaluate the combined impact of multiple media schedules.

As explained earlier, the random combination method estimates the rating or reach of a pair of different media vehicles, A and B, as follows:

$$R_{A,B} = R_A + R_B - (R_A)(R_B) \tag{11-1}$$

This can also be expressed as:

$$R_{A,B} = GRPs_{A,B} - Duplication_{A,B}. \tag{11-2}$$

That is, the duplication between two vehicles is assumed to be the product of the two ratings. This reasoning can be extended to the situation involving two media categories instead of two vehicles. Since the sum of an exposure distribution is equal to 1.00, the product of two separate exposure distributions must also equal 1.00. Therefore, it should be possible to multiply two exposure distributions in order to derive a combined exposure distribution. Here is how it can be done.

You should recall the unweighted ADPLAN exposure distributions for the full information magazine schedule and the television schedule which were estimated in Chapters Eight and Nine.

Now, to multiply the two exposure distributions, one eliminates the ''%'' signs by moving the decimals two places to the left for each exposure level. Then a matrix is set up with the television exposure distribution on the left and the magazine exposure distribution across the top as in Table 11.2.

After this, the next step is to multiply each column percent by each row percent to get the random ''duplication'' between each frequency level in the magazine schedule and each frequency level in the television schedule, filling in the entire matrix, as in Table 11.2.

Since the 63 cells in the matrix must sum to 1.00, the combined exposure distribution can be obtained for each frequency level by adding together the percent-

TABLE 11.1 Magazine and Television Exposure Distributions

f	Magazines	Television
0	40.59%	38.00%
1	20.35	27.68
2	13.93	17.13
3	10.13	9.50
4	7.32	4.71
5	4.96	2.03
6	2.71	0.73
7		0.20
8		0.03
Sum:	100.00%	100.00%

TABLE 11.2 Combining Magazine and Television Exposure Distributions
Magazine (Across) and Television (Down)

f		0	1	2	3	4	5	6
	%	.4059	.2035	.1393	.1013	.0732	.0496	.0271
0	.3800	.1542	.0773	.0529	.0385	.0278	.0188	.0103
1	.2768	.1124	.0563	.0386	.0280	.0203	.0137	.0075
2	.1713	.0695	.0349	.0239	.0174	.0125	.0085	.0046
3	.0950	.0386	.0193	.0132	.0096	.0070	.0047	.0026
4	.0471	.0191	.0096	.0066	.0048	.0034	.0023	.0013
5	.0203	.0082	.0041	.0028	.0021	.0015	.0010	.0006
6	.0073	.0030	.0015	.0010	.0007	.0005	.0004	.0002
7	.0020	.0008	.0004	.0003	.0002	.0001	.0001	.0001
8	.0003	.0001	.0001	.0000	.0000	.0000	.0000	.0000

ages along each diagonal of the matrix, as illustrated for a frequency of three in Table 11.2. Each diagonal contains the probabilities for alternative ways of being exposed 1, 2, 3, ..., 14 total insertions in the schedule. The procedure leading to a combined exposure distribution is illustrated in Table 11.3.

TABLE 11.3 Combined Magazine and Television Exposure Distribution

Exposure Distribution

f	%	=	Sum of Table 11.2 Diagonals
0	15.42	=	.1542
1	18.97	=	.1124 + .0773
2	17.88	=	.0695 + .0563 + .0529
3	15.05	=	.0386 + .0349 + .0386 + .0385
4	11.82	=	.0191 + .0193 + .0239 + .0280 + .0278
5	8.75	=	.0082 + .0096 + .0132 + .0174 + .0203 + .0188
6	5.99	=	.0030 + .0041 + .0066 + .0096 + .0125 + .0137 + .0103
7	3.28	=	.0008 + .0015 + .0028 + .0048 + .0070 + .0085 + .0075
8	1.64	=	.0001 + .0004 + .0010 + .0021 + .0034 + .0047 + .0046
9	0.75	=	.0001 + .0003 + .0007 + .0015 + .0023 + .0026
10	0.31	=	.0000 + .0002 + .0005 + .0010 + .0013
11+	0.15	= 1.00	− .1542 − .1897 − .1788 − .1505 − .1182 − .0875
			− .0599 − .0328 − .0164 − .0075 − .0031
Sum:	100.00		

The 11+ exposure level includes those who are exposed 11 or more times. When an exposure distribution is not completely enumerated, it is often referred to as a "truncated" exposure distribution. For large exposure distributions it is usually more convenient to truncate them at 10 or 11 or more exposures. The 11+ exposure level can be computed, for example, as 100 percent less the percentage for each exposure level below 11.

There are at least two major problems with this method of combining exposure distributions. First, it assumes that television exposures are equivalent to magazine exposures. But if the objective of Kellogg's All-Bran advertising is "correct recall" of principal product benefits, the two media categories are likely to contribute differently toward that objective. As a result each media category exposure distribution must be weighted in accordance with its contribution to advertising goals before it is combined with other media category exposure distributions. Chapter Three demonstrated how this can be accomplished.

The second problem has to do with the amount of duplication between media categories. One may recall that the rating or reach of vehicles A and B can be estimated as follows:

$$R_{A,B} = R_A + R_B - (k)(R_A)(R_B)$$

As stated before, k is the correction factor for interdependence such that if duplication between media vehicles is greater or less than would be expected on the basis of chance, then k would be greater or less than 1.00. Likewise, when the duplication between media categories is greater or less than would be expected on the basis of chance, the cells of the Table 11.2 matrix that involve duplication between exposures should be increased or decreased by "k" and the zero cell and the marginal cells should also be increased or decreased so that all cells sum to 1.00.

To illustrate how this would work as a practical matter, assume that a media planner wanted to estimate the reach of two vehicles, A and B, and further assume that the rating of A is .2 and the rating of B is .3. Using the random combination method:

$$R_{A,B} = .2 + .3 - (.2)(.3)$$
$$= .5 - .06$$
$$= .44$$

This problem could also be solved using the matrix method illustrated in Table 11.2. Here is how this is done.

f	Exposure Distributions	
	Vehicle A	**Vehicle B**
0	80.0%	70.0%
1	20.0%	30.0%
	100.0%	100.0%

Using these exposure distributions, the matrix is presented as follows.

Vehicle A

		0	1
f		0	1
	%	.8	.2
0	.7	.56	.14
1	.3	.24	.06

Vehicle B

Summing the diagonals of the matrix yields the following combined exposure distribution.

Combined Exposure Distribution

f	%		**Sum of Matrix Diagonals**
0	.56	=	.56
1	.38	=	.24 + .14
2	.06	=	.06

There is nothing difficult or surprising about this example. It merely serves as a point of departure for examining the impact of duplication that is greater or less than would be expected on the basis of chance.

If one assumes that the media planner learns that the correction factor for inter-dependence of vehicles A and B is approximately 1.50, re-estimating the reach of A and B gives:

$$R_{A,B} = .2 + .3 - (1.5)(.2)(.3)$$
$$= .5 - .09$$
$$= .41$$

The exposure distributions for each vehicle remain unchanged.

f	**Exposure Distributions**	
	Vehicle A	**Vehicle B**
0	80.0%	70.0%
1	20.0%	30.0%
	100.0%	100.0%

But the duplication between vehicle A and B is now .09, not .06 as it was initially.

Vehicle A

f		0	1
	%	.8	.2
0	.7	.59 = 1-.41	.11 = .2-.09
1	.3	.21 = .3-.09	.09

Vehicle B

As a result, all of the cells in the new matrix are different than they were in the previous example. Of course, the "0,0" cell will be non-reach, or 1 - .41 = .59. The two remaining cells will be equal to the marginal minus the duplication; .21 and .11 respectively.

Although the reasoning here is based on reach and duplication of particular vehicles, it is similar to the reasoning required to deal with duplication between media categories. Vehicles A and B could just as easily be magazine and television schedules, respectively. Evaluating typical schedules does become considerably more complex, however, but the objective is identical to the example shown above.

ESTIMATING DUPLICATION BETWEEN MEDIA CATEGORIES

If a media planner is willing to assume that the media schedule being evaluated is "representative" of the media categories involved, then media quintile data and media imperative data can be used to estimate the degree of duplication between the media categories to see whether it is greater or less than would be expected on the basis of chance. This information can then be used to adjust the matrix when estimating combined exposure distributions.

SMRB, Volume P-20 (1985), reports the following Media Quintile data for magazines and television for female homemakers who use cold breakfast cereals.

	Magazine	TV-Total
Quintile 1	19.8%	20.4%
Quintile 2	22.4	20.3
Quintile 3	16.1	19.9
Quintile 4	18.8	19.5
Quintile 5	23.0	19.9

Each quintile includes approximately 20 percent of the target in various media usage groups. For example, the SMRB Technical Appendix indicates that females grouped in Magazine Quintiles 1 and 2 read six or more magazines per month. Females grouped in Television Quintiles 1 and 2 view 107 or more half-hours of television per month.

Sometimes media quintile data can give media planners clues as to the most useful media categories against a particular target. The objective would be to find a good match between Media Quintiles 1 and 2 and heavy users of the product category. For the time being, however, the objective here is quite different. The quintile data are used to estimate the degree to which the duplication between media categories is greater or less than would be expected on the basis of chance. To do so, the concept of "dual" audience must first be introduced.

SMRB defines the dual audience between two media categories as various aggregates of the upper quintiles of the two media categories. In the case of "magazines and all day TV half-hours," SMRB defines the dual to be those target persons in the upper two quintiles of both media categories plus those who are in the third quintile of both media categories.

FIGURE 11.1   Definition of Dual Audience

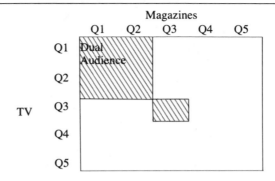

The shaded area in Figure 11.1 represents the dual audience. In this example, SMRB estimates that 19 percent of the All-Bran target audience is in the "Magazine - Television: Dual" (SMRB, 1985, Volume P-20, p. 37). This is the actual target percent estimated to be exposed heavily to both media categories. What percent of the target would one expect to be exposed heavily to both media categories on the basis of chance alone?

Using the definition of the dual audience given in Figure 11.1, and the quintile data presented earlier, this can be estimated quite easily.

The percentage in each of the cells represents the product of the respective media category quintile percentages. Summing the percentages in the five cells gives an estimate of the dual that would be expected on the basis of chance.

$$\text{Dual}_R = .0404 + .0457 + .0402 + .0455 + .0320$$
$$= .2038$$
$$= 20.38\%$$

where Dual_R = random dual.

One will recall that the actual dual (Dual_A) is 19 percent. Consequently, the ratio of random dual (Dual_R) to the actual dual (Dual_A) is given by:

$$\text{Ratio} = \text{Dual}_R/\text{Dual}_A \qquad\qquad (11\text{-}3)$$
$$= 20.38\%/19\%$$
$$= 1.073$$

That is, the dual estimated on the basis of chance is 1.073 times greater than the actual dual. Therefore, the cells in Table 11.2 reflect too much duplication, which means it is likely that the amount of duplication between the magazine and television schedules is less than estimated in Table 11.2. That is, the matrix procedure, which is based on the assumption of random duplication, will probably overestimate duplication and frequency and underestimate reach in this example.

As it turns out, ratios based on Equation 11-3 can be used to adjust matrices such as Table 11.2 to account for duplication that deviates from that which would

FIGURE 11.2 Estimating Random Dual Audience

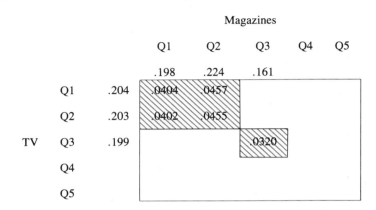

be expected on the basis of chance. This should lead to more realistic estimates of reach and frequency.

The work required to adjust Table 11.2 using the ratio of 1.073 based on Equation 11-3 can be quite tedious and difficult to follow on an intuitive basis. Happily, ADPLAN will handle the mathematics quite nicely. Therefore, more trusting souls may wish to skip the section which follows and move on to Chapter Twelve.

NONRANDOM MIXED MEDIA DUPLICATION

The previous section considered an intuitive example showing how to adjust simple matrices when duplication between media categories is not random. For larger schedules, the problem of computing the combination of pairs of exposure distributions in the face of nonrandom duplication is considerably more complex.

Here are the steps that should be followed:

1. Compute the Ratio of random duplication to actual duplication. Ratio = $Dual_R/Dual_A$. The ratio must be greater than the highest reach of the two schedules being combined. If it is not, then it may be preferable to increase it before proceeding so that it is at least one percentage point larger than the highest reach of the two schedules being combined.

2. Use the Ratio to re-estimate the percent of the target not exposed to each schedule.

$$P^*_0 = P_0 - 1.0 + Ratio$$

where: P^*_0 = Re-estimated percent of the target not exposed to a particular media schedule.

P_0 = Original percent of the target estimated not to be exposed to a particular media schedule.

3. Multiply the pairs of revised exposure distributions in the usual fashion and, for each matrix cell percentage, divide the result by the Ratio.

$$P^*_{ij} = (P_i)(P_j)/Ratio$$

where: P_i = percent of the target exposed n times to the first of a pair of media schedules where i = 0, 1, 2,..., 11+.

P_j = percent of the target exposed n times to the second of a pair of media schedules where j = 0, 1, 2,..., 11+.

P_{ij} = percent of the target exposed i + j times to a pair of media schedules where i = 0, 1, 2,..., 11+ and j = 0, 1, 2,..., 11+.

4. Recompute the new "0,0" cell of the matrix (that is, i=0, j=0).

$$P_{0,0} = ((P^*_{0,})(P^*_{,0})/Ratio) + 1 - Ratio$$

where: $P^*_{0,}$ = original estimate of the percent of the target not exposed to media schedule i.

$P^*_{,0}$ = original estimate of the percent of the target not exposed to media category schedule j.

A SIMPLE EXAMPLE

Returning now to the simple example that was solved by inspection, readers can proceed through the four steps to insure that they arrive at the same result.

1. One will recall that random duplication is equal to 6.0 percent and actual duplication is equal to 9.0 percent.

   Ratio = 6.0%/9.0% = .666

   This is larger than the reach of .2 or .3 for the two "vehicles," respectively. Therefore, it is appropriate to continue the process using the ratio of .666.

2. Recomputing the percent not exposed to each vehicle, one would obtain:

   $$P^*_{0,} = .8 - 1 + .666$$
   $$= .466$$
   $$P^*_{,0} = .7 - 1 + .666$$
   $$= .366$$

The revised exposure distributions follow.

f	Exposure Distributions	
	Vehicle A	**Vehicle B**
0	46.6%	36.6%
1	20.0	30.0
Sum:	66.6	66.6

One should note that each of the exposure distributions now sums to the ratio (66.6%). Multiplying the distributions gives the results in Figure 11.3.

The numbers in the matrix represent the completion of steps three and four. That is, the revised exposure distributions have been multiplied in the usual fashion and the result in each cell has been divided by the ratio of .666. In addition, to

FIGURE 11.3   Accounting for Mixed Media Nonrandom Duplication

		Vehicle A	
f		0	1
Vehicle B	%	.466	.200
0	.366	.59 = ((.366)(.466)/.666) + 1-.666	.11 = (.366)(.2)/.666
1	.300	.21 = (.3)(.466)/.666	.09 = (.3)(.2)/.666

estimate the probability of not being exposed to either schedule, one adds 1 - .666 to the ''0,0'' cell. Readers will recognize this result as being identical to that obtained by inspection. The value of the more detailed approach, of course, is that it will allow for the systematic solution of larger problems.

A REALISTIC EXAMPLE

To insure that the procedures described so far are clear, they will now be applied to more complex problems involving the magazine and television schedules presented earlier.

1. Readers will recall that:
   $$\text{Ratio} = \text{Dual}_R/\text{Dual}_A$$
   $$= 20.38\%/19\%$$
   $$= 1.073$$
   One can see that 1.073 is indeed greater than the reach of either schedule.

2. Recomputing the percent not exposed to each media category gives:
   $$P^*_{0.} = .4059 - 1 + 1.073$$
   $$= .4789$$
   $$P^*_{.0} = .38 - 1 + 1.073$$
   $$= .453$$

The revised exposure distributions follow:

f	Exposure Distributions Magazines	Television
0	47.89%	45.30%
1	20.35	27.68
2	13.93	17.13
3	10.13	9.50
4	7.32	4.71
5	4.96	2.03
6	2.71	0.73
7		0.20
8		0.03
Sum:	107.30	107.30

TABLE 11.4 Combining Magazine and Television Exposure Distributions: Nonrandom Duplication

		Magazine (Across) and Television (Down)						
f		0	1	2	3	4	5	6
	%	.4789	.2035	.1393	.1013	.0732	.0496	.0271
0	.4530	.1292	.0859	.0588	.0428	.0309	.0209	.0114
1	.2768	.1235	.0525	.0359	.0261	.0189	.0128	.0070
2	.1713	.0765	.0325	.0222	.0162	.0117	.0079	.0043
3	.0950	.0424	.0180	.0123	.0090	.0065	.0044	.0024
4	.0471	.0210	.0089	.0061	.0044	.0032	.0022	.0012
5	.0203	.0091	.0039	.0026	.0019	.0014	.0009	.0005
6	.0073	.0033	.0014	.0009	.0007	.0005	.0003	.0002
7	.0020	.0009	.0004	.0003	.0002	.0001	.0001	.0001
8	.0003	.0001	.0001	.0000	.0000	.0000	.0000	.0000

Each of the exposure distributions now sums to ratio (107.30). Multiplying the two exposure distributions, one obtains the results in Table 11.4.

The work leading to the final percentages is not depicted in the matrix above due to space constraints. Let it suffice at this point to illustrate the computations for the first two cells.

$$P^*_{0,0} = ((.4530)(.4789)/1.073) + 1 - 1.073$$
$$= .1292$$
$$P^*_{1,0} = (.4530)(.2035)/1.073$$
$$= .0859$$

Since the ratio of the random dual to actual dual is greater than 1.00, it stands to reason that reach will increase using this method because the unadjusted random combination method understated reach and overstated duplication.

The combined exposure distribution follows in Table 11.5, which is adjusted to account for nonrandom duplication.

EVALUATING THREE OR MORE MEDIA CATEGORIES

In theory, it should be possible to evaluate the impact of schedules involving two or more media categories as long as the inherent differences between media categories have been taken into account through weighting procedures, and as long as all media categories are assigned the same general communications objective. Those who wish to pursue further the intricacies of the problem should see Rust,[2] Rust and Leone,[3] and Lancaster and Katz.[4]

To combine more than two media category exposure distributions, one would simply combine the first two in the usual manner. Then the resulting exposure distribution can be combined with the third media category exposure distribution, and so on. If one deals with truncated exposure distributions, this procedure is manageable. Difficulty arises when attempts are made to account for non-random

TABLE 11.5 Magazine and Television Exposure Distribution: Non-Random Duplication

Exposure Distribution

f	%	=	Sum of Table 11.4 Diagonals
0	12.92%	=	.1292
1	20.94	=	.1235 + .0859
2	18.78	=	.0765 + .0525 + .0588
3	15.36	=	.0424 + .0325 + .0359 + .0428
4	11.83	=	.0210 + .0180 + .0222 + .0261 + .0309
5	8.63	=	.0091 + .0089 + .0123 + .0162 + .0189 + .0209
6	5.81	=	.0033 + .0039 + .0061 + .0090 + .0117 + .0128 + .0114
7	3.07	=	.0009 + .0014 + .0026 + .0044 + .0065 + .0079 + .0070
8	1.53	=	.0001 + .0004 + .0009 + .0019 + .0032 + .0044 + .0043
9	0.70	=	.0001 + .0003 + .0007 + .0014 + .0022 + .0024
10	0.29	=	.0000 + .0002 + .0005 + .0009 + .0012
11+	0.14	=	1.0 − .1292 − .2094 − .1818 − .1536 − .1183 − .0863
			− .0581 − .0307 − .0153 − .0070 − .0029
	100.0%		

overlap among more than two media categories. What ratio of random to actual dual should be used?

It is recommended that the ratio of random to actual dual be computed for all possible pairs of media categories in the schedule. Then divide the sum of the ratios by the total number of media category pairs in the schedule to get the average ratio. However, this average probably will approach 1.00 as the number of media categories increase. Consequently, it may be just as fruitful to use a ratio of 1.00 when more than two media categories are involved, at least until more research has been conducted on the topic.

USING *ADPLAN* TO EVALUATE MIXED MEDIA SCHEDULES

It is possible with ADPLAN to combine two or more separate media category schedules, enabling the user to evaluate the combined effects. When offered the alternatives at the end of an ADPLAN interaction, one selects "5" to combine two or more schedules. At this point, ADPLAN will list all created schedules and summarize each one including medium, target size, campaign period, total schedule cost, weighted effective reach (3+), weighted CPM, and the number of ads. After the listing of previous schedules, ADPLAN will prompt the user for the number of schedules to be combined. For this example, two schedules are used. ADPLAN then asks for the schedule numbers to be combined.

Here, the consumer magazine (full information) and the network television schedules are used (see Chapters Eight and Nine). An adjustment ratio for duplication between media categories must be entered. If random, one simply enters "1." If duplication is greater than chance, the number will be a decimal less than one, or if it is less than chance, a number above one is entered.

This ratio can be estimated by computing the ratio of the random dual to the actual dual for each pair of media categories being evaluated, as illustrated above.

For this example a ratio of 1.073 (20.38%/19%) is used. The program will then provide a combined schedule, including exposure distributions plus summary and vehicle evaluations.

Here is a sample interaction with ADPLAN which illustrates how to analyze the combined effects of two or more media categories.

```
 1 = Review LAST schedule
 2 = Modify LAST schedule
 3 = Create NEW schedule using parts of LAST schedule
 4 = Create NEW schedule from scratch
 5 = Combine two or more schedules
 6 = Save raw data on disk file
 7 = Get raw data on disk file
 8 = Save table on disk file
 9 = Print table
10 = Select Optimum Schedule
11 = Return to DOS
12 = Stop, return to DOS


Your choice? 5

You have created 2 schedules:
```

| | | | | Weighted | | |
Schedule #/Medium	Target Size	Period	Cost	Reach 3+	CPM	Ads
1 CONSUMER MAGAZI	69,405,000	January 19	$535,245	13.19%	$9.86	6
2 NETWORK TV	69,405,000	January 19	$499,130	12.55%	$7.86	8

```
Combine how many (e.g., 2 to 10)? 2

        Schedule  1? 1
        Schedule  2? 2

Enter adjustment for duplication between media categories.

        Ratio = 1  (random duplication)
        Ratio < 1  (duplication greater than chance, e.g., .95)
        Ratio > 1  (duplication less than chance, e.g., 1.05)

Enter ratio between 0.66 and 2? 1.073


---------------------------------+-----------------------------------------
ADPLAN RESULTS:  CONSUMER MAGAZINES, NETWORK TV

Name = Kent Lancaster          Target ID = Female Homemakers
Brand = Kellogg's All-Bran     Target Size = 69,405,000
Period = January 1988
```

Frequency (f) Distribution	Unweighted		Weighted	
f	% f	% f+	% f	% f+
0	12.92%	100.00%	36.71%	100.00%
1	20.94%	87.08%	20.51%	63.29%
2	18.78%	66.14%	15.11%	42.79%
3	15.36%	47.36%	10.62%	27.68%
4	11.83%	32.00%	7.20%	17.06%
5	8.63%	20.17%	4.72%	9.85%
6	5.81%	11.54%	2.87%	5.14%
7	3.07%	5.72%	1.25%	2.27%
8	1.53%	2.65%	0.60%	1.03%
9	0.70%	1.12%	0.27%	0.43%
10	0.29%	0.42%	0.11%	0.16%
11+	0.14%	0.14%	0.05%	0.05%

Duplication Ratio = 1.07, Combined Weight (recall) = 72.7%

Summary Evaluation	Unweighted	Weighted
Reach (1+)	87.08%	63.29%
Effective Reach (3+)	47.36%	27.68%
Average Frequency	3.15	2.68
Gross Rating Points	274.40	169.77
Gross Impressions (000)	190,447.31	117,826.78
CPM/Gross Impressions	$5.43	$8.78
Cost Per Rating Point	$3,769.59	$6,092.91

Vehicle List	Rating	Cume	Ad Cost	CPM	Ads	Total Cost
1. CONSUMER MAGAZINES			Totals:	$9.86	6	$535,245
Reader's Diges	26.60	34.10	$108,800	$11.23	1	$108,800
TV Guide	25.40	32.20	$89,300	$9.65	4	$357,200
Good Housekeep	20.80	27.70	$69,245	$9.14	1	$69,245
2. NETWORK TV			Totals:	$7.86	8	$499,130
Young and Rest	8.80	14.12	$22,510	$5.05	2	$45,020
All My Childre	8.40	13.49	$21,487	$5.05	2	$42,974
Dallas	23.80	34.53	$107,528	$8.92	2	$215,056
Bill Cosby Sho	21.70	32.03	$98,040	$8.92	2	$196,080
			Totals:	$8.78	14	$1,034,375

CONCLUSION

Few of the ideas presented in this chapter have been published elsewhere. The selected references listed below may be of some help for those who wish to pursue the topic. While it is clear that considerably more research is needed regarding the theory and practice of evaluating the combined impact of multiple media categories, it is hoped that the material presented in this chapter will be sufficient to stimulate others to make such an effort. Some potentially fruitful avenues for future research on these topics are presented in Chapter Fifteen.

ENDNOTES

1. The authors are grateful to John D. Leckenby for introducing several of the substantive concepts presented here. The authors are responsible, of course, for any liberties taken with the method.

2. Roland T. Rust, *Advertising Media Models: A Practical Guide* (Massachusetts: Lexington Books, 1986).

3. Roland T. Rust and Robert T. Leone, "The Mixed-Media Dirichlet Multinomial Distribution: A Model for Evaluating Television-Magazine Schedules," *Journal of Marketing Research* 21 (1984), pp. 89-99.

4. Kent M. Lancaster and Helen Katz, "Evaluating the Combined Impact of Multiple Advertising Media Categories," *Proceedings of the American Academy of Advertising,* 1988 Annual Conference, Chicago, Illinois, April 1988.

CHAPTER TWELVE

Developing Optimum Media Plans

This text has shown how to analyze marketing-communications situations and to evaluate comprehensive media plans. You can now examine competitive advertising media expenditures and set marketing, advertising, and media goals. You should know how to evaluate media plans designed to reach goals in terms of advertising message quality and the usual media evaluation factors. These all have been necessary, but not sufficient steps to allow the confident development of comprehensive media plans that have been considered and defended in light of all reasonable alternatives.

Here are a few questions that might present some uncertainty at this point. The client has $6,000,000 to spend on media. Which media categories should be used and in what proportions? What effective reach would be delivered by a $6,000,000 yearly campaign on a monthly basis? How much effective reach can be expected from $500,000, $1,000,000 or $2,000,000 of monthly expenditures in network television or magazines? How many GRPs will be needed to schedule on a monthly basis to effectively reach 50 percent of the target using network radio? A $1,000,000 magazine schedule delivers 22 percent effective reach (3+) against the target with a CPM of $9.55. Can it be improved? If so, how?

There is a very simple reason that these questions might pose some difficulty. To answer them intelligently requires experience. Planners would have to evaluate a number of different schedules, ranging from, say, $100,000 to $2,500,000 per month, in all major media categories and combinations of categories. Doing so would give an indication of what effective reach might be delivered, among other media evaluation factors, for a fixed expenditure in each major media category. This process would also help to show how effective reach might increase within a particular media category as media expenditures increase. It would be helpful too if such data were available for a variety of reasonable target audiences and message weights. Such ''experience'' would allow planners to identify quickly the optimum media strategies for a particular brand and to improve on the alternatives selected.

This chapter explains the significance of such relationships and tradeoffs. The objective is to guide you in developing similar insights on your own in the future when confronting a variety of different and changing advertising media planning circumstances.

MAXIMIZING EFFECTIVE REACH

One of the first notions that many students of advertising learn is of the inverse relationship between reach (1+) and average frequency. That is, given a fixed budget or GRP level, average frequency is sacrificed at the expense of reach, and vice versa. This can be seen in two well known formulas.

$$\text{Reach}(1+) = \text{GRPs}/\bar{f} \qquad\qquad (12\text{-}1)$$
$$\bar{f} = \text{GRPs}/\text{Reach}(1+) \qquad\qquad (12\text{-}2)$$
$$\text{where: } \bar{f} = \text{average frequency}$$

Clearly, if GRPs are fixed, then at any given GRP level, increases in reach are associated with decreases in average frequency. For example, if GRPs equal 200 and reach (1+) is 50, then average frequency is 4 (4 = 200/50). But if reach is 75, then average frequency is 2.6 (2.66 = 200/75). You might work through some examples on your own and also vary the level of average frequency for fixed levels of GRPs.

This reasoning is the basis of the often stated axiom that, given a fixed budget, one cannot maximize both reach (1+) and frequency. Of course, if budgets are not fixed, then the statement does not apply and high levels of both reach and frequency should be possible. The remainder of this chapter will go beyond published research and explore more sophisticated procedures for maximizing not only reach (1+) or average frequency, but effective reach (3+) as well.

If the planner's objective is to maximize reach (1+), what decision rules would be followed? It is better to begin by asking another question. Generally speaking, which is greater, audience duplication *within* a media vehicle, or audience duplication *between* media vehicles; duplication within media categories or duplication *between* media categories? Of course, given the habitual media usage patterns of most members of major target audiences, duplication *within* media vehicles and categories is greater than duplication *between* them. So, to maximize reach (1+) given a fixed media budget, one wants to minimize duplication, which will minimize average frequency. Therefore, a planner would tend to schedule only one insertion in each appropriate vehicle in a media category, then add additional media categories, as appropriate, until the budget is exhausted. Assuming that the most efficient vehicles have been selected in terms of CPM and message impact, reach (1+) could not be higher.

To maximize frequency, then, the opposite strategy would be followed: selecting a narrow range of media categories and vehicles and placing the maximum number of insertions per period in each. This strategy maximizes duplication, hence average frequency.

This is a useful foundation to work from. As you already know, most advertisers are not interested in maximizing reach (1+) or average frequency but, rather, effective reach. This, however, complicates the decision rules because now one must blend a minimum level of frequency with the maximum level of reach at that frequency level. How should one proceed?

First, the most cost effective media categories and vehicles within those categories must be identified, given the objective and target audience. Once this is done, how many insertions should be placed in each vehicle?

Here it will be assumed that the aim is to maximize effective reach (3+) as opposed to 2+, 4+ or some other frequency levels. To augment the contribution of a given vehicle to effective reach (3+), exactly three insertions should be placed *within* each vehicle. This approach takes advantage of the high levels of within-vehicle duplication versus the relatively low levels of between-vehicle duplication. For a given vehicle, fewer than three insertions will add little or nothing to effective reach. And more than three insertions will not increase effective reach significantly, but only add to average frequency. So the three insertions are placed in each appropriate vehicle within the most important media category, then in the second most important media category, and so on, until the budget is exhausted. Assuming that the most cost effective media categories and vehicles are chosen, effective reach (3+) generally cannot be higher. These tradeoffs are depicted in Figure 12.1.

Clearly, if some other frequency cutoff besides 3+ is desired, then the number of insertions per vehicle would be equal to that cutoff (for example, 2+, 4+, 5+, etc.).

Now, this decision rule seems to work in most media categories most of the time. However, it is not supported by much empirical research. Limited research by the authors suggests that for prime time network television, the strategy described above will maximize effective reach (3+) up to about 540 GRPs. Beyond that, the decision rule for maximizing reach *(1+)* in fact leads to higher levels of

FIGURE 12.1 Effective Reach (3+): Three Insertions Within a Vehicle versus One Insertion Each in Three Different Vehicles

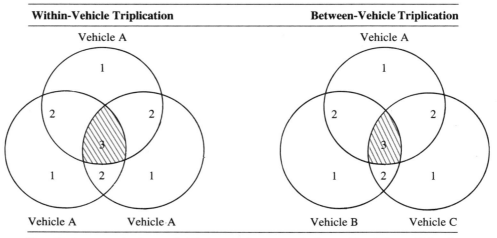

Note: Circles represent ratings against the target and are assumed to be equal for all three vehicles, A, B, and C. Numbers in circles represent the frequency delivered by various combinations of vehicles (that is, 1, 2, and 3).

reach (3+)! A tentative explanation for this observation is that for large schedules, adding new vehicles to a schedule adds more new target members to the effective reach range than does increasing the number of insertions per vehicle. That is, for large schedules, cross-vehicle duplication adds more to reach (3+) than within-vehicle duplication does.

A useful line of research would be to explore further possible decision rules for maximizing reach (n+) in each media category. For now, the best approach seems to be the rules described above. You should use the outcome of the rules as a benchmark and then experiment to see whether schedules exist that yield even greater effective reach.

There are a number of interesting implications of these decision rules for maximizing effective reach (3+). For example, if *monthly* schedules are being evaluated, the rules favor weekly magazines over monthly issues because it is possible to place three insertions in a weekly magazine each month, but only one insertion is possible in a monthly publication. And since the number of weeklies is limited, magazines may be at a disadvantage in a schedule evaluated on a *monthly* basis when considered in relation to media categories with more flexible distribution patterns.

The authors have also observed that for any fixed advertising expenditure or GRP level, there exists a large number of reasonable alternative schedules, several of which will have obtained a maximum effective reach plateau for that target, expenditure, GRP level, and media mix. However, only one such schedule will have the minimum cost. The art and science of media planning, of course, is to identify that schedule. The next few sections of this chapter explain how AD-PLAN can be used to do just that.

SELECTING OPTIMUM SCHEDULES

The high cost and complexity of advertising schedules and the large number of available options make it desirable to remove some of the subjectivity and tedium from the media planning process. To make this point vivid, an advertiser considering a simple monthly magazine schedule, out of a pool of 30 feasible publications meeting editorial environment and targeting requirements, essentially must consider over one billion schedules when narrowing the possibilities down to the few feasible alternatives that maximize campaign goals within budget constraints. Why over one billion possible schedules? There are two outcomes for each monthly magazine in a monthly schedule, either to use a particular publication or not to do so. Therefore, the total number of possible schedules equals two raised to the 30th power (that is, $2^{30} = 1,073,741,800$). If ten *weekly* magazines are involved in a monthly schedule, the choices for each are not to run any advertisement or to run up to 4.3, the average number of weeks in a month. Technically, this presents the planner with over 17 million possible schedules from which to choose (that is, $(4.3 + 1)^{10}$). Now one can imagine how the options explode when one is also considering 60 prime time and 25 daytime broadcast television network programs, 12 cable television networks, 16 radio networks, four national newspapers, and three newspaper supplements, with *each vehicle* having between 4.3 and perhaps as many as 30 or more possible insertions per month.

It is important for one to be able to estimate and control the number of feasible schedules when developing optimum media plans. In general, the total number of possible schedules can be estimated by using the product operation shown in Equation 12-3.

$$\text{Total schedules} = \prod_{i=1}^{m} (n_{u,i} - n_{l,i} + 1) \qquad (12\text{-}3)$$

where n is the number of insertions in vehicle i and where $i = 1, 2, ..., m$ total vehicles in the data base. The subscripts u and l represent the upper and lower insertion constraints per vehicle respectively. When the maximum and minimum number of insertions in each vehicle are the same, Equation 12-3 can be reduced to Equation 12-4.

$$\text{Total schedules} = (\bar{n}_u - \bar{n}_l + 1)^m \qquad (12\text{-}4)$$

where all terms are as defined in Equation 12-3 and where $\bar{n}$ is the average number of insertions per vehicle.

Certainly in most instances a relatively small subset of schedules satisfy budget and insertion constraints, but how is a planner to know with confidence which of the overwhelming number of possibilities is best under the circumstances? The optimization problem is rarely a simple linear combination of the number of advertisements multiplied by their costs since planners are most interested in schedule reach, frequency and effective reach.[*] That is, they want to know how many different people are exposed to messages at frequency levels necessary to communicate certain information. These media planning factors require taking into account within- and between-vehicle audience duplication, which will vary considerably, systematically, and non-linearly, depending on the particular combination of vehicles in a selected schedule. Indeed, there are 435 cross-pairs (the reach of one insertion in two different vehicles) in a schedule involving 30 vehicles (e.g., $_{30}C_2 = 435$), while in one with ten there are 45 (that is, $_{10}C_2 = 45$).

AVAILABLE MODELS

Computers can efficiently support software with such optimizing capability. For years Interactive Market Systems, Inc. (IMS) and Telmar Communications, among others, have provided advertisers and advertising agencies with access to mainframe and personal computer data bases and software that help optimize schedules. However, these often are prohibitively expensive for students, faculty, and many small advertisers, agencies and media organizations, all of whom nevertheless face challenging media planning problems and therefore desire such optimizing capability.[2]

The literature on media selection, evaluation, and optimization has a long and rich history, much too extensive to review adequately here. Excellent reviews of this literature can be found elsewhere.[3] Because of their comprehensiveness and complexity, no doubt, to the authors' knowledge none of these systems have yet been adapted to microcomputers or otherwise packaged and distributed for broad use by researchers, educators, or practitioners.

ADPLAN OPTIMIZATION CAPABILITY

ADPLAN allows one to identify optimum advertising media plans. Although the program does not yet capture explicitly all of the complexity of established or commercial mainframe or microcomputer models, it nevertheless has strong features that emphasize the most important dimensions of the media planning process. It will exceed the requirements of most educators and small to modest size advertisers, agencies and media organizations.

ADPLAN will select optimum schedules involving up to 30 vehicles in all major advertising media categories, including broadcast and cable networks, spot and local television and radio, national and local newspapers and supplements, and consumer and business magazines. ADPLAN will also evaluate outdoor and direct mail schedules, but these do not directly involve optimization since the program assumes only one such vehicle per target audience. In addition, users may evaluate the combined effects of any combination of optimum schedules within multiple advertising media categories, such as network television and consumer magazines taken together.

The program helps users build and store data bases for each media category from which optimum schedules can be selected. These data bases contain vehicle names (e.g., *Reader's Digest*), cost per advertisement (e.g., $104,600), and target audience rating points (e.g., 26.6 percent). The user can also control the minimum and maximum allowable vehicle insertions per planning period (e.g., 0 to 1 insertions per month). Choosing a minimum number of insertions greater than zero will force that vehicle into the solution, assuming other constraints are satisfied.

The number of allowable insertions will depend on the planning time frame and media category involved. A narrow time frame, such as monthly, is recommended, to support forecasts of specific advertising effects and to take into account target audience forgetting and competitive advertising messages.[4] The number of insertions per month can vary from one, for monthly magazines, to 30 or more for network radio. Quarterly or annual evaluations will increase the number of insertions by factors of three and 12, respectively. But these will overstate the likely effects of media schedules since they unrealistically assume 100 percent advertising carry-over, or no advertising decay, from one month to the next.

OPTIMIZATION CONSTRAINTS

Once the user has prepared a media category data base, ADPLAN will search for the best schedule given the budget and insertion constraints and the primary and secondary optimization factors. ADPLAN requires lower and upper bounds on the budget. It is unlikely that the cost of an optimum schedule will exactly meet the upper budget limit because differences in total schedule cost from one possible solution to another will be in multiples of the typical vehicle cost. The lower budget constraint accounts for this variation in total schedule cost. It also speeds the search for a solution by eliminating schedules on the basis of cost alone without completing an extensive reach and frequency analysis for each of these options. The narrower the gap between the lower and upper budget constraint, the faster the solution. Of course, if the gap is too narrow, a solution may not be feasible, given the unevenness of vehicle costs.

The user can select a primary and secondary factor for schedule optimization from five alternatives. These include the following factors which are weighted to account for message exposure or effects.

1. Reach (1+)   Percent of the target audience exposed one or more times to the advertisements in a schedule.
2. Reach (3+)   Percent of the target audience exposed three or more times to the advertisements in a schedule.
3. Average frequency   Mean number of times those reached (1+) by a schedule are exposed to its messages.
4. Gross rating points (GRPs)   Sum of all of the rating points delivered by a schedule.
5. Cost-per-thousand impressions (CPM)   Total schedule cost divided by gross impressions in thousands.

For instance, the user could have ADPLAN search a magazine data base with 25 vehicles for a schedule that costs between $475,000 and $500,000 with the highest possible reach (1+). Whenever ADPLAN finds more than one schedule that satisfies both conditions, it will then choose from this group the one with the lowest CPM, if that is the user's preference as a secondary optimization factor.

The program selects the best schedule from all the possible schedules generated based on the range of feasible insertions per vehicle. Thus, if there are no minimum insertions per vehicle, zero to n total insertions in the first vehicle are considered in turn, with zero to n total insertions in the second, and so on, for all vehicles in the data base. The total cost of each schedule is then checked against the upper and lower budget constraint to determine whether further analysis is needed.

SHORTCUTS

ADPLAN has a number of useful options that help users manage the optimization process. No matter which of the five optimization criteria are selected, the budget constraint dictates that the optimum schedule include the most efficient vehicles in terms of CPM. Inefficient vehicles will be included only if 1) the user forces them into the solution with a lower insertion constraint greater than zero, or 2) there is just enough slack between the cost of the optimum schedule and the budget constraint to include one more insertion in an otherwise less desirable vehicle. ADPLAN takes this tendency toward efficient vehicles into account by allowing the user to first sort vehicles by CPM. In this way the solution can generally be obtained early in the optimization process, among the most efficient vehicles. Consequently, evaluating all possible schedules outside of the pool of the most efficient ones may not improve the results. ADPLAN therefore also allows the user to exit the optimization search after a predetermined number of schedules have been evaluated and before all possible schedules have been considered. Of course, using this technique does not guarantee that the results are optimal and it relies heavily on user experience and judgment. But the approach can save considerable computer time and the results will be the most preferred.

When the optimum schedule is likely to contain a large number of vehicles and/or insertions, it may be helpful to raise the lower limit on the most efficient vehicles. This will reduce the number of schedules ADPLAN must consider significantly, particularly when the most efficient vehicles are to be used heavily anyway.

Although the program will not determine the optimum budget proportion to devote to each media category, users can easily experiment with various allocation scenarios to see which combination is best. A useful point of departure might be the "economic equilibrium" described by Little and Lodish.[5] This approach generates proportional exposure values based on the reciprocal of the overall CPM for the respective media categories.

What follows is a sample interaction with the optimizing subroutine of ADPLAN, revealing its essential features, procedures, and results.

SAMPLE OPTIMIZATION PROBLEM

To demonstrate the program's capabilities, the following hypothetical situation is considered. A media planner for Kellogg's All-Bran is interested in reaching female homemakers who use cold breakfast cereals. According to SMRB (Volume P-20, 1985) the target audience size is 69,405,000. The top 12 rated magazines against the target market are listed in Table 12.1, along with each magazine's rating, cost per full-page, four-color advertisement, and the maximum number of insertions per month, using June 1988 as the planning period, a month with five weeks. The annual advertising appropriation is $12 million, with $1 million to be spent each month and with a 50:50 split between consumer magazines and network television.

These data are entered into ADPLAN and stored as ASCII file MAG.DAT using the procedures shown in the Appendix of this chapter.

☐ Selecting Optimum Schedules

After one selects the optimizing subroutine (10), the optimization menu is then displayed. It shows the total possible schedules in the data base (110,592 in this instance), and it allows the user to change the minimum and maximum insertions per vehicle, alter the total number of schedules to be run, sort vehicles by CPM (including all cross-pair audience ratings if applicable), select optimization criteria, or return to the main menu. For convenience, the minimum number of insertions per vehicle is assumed to be zero unless it is overridden using that subroutine. Raising the minimum number of insertions for any vehicle will force it into the solution, assuming other constraints are satisfied. This is useful when there are relatively strong qualitative reasons for including a vehicle in a schedule, such as editorial environment, audience involvement, or trade acceptance, for example. Changing the number of schedules to be run to a number less than 110,592 will cause the results to be displayed before all possibilities are considered. If this is done, it is recommended that vehicles are first sorted by CPM to increase the chances that the results are optimum. To provide ADPLAN speed benchmarks, all possible schedules are considered here, so the fourth option is chosen to select optimization criteria and an optimum schedule. It should be noted, however, that the optimum schedule was in fact obtained within the first 2,000 attempts. The remaining 108,592 schedules did not improve results.

ADPLAN then requests the lower and upper budget constraints. Here, a lower constraint of $475,000 is used with an upper limit of $500,000. Next, the primary and secondary optimization factors are requested. In this instance, reach $(1+)$ and CPM, respectively, are selected.

□ Output

The program reports the total number of schedules to be run, the total schedules evaluated at the time of the report, the current status of the primary and secondary optimization factors, and the total elapsed time since optimization was initiated. Status reports are provided to assure the user that the program is functioning properly in view of the large number of schedules typically evaluated. Such reports are revised every 1,000 or 2,000 schedules, depending on whether the total number of schedules to be evaluated is less or greater than 10,000.

TABLE 12.1 Magazine Data Base

	Magazine	Rating	Cost	Maximum Insertions
1.	Reader's Digest	26.6%	$104,600	1
2.	TV Guide	25.4	95,900	5
3.	Family Circle	20.8	75,280	1
4.	Good Housekeeping	20.8	80,025	1
5.	Better Homes & Gardens	20.4	95,400	1
6.	Woman's Day	19.4	66,960	1
7.	McCall's	16.8	60,800	1
8.	People	15.2	61,345	5
9.	Ladies Home Journal	14.7	61,300	1
10.	National Geographic	12.9	117,715	1
11.	Time	10.9	114,955	5
12.	Redbook	10.2	55,255	1

Note: Ratings obtained from SMRB, Volume P-20, pp. 38-39, 1985; base is female homemakers who use cold breakfast cereals; costs obtained from *Leo Burnett 1986 Media Cost and Coverage*, pp. 17-18. Minimum insertions = 0 for each vehicle.

Figure 12.2 displays the solution ADPLAN offers for this problem after considering 110,592 possible schedules. It shows that, given the planning constraints, the highest possible weighted reach (1+) is 36.52 percent. And of all schedules with the same reach, this one has the lowest weighted CPM at $10.20. Five magazines are selected from the data base (see Table 12.1), including the top three and those ranked seventh and eighth. Four of the vehicles are monthly and have one insertion, while the weekly *TV Guide* has two. The schedule cost is in fact close to the upper budget limit of $500,000 at $499,440.

Since ADPLAN is using an iterative, limited information, consumer magazine subroutine, the processing time is at a maximum. For convenience, the output displays the data file analyzed (for example, MAG.DAT), the total number of schedules considered (for example, 110,592) and the total elapsed time (such as, 00:07:45). This will give the user some ADPLAN speed benchmarks for his or her hardware configuration, media categories analyzed (which utilize variously complex computations), data base size, width of budget constraints, and optimization criteria desired.

ENHANCING SPEED

Table 12.2 provides some benchmarks for a variety of popular machines available to the authors using the example described in this study. ADPLAN demonstrates differences in processing speed across hardware configurations, *underscoring the importance of using fast machines, and/or ones equipped with math coprocessors* for large optimization tasks.

Therefore, to keep processing time to a minimum when using the ADPLAN optimization subroutine, it is recommended that the user access the fastest avail-

TABLE 12.2 ADPLAN Optimizing Speed across Popular Hardware Configurations*

Hardware Configuration	Processing Time (hh:mm:ss)	Schedules Run Per Minute
IBM PS 60, Math Coprocessor	00:04:51	22,802
Macintosh II	00:06:07	18,081
PC's Limited Turbo, 6.66 MZ, Math Coprocessor	00:07:45	14,270
Compaq 286, Math Coprocessor	00:09:04	12,198
IBM AT, Math Coprocessor	00:10:33	10,483
IBM PC, Math Coprocessor	00:12:44	8,685
Macintosh SE	00:18:37	5,941
Macintosh Plus	00:21:43	5,093
IBM PS 80	00:37:54	2,918
IBM PS 50, 10 MZ	00:43:33	2,540
IBM PC	03:40:09	502

*Processing time varies dramatically, depending on the hardware configuration, media categories analyzed (due to differences in the complexity of the computations), the relative width of the upper and lower budget constraints and the combination of criteria to be optimized. The schedule analyzed here is described in Table 12.1 and the corresponding text.

FIGURE 12.2 Sample Optimization Results

```
-----------------------------------------------------------------------
ADPLAN RESULTS:  CONSUMER MAGAZINES

Name = Kent Lancaster        Target ID = Female Homemakers - Users
Brand = All-Bran             Target Size = 69,405,000
Period = June 1988

        Frequency (f)  Unweighted              Weighted
        Distribution  ---------------         ---------------
            f          % f     % f+            % f     % f+
        -----------   ------  ------          ------  ------
            0         30.44%  100.00%         63.48%  100.00%
            1         30.74%   69.56%         16.14%   36.52%
            2         21.10%   38.82%         11.08%   20.38%
            3         11.32%   17.71%          5.94%    9.30%
            4          4.74%    6.40%          2.49%    3.36%
            5          1.43%    1.66%          0.75%    0.87%
            6          0.24%    0.24%          0.13%    0.13%

BBD Factors:  Rl = .224, RE = .682, A = 2.01934, B = 6.995571
Weight (exposure) = 52.5%

        Summary Evaluation         Unweighted        Weighted
        ------------------         ----------        --------
        Reach (1+)                   69.56%           36.52%
        Effective Reach (3+)         17.71%            9.30%
        Average Frequency             1.93             1.93
        Gross Rating Points         134.40            70.56
        Gross Impressions (000)  93,280.34        48,972.17
        CPM/Gross Impressions        $5.35           $10.20
        Cost Per Rating Point     $3,716.07        $7,078.23

Vehicle List    Rating  Cume    Ad Cost     CPM     Ads   Total Cost
------------    ------  ----    --------   -------   ---   ----------
Reader's Diges   26.60  N/A    $104,600    $10.79    1      $104,600
TV Guide         25.40  N/A     $95,900    $10.36    2      $191,800
Family Circle    20.80  N/A     $75,280     $9.93    1       $75,280
Woman's Day      19.40  N/A     $66,960     $9.47    1       $66,960
McCall's         16.80  N/A     $60,800     $9.93    1       $60,800
                                --------   -------   ---   ----------
                        Totals:            $10.20    6      $499,440

Data File = MAG.DAT, Options = **110,592, Time Used = 00:07:45
---------------------------  ------------------------------------
```

able machine and reduce the data base to the fewest feasible vehicles by removing those that are inefficient or least effective. This can be done by evaluating all vehicles in the data base, then inspecting each vehicle's CPM, rating, cume or other criteria. One simply deletes unwanted vehicles by selecting from the ADPLAN main menu the second option, "Modify LAST schedule." It is also important to insure that the maximum allowable insertions per vehicle do not exceed what is feasible or necessary. When optimizing, it is best to keep the gap between the lower and upper budget constraints as narrow as possible, to eliminate a complete reach and frequency analysis of schedules that cost too little or too much.

When optimizing media categories that involve a large number of insertions per vehicle, such as network radio, it may be wise to reduce the number of insertions considered by narrowing the time frame to one typical week instead of one month. For example, a network radio data base involving six networks and 30 potential monthly insertions per network would require ADPLAN to consider 887,503,680 schedule options (e.g., $887,503,680 = (30+1)^6$). Considering a typical weekly schedule instead of a monthly one would reduce the problem to one million schedule options, assuming nine maximum insertions per network (that is, $1,000,000 = (9+1)^6$). This could be solved on ADPLAN in about one hour, again depending on the hardware configuration used. One could then generate a monthly schedule by using four to five times the number of one-week insertions per vehicle shown in the optimum schedule, depending on the number of weeks in the month. Of course, this will not provide an exact monthly optimum because it does not account fully for within- and between-vehicle duplication as optimizing an entire monthly schedule would do. The closer the artificially narrow budget constraint is to the desired budget limit, the closer the projected solution will be to the exact optimum. Often the differences are not significant in relation both to the amount of computation time saved and to other sources of media planning error, such as planning future schedules using recent, but historical data.

This approach to reducing the problem size could be misleading when the budget constraint is low in relation to vehicle costs. Such a situation might exist for consumer magazines or prime time network television, for example. To satisfy low budget constraints ADPLAN may be forced to choose vehicles with low absolute cost, which also will probably have lower ratings than other, perhaps more efficient vehicles in the data base. The resulting solution would then contain a disproportionately large number of low-rated and relatively inefficient vehicles.

RESEARCH IMPLICATIONS

To the authors' knowledge, ADPLAN is the only microcomputer-based, multi-media planning optimizing model that is widely and inexpensively available to educators, students, and small businesses. Previously, such capability could only be had at considerable expense through commercial media software houses. In addition to making the media planning process easier while improving the quality of recommendations, there are a number of interesting research opportunities presented by ADPLAN capability.

☐ Optimum Schedule Characteristics

What are the general characteristics of optimum schedules? Do they have a large number of insertions within a few vehicles, or do they have one insertion in each of numerous alternatives? And within a media category, how does relative schedule size affect the decision rules? How do the rules vary across media categories? What guidelines pertain to maximizing reach (1+) versus reach (3+) or reach (n+)? What mix of high versus low rated vehicles leads to optimum schedules? How does advertising carry-over affect optimum schedule choice? Does flighting and pulsing of advertising weight affect the character of optimum schedules?

Other questions that might be asked of ADPLAN are: What is the reach of a minimum CPM schedule, or the CPM of a maximum reach schedule? What is the average frequency of a maximum reach schedule, or the reach of a maximum frequency schedule? Researchers might wish to set up grids similar to Table 12.3, which is based on an analysis of the magazine data previously described. AD-PLAN was run five times, alternating the primary and secondary optimization criteria as shown.

The table shows that for some criteria the results are identical, while for others they are different. The circled figures emphasize the classic reach-frequency tradeoff given a fixed budget, few examples of which exist in the literature. The similarities among the remaining criteria stem from the restrictive budget constraints and the relatively small data base. There is not much room to maneuver. More research results of this kind are needed, using various expenditure levels within and across media categories, in order to develop generalizations regarding tradeoffs among optimization criteria.

☐ Broader Capability

ADPLAN should also be expanded to accommodate a task-objective approach to media planning. This would allow the user to specify a goal, such as a desired level of effective reach (3+), then have ADPLAN assemble the most efficient schedule that would achieve this objective. ADPLAN should also enable the user to specify lower and upper bounds on goals.

TABLE 12.3 Tradeoffs among Optimization Criteria

ADPLAN Results	Primary Optimization Criteria				
	Reach(1+)	Reach(3+)	Frequency	GRPs	CPM
Reach (1+)	36.52%	36.52%	30.65%	36.52%	36.22%
Reach (3+)	9.30%	9.30%	8.41%	9.30%	9.21%
Average frequency	1.93	1.93	2.02	1.93	1.93
GRPs	70.56	70.56	61.79	70.56	69.93
CPM	$10.20	$10.20	$11.29	$10.20	$10.11
Schedule cost	$499,400	$499,400	$484,080	$499,400	$490,740
Secondary Optimization Criteria	CPM	CPM	CPM	CPM	Reach(1+)

More work is required to improve the model's efficiency as well. For example, what optimization shortcuts are practical? Can processing time be reduced with acceptable margins of error by, say, cutting in half the budget constraints and the maximum allowable insertions per vehicle, where appropriate, then doubling the result? If such error is systematic, perhaps correction factors are practical. More abstractly, it would be useful to examine the distributions of optimization results, such as the distribution of reach (3+) across all possible schedules in a data base. When are they normally distributed and when and how are they skewed? How tight are the distributions around the optimum solution, where tight distributions suggest numerous satisfactory solutions? At present it is still not known under what circumstances these approaches might prove useful.

Also needed are algorithms that help planners develop optimum schedules across multiple media categories and subcategories. It is probable that models similar to ADPLAN can, for example, help planners decide on the optimum magazine/television mix or on an ideal television daypart mix in addition to determining the best schedule within each media category.

These and other implications of ADPLAN are worthy of greater exploration for they will lead media planners to rules and guidelines that are helpful in developing data bases for media plan optimization. ADPLAN thus stretches to the limit current microcomputer technology and programming finesse. Nevertheless, further work is required to speed up the optimization process to identify and eliminate schedules more quickly that cannot satisfy budget constraints and optimization criteria. Here, work on heuristics, such as that of Pearl,[6] may provide fruitful avenues of research.

In the long run it is improbable that ADPLAN will lead to lazy or untidy media planning because of its brute force approach to schedule optimization. Rather, it is more likely to elevate the quality of the decision making process and intensify the search for rules for shaping optimum schedules. The recent massive proliferation of microcomputers and tandem geometric increases in memory, speed and power, coupled with diffusing ability and experience with using them, bodes well for the widespread research, development, distribution and use of inexpensive, user-friendly, yet comprehensive optimization models. Such capability can only enhance what is known about when and how advertising works, and improve the decision making process.

COMPARING MEDIA CATEGORIES GIVEN FIXED EXPENDITURES

This section will provide some benchmark media evaluation factors based on optimization procedures already discussed. Here expenditures will be fixed, then the optimum results identified across media categories. The next section will show the effects of allowing the budget to change.

Students enrolled in an undergraduate advertising media planning course were given the following assignment. They were asked to maximize effective reach (3+) in each of 13 major advertising media categories against 67,502,000 female homemakers who are users of cold breakfast cereals (Mediamark Research, Inc.,

Volume P-15, 1984). Advertising expenditures were fixed at $500,000 in each media category, and reasonable message weights were also assigned that were similar to those used throughout this text.

Students used cost data presented in the *Leo Burnett 1984 Media Costs and Coverage* guide. Local and spot media schedules were confined to the top ten U.S. markets. The outdoor audience data were obtained from SMRB, Volume P-20, 1983. Schedules were evaluated using ADPLAN.

Table 12.4 presents some *weighted* results from their effort. The table lists the *maximum* number of ads, reach (1+), reach (3+), average frequency and gross rating points that any student was able to achieve in each media category. The table also lists the *minimum* cost factors achieved, including cost-per-thousand impressions, cost-per-rating point, and cost-per-effective reach (3+) point.

There are a number of useful conclusions to be derived from the data presented here. First, the table provides a benchmark for all major media evaluation factors and media categories in relation to an expenditure of $500,000. If one needs to know what the factors would be for an expenditure level other than $500,000, such as $1,000,000, a rough approximation could be obtained by doubling the first

TABLE 12.4 *Weighted* Media Evaluation Factors Obtained from $500,000 Expenditures in Major Advertising Media Categories

Target: Female Homemakers Who Are Users of Cold Breakfast Cereals (N = 67,502,000)

Media Category	Number of Ads	Reach (1+)	Reach (3+)	Fre-quency	GRPs	CPM	CPP	CPEP
1. Local Newspapers	6	26.5	14.0	2.9	76.6	$58.82	$ 7343	$40116
2. National Newspapers	16	11.9	3.3	2.1	25.1	30.73	20742	158474
3. Newspaper Supplements	4	11.6	2.3	1.7	19.9	38.19	25780	226724
4. Magazines (Ltd. Data)	9	47.9	19.1	2.3	112.1	7.10	4792	28135
5. Network TV (Prime time)	7	29.9	11.7	2.5	74.5	11.25	7593	48300
6. Network TV (Daytime)	29	42.3	17.9	2.6	111.7	6.75	4558	28430
7. Spot TV (Prime time)	13	48.9	19.7	2.6	125.4	31.87	4118	21269
8. Spot TV (Daytime)	81	47.8	38.5	5.9	283.5	13.67	1766	13001
9. Cable TV	680	38.2	18.3	3.4	130.9	5.66	3820	27386
10. Network Radio	248	23.0	12.8	4.7	107.6	6.90	4659	39107
11. Spot Radio	546	28.7	18.7	5.6	160.5	24.18	3125	26824
12. Outdoor	30	37.4	30.4	11.8	440.3	8.51	1100	15917
13. Direct Mail	1	9.2	0.0	1.0	9.2	148.94	103838	N/A
14. Magazines (Ltd. Data)& Network Television (Ratio = .9524)	16	62.8	32.4	3.0	186.6	8.76	5910	34030

Note: The results presented in this table assume the following vehicle weights for the various media categories: Magazines, 52.5%; Network TV, Prime time, 80.0%; Network TV, Daytime, 55.0%; Spot TV, Prime time, 72.5%; Spot TV, Daytime, 50.0%; Cable TV, 62.5%; Network Radio, 40.0%; Spot Radio, 37.5%; Newspapers and Supplements, 35.0%; Outdoor Posters, 47.5%; Direct Mail, 60%. Local and spot media have been evaluated within the Top Ten U.S. Markets as defined by the *Leo Burnett 1984 Media Costs and Coverage* guide. Advertising costs are based on data presented in the *Leo Burnett* cost guide assuming 30-second broadcast commercials, full-page and four-color magazine and newspaper supplement ads and 85 SAU column inch newspaper ads. Audience data were obtained from Mediamark Research, Inc., Volume P-15, 1984, and Simmons Market Research Bureau, *1983 Survey of Media and Markets,* Volume P-20. The following individuals deserve recognition for achieving maximum effective reach, given the budget constraint, in the various media categories: Patricia J. Eckle, Edward C. Gold, Jeff A. Lamb, Sylvia M. Carlton, Lisa B. Kizer, Deborah C. Rojek and Tracey L. Tharp.

five columns, with only slight increases in the last three columns. One must keep in mind that reach (1+) and reach (3+) can never exceed 100% and that, since there are generally diminishing returns in reach (1+) and reach (3+) from increases in expenditures or GRPs, doubling expenditures will not usually double reach (1+) or reach (3+). Nevertheless, Table 12.4 will give you some expectations before you actually begin evaluating your own schedules.

One aspect that already may be surprising is how little effective reach (3+) can be purchased for $500,000. The highest level achieved by any national media schedule is 19.1 percent for magazines. (One should remember that the local and spot media categories were confined to the top ten markets only. Consequently, it would be expected that the percent of the target effectively reached by those media categories is substantially higher than in the other media categories where $500,000 are spread across the entire country.) The low levels of effective reach (3+) are consistent across media categories despite wide variation in the number of ads and in GRPs. This is due in large measure to the leveling effect of the message weights that were selected in evaluating the various media categories. *It is clear that high quality advertising messages can pay dividends to advertisers in terms of enhancing media weight.*

The last column of Table 12.4 presents a new concept: cost-per-effective reach (3+) point (CPEP). CPEP is nothing other than total schedule cost divided by the total effective reach (3+) points delivered by a schedule.

$$\text{CPEP} = (\text{Total Schedule Cost})/\text{Reach } (3+) \tag{12-5}$$

CPEP is a useful planning tool. If the levels of effective reach (3+) required by a particular campaign are known, one can multiply reach (3+) by CPEP for a particular media category to determine total schedule cost. For example, if an effective reach of 50 percent against the target from a prime time network television schedule is needed, then approximately $2.42 million are required (that is, $2,415,000 = 50 \times \$48,300$).

With a little effort, you can probably surpass the benchmarks presented in Table 12.4 by one, or some combination, of the following possibilities.

1. Identify more cost-effective vehicles (i.e., vehicles with low CPM) and include these in the schedule in place of the vehicles with the highest CPM. Of course, this assumes that the editorial environments of the new, more efficient vehicles are compatible with campaign objectives and image.
2. Increase message effectiveness, which will allow use of higher media weights.
3. Decrease ad size or the length of commercials. This generally will reduce ad cost at a faster rate than message impact (media weight) is diminished.

Unless the advertising budget is restricted severely, step three above should be a measure of last resort. But, unfortunately, there are often situations where all three measures are required.

Finally, data may be required similar to that presented in Table 12.4 for a broader range of target audiences, such as adults, males, females and all female homemakers, for example. But after seeing the table and how it is organized, one could easily prepare one for any target audience. Nevertheless, such tables would probably look similar for all female homemakers, females and even males. It would also be similar for adults, except the CPM column, where CPM values would be cut approximately in half. You might think about why such similarities exist for this broad range of targets. In explaining this outcome, you might also come to understand why advertisers and agencies often evaluate media plans using the broadest possible target audiences.

COMPARING MEDIA CATEGORIES GIVEN VARIABLE EXPENDITURES

The previous section compared media categories in terms of their likely media evaluation factors, assuming particular ad sizes and lengths, various media weights, and a fixed expenditure of $500,000. Yet there are other useful ways of doing this comparison.

Figure 12.3 compares media categories in terms of the likely *unweighted* effective reach (3 +) delivered at various GRP levels. Unweighted effective reach (3 +) is used to keep the curves separated in the figure to the fullest possible extent. Had weights been used, the reach curves would tend to converge, due to the leveling effect of the weights, and it would be difficult to identify the curve belonging to a particular media category. Using unweighted reach curves also allows one to apply whatever weight is chosen to a particular media category after points of interest are located on the axes.

Before using the curves, readers should notice how the figure is organized. Various levels of reach (3 +) are displayed along the vertical axis that range from 10 to 80. The horizontal axis depicts gross rating points ranging from 100 to 500. There is a line or curve for each major media category. The curve shows the relationship between unweighted reach (3 +) and gross rating points for a selected media category. For example, 100 prime time network television GRPs are estimated to reach approximately 15 percent of the target three or more times, while 500 GRPs in the same category should deliver approximately 67 unweighted reach (3 +) points.

Next, one should notice the overall characteristics of the curves. With two exceptions, all media categories display strongly diminishing returns in effective reach (3 +) as GRPs increase. That is, as GRPs rise, reach (3 +) does not go up proportionately. The two exceptions, which display increasing returns in reach (3 +) as GRPs increase, include media categories evaluated using the limited information algorithm (for example, newspaper supplements, national newspapers and magazines) and prime time television.

You should also compare the high levels of reach (3 +) predicted in media categories evaluated using the limited data procedures, to the relatively low levels predicted by the full data magazine curve. It appears that there actually may be more duplication within and between vehicles than would be predicted by the limited information model. The differences between the two procedures were highlighted in Chapter Eight. The variation in the estimated reach (3+) appears to increase as schedule size increases. It is believed that this problem arises because the limited information model was developed using schedules with a maximum of two insertions per vehicle. The limited data model is used still, however, because it saves a great deal of time, trouble, and expense in gathering self- and cross-pair audience data, which may even be unavailable in many circumstances. But when it is used, one must keep in mind that it probably overstates schedule reach (3+). The prime time television curve displays constant returns largely because it was estimated over too few GRPs to exhibit strongly diminishing returns.

Next, one can see that at any given level of GRPs, the media categories can be ranked in terms of the level of reach (3+) delivered. Print media estimates based on single insertion ratings only, for example, appear to deliver higher levels of reach (3+) than the broadcast media. Furthermore, since print readership levels

FIGURE 12.3 **Effective Reach (3+) versus Gross Rating Points for Selected Advertising Media Categories**

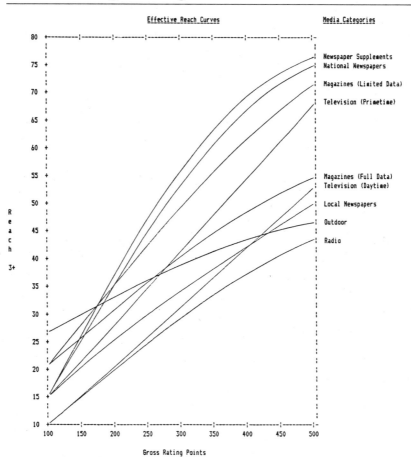

generally are higher for broad targets and typical ads than similar measures for broadcast commercials, weighted effective reach (3+) is likely to be higher for print than for broadcast media at all GRP levels.

How can the weighted estimates of effective reach (3+) be derived using the curves depicted in the figure? Say that planners in the initial media planning stages for a particular brand want to know approximately how much it will cost to effectively reach 20 percent of the target using prime time network television. They could place a straight edge horizontally from the approximate location of reach (3+) equal to 20 percent until it crosses the prime time television curve, then mark the intersection on the curve. Now by running the straight edge vertically at the point of intersection and noting approximately where it crosses the GRP axis, one finds that roughly 150 *weighted* GRPs are required to effectively reach 20 percent of the target. Using the *weighted* cost-per-point (CPP) data from Table 12-4, one would estimate that such a schedule would cost an advertiser approximately $1.14 million ($1,138,950 = 150 × $7,593).

Since the weighting system used throughout this text is linear, readers can move freely between weighted and unweighted factors. For example, one may divide the required weighted effective reach and GRPs by the weight chosen to discount vehicle ratings. Assuming a weight of .80 means it is necessary to achieve an *unweighted* effective reach (3+) of 25 percent (25% = 20%/.80) or 187.5 unweighted GRPs (187.5 = 150 weighted GRPs/.80).

To estimate the *combined* effective reach of two or more media categories, one can simply add together the weighted or unweighted effective reach estimates of each media category and subtract random duplication.

$$\text{Reach}(n+)_{ij} = \text{Reach}(n+)_i + \text{Reach}(n+)_j - (\text{Reach}(n+)_i \ (\text{Reach}(n+)_j \qquad (12\text{-}6)$$

where: $\text{Reach}(n+)$ = either weighted or unweighted reach at a particular frequency level and above (n+),

i and j = individual media category schedules i and j.

The result of Equation 12-6 might then be combined with yet another media category reach $(n+)_k$ to estimate the likely reach$(n+)_{ijk}$ of three advertising media category schedules to be implemented simultaneously, and so on.

HOW REACH (3+) CURVES ARE ESTIMATED

The curves depicted in Figure 12.3 required considerable effort to generate. And since similar curves are used heavily in industry, it will be helpful to understand how they are derived. Those not familiar with regression analysis techniques should read Chapter Fourteen before this section of the chapter.

Students enrolled in an advanced advertising media planning and research course were assigned to develop reach (3+) curves for a selected media category. The target was female homemakers who use cold breakfast cereals. Students were asked to develop approximately 25 reasonable schedules, where appropriate, for their media category, with GRPs ranging from the lowest that was practical in their media category to at least 600. The schedules were to be evaluated using ADPLAN.

Students then developed a data base containing the 25 estimates of reach (3+) coupled with the 25 GRP levels. Using techniques described in Chapter 14, students were asked to estimate reach (3+) as a function of GRPs. A variety of functional forms was estimated, including linear, log-linear, double-log, and quadratic, among others, that appeared likely to most closely express the relationship for a particular media category.

The best equations were selected for each media category using a variety of criteria, including face validity, R^2, relative simplicity, and the relative significance of the regression coefficients, among others. These equations are listed in Table 12.5, by media category.

Future research efforts will probably yield better equations for each media category. Nevertheless, all of the equations presented appear to represent the data well. The lowest R^2 is .917, for daytime network television, while most estimates of R^2 exceed .95.

The equations listed in Table 12.5 are those used to support Figure 12.3. Various levels of GRPs are substituted in each equation, ranging from 100 to 500. Each equation is then evaluated at each GRP level to see what amount of reach (3+) is predicted. For example, what level of reach (3+) could be expected from 300 GRPs in local newspapers? The specific local newspaper estimating form is presented as Equation 12-7.

$$lnReach(3+) = -.887 + .775(lnGRPs) \tag{12-7}$$

Converting Equation 12-8 to its multiplicative form in order to estimate reach (3+) instead of the natural logarithm of reach (3+) gives Equation 12-8.

$$Reach(3+) = e^{-.878}GRP^{.775} \tag{12-8}$$

Substituting 300 GRPs (and 2.71828 for the natural logarithm base $= e$) into Equation 12-8 gives:

$$Reach(3+) = 2.71828^{-.878}300^{.775}$$
$$= (.416)(83.13)$$
$$= 34.5\%$$

From this it is seen that the reach $(3+)$ of 34.5 percent is also the figure predicted using the local newspaper curve in Figure 12.3.

You should follow this procedure for all other double-log equations in Table 12.5, including prime time and daytime television, radio, and outdoor. The four quadratic equations listed in the table are more straightforward to evaluate and require slightly different procedures. For example, what unweighted effective reach $(3+)$ is predicted if 300 GRPs are scheduled in national newspapers? The national newspaper reach $(3+)$ curve is presented as Equation 12-9.

$$\text{Reach}(3+) = -17.076 + .317(\text{GRP}) - .00025(\text{GRP}^2) \qquad (12\text{-}9)$$

Substituting 300 GRPs into Equation 12-9 leads to:

$$
\begin{aligned}
\text{Reach}(3+) &= -17.076 + .317(300) - .00025(300^2) \\
&= -17.076 + 95.1 - .00025(90000) \\
&= 78.024 - 22.5 \\
&= 55.5\%
\end{aligned}
$$

TABLE 12.5 Regressions of Reach(3+) on GRPs for Selected Advertising Media Categories

Media Categories (GRP Ranges)	Regression Equations			R^2	F	N
Loc. Newspapers (GRP = 30-1500)	lnreach(3+) = −	.878 + (.142)	.775(lnGRP) (.025)	.952	998	52
Nat. Newspapers (GRP = 38-647)	Reach(3+) = −	17.076 + (1.211)	.317(GRP) (.0084) − .00025(GRP^2) (.00001)	.984	3577	120
Newspapers Supp. (GRP = 43-653)	Reach(3+) = −	16.887 + (3.577)	.330(GRP) (.024) − .00027(GRP^2) (.00003)	.985	388	15
Magazines (Full) (GRP = 78-789)	Reach(3+) =	7.859 + (1.346)	.134(GRP) (.007) − .00007(GRP^2) (.000007)	.995	1543	20
Magazines (Ltd.) (GRP = 44-1321)	Reach(3+) =	1.459[n] + (3.966)	.198(GRP) (.013) − .0001(GRP^2) (.00001)	.945	232	30
TV (Prime time) (GRP = 61-613)	lnreach(3+) = −	2.322 + (.302)	1.062(lnGRP) (.052)	.923	410	36
TV (Daytime) (GRP = 30-595)	lnreach(3+) = −	3.125 + (.271)	1.156(lnGRP) (.050)	.917	575	54
Radio (GRP = 12-849)	lnreach(3+) = −	1.466 + (.166)	.849(lnGRP) (.029)	.986	846	14
Outdoor (GRP = 465-1848)	lnreach(3+) =	1.555 + (.051)	.375(lnGRP) (.007)	.994	2564	18

Note: Standard errors of coefficients are in parentheses; all coefficients, R squares and F ratios are significant at the .10 level except where noted otherwise by "n"; ln = natural logarithm to base e = 2.71828; Reach(3+) = percentage of target female homemakers who are exposed to advertising media schedules three or more times; GRP = gross rating points. Schedules are designed to be representative of those likely to be run against the target, including schedules with few vehicles and insertions and with many vehicles and insertions. The equations are predictive of likely schedule (unweighted) reach(3+) only over the range of gross rating points noted for each equation. All data are derived from *Simmons Market Research Bureau, 1983 Survey of Media and Markets,* volumes P-20 and M-4, for 69,719,000 U.S. female homemakers who use cold breakfast cereals. The following individuals deserve recognition for assistance in data processing: Dongseung Kim, Gary C. Walgren, James A. Edfors and Robert L. Bruce.

Again, 55.5 percent effective reach (3+) is approximately the percentage estimated by the national newspaper curve depicted in Figure 12.3.

Figure 12.3, then, merely superimposes evaluations of all of the equations in Table 12.5 on to one set of reach (3+) and GRP axes. This makes it easy to compare the various media categories as a preliminary step to developing a media plan.

One should keep in mind, however, that there could be substantial differences between the predictions made by Figure 12.3 or Table 12.5 versus actual schedules that are developed and evaluated. There are several reasons for this. The estimates presented here are based on a broad range of reasonable alternatives. But any fixed level of GRPs in a particular media category can be achieved by using any combination of the following dimensions:

1. Number of vehicles: few versus many.
2. Number of insertions per vehicle: one versus many.
3. Vehicle ratings: low versus high.

For example, a schedule with several insertions in a few highly rated vehicles is likely to achieve greater reach (3+) at low levels of GRPs than a schedule with identical GRPs but with one insertion each in many low rated vehicles.

These factors could be taken into account in developing equations. Doing so would increase substantially the accuracy of the predictions. However, it is not possible to depict such multivariate equations in the manner of Figure 12.3. At this point, it is more important to have a clear picture of the possibilities than to have more accurate equations.

Nevertheless, by using Table 12.4 and Figure 12.3 in tandem, you should have some useful benchmarks for comparison as you develop and evaluate your own media plans. If the estimates presented can be matched or exceeded, then progress is being made.

ENDNOTES

1. Peggy J. Kreshel, Kent M. Lancaster and Margaret A. Toomey, "How Leading Advertising Agencies Perceive Effective Reach and Frequency," *Journal of Advertising*, 14:3 (1985), pp. 32-38, 51; Kent M. Lancaster, Peggy J. Kreshel and Joya R. Harris, "Estimating the Impact of Advertising Media Plans: Media Executives Describe Weighting and Timing Factors," *Journal of Advertising*, 15:3 (September 1986), pp. 21-29, 45.

2. David R. Gusse and Kent M. Lancaster, "Using on-line data services makes course more realistic," *Journalism Educator*, (Autumn 1983), pp. 6-10, 38.

3. David A. Aaker and John G. Myers, *Advertising Management*, New Jersey: Prentice Hall, Inc., 1987; Samuel C. Craig and Avijit Ghosh, "Maximizing Effective Reach in Media Planning," *Proceedings, 1985 American Marketing Association Educators' Conference*, Series No. 51, Robert F. Lusch et al. (eds.), pp. 178-182; Dennis Gensch, *Advertising Planning: Mathematical Models in Advertising Media Planning*, Amsterdam: Elsevier Scientific Publishing Company, 1973; John D.C. Little and Leonard M. Lodish, "A Media Planning Calculus," *Operations Research*, 17:1 (January-February, 1969), pp. 1-

35; Anthony F. McGann and J. Thomas Russell, *Advertising Media: A Managerial Approach* (2nd ed.), Homewood: Irwin, 1988; Roland T. Rust, "Selecting Network Television Advertising Schedules," *Journal of Business Research*, 13 (December 1985), pp. 483-494; Roland T. Rust, *Advertising Media Models: A Practical Guide*, Massachusetts: Lexington Books, 1986.

4. Kent M. Lancaster, "Planners as Forecasters," *Marketing and Media Decisions*, 22:7, July 1987, p. 160; Kent M. Lancaster and Peter E. Helander, "Forecasting Advertising Effects Using Media Exposure Distribution Models: Some Test Market Results," *Proceedings of the 1987 Annual Conference of the American Statistical Association*, Section on Business and Economic Statistics, Subsection on Statistical Applications in Marketing, San Francisco, California, August 1987; Kent M. Lancaster, Peggy J. Kreshel and Margaret A. Toomey, "Estimating the Communication Impact of Advertising Media Plans," *Proceedings of the Atlantic Marketing Association Annual Conference*, Orlando, Florida, October 8-11, 1986, pp. 31-39.

5. John D.C. Little and Leonard M. Lodish, op. cit.

6. Pearl, Judea, *Heuristics: Intelligent Search Strategies for Computer Problem Solving*, Massachusetts: Addison-Wesley Publishing Company, 1984.

APPENDIX 12-A SAMPLE *ADPLAN* OPTIMIZATION INTERACTION*

```
                  For Advertising Media Planning and Evaluation

                     (C) Copyright 1988, Kent M. Lancaster
                            Department of Advertising
                     University of Illinois at Urbana-Champaign
                            Urbana, Illinois 61801

                           Press any key to continue.

Get ADPLAN data file (1=yes, 2=no)? 2

Type your name                        ? Kent Lancaster
Enter brand name                      ? All-Bran
Campaign Period (e.g., June 1988)     ? June 1988

Describe the geographic coverage of your schedule

    1 = National schedule
    2 = National schedule evaluated in a particular region
    3 = Regional schedule

Your choice? 1

Describe your target (e.g., Female Homemakers)   ? Female Homemakers -
                                                   Users

Type target size (e.g., 67502000)                ? 69405000

Select the media category you want to use.
```

```
1=Consumer Magazines      5=Local Newspapers    9=Network Radio
2=Business Publications    6=Network TV          10=Spot Radio
3=National Newspapers      7=Spot TV             11=Outdoor
4=Newspaper Supplements    8=Cable TV            12=Direct Mail
```

Your choice? 1

Available audience data:

```
1 = Single insertion ratings only
2 = Single insertion ratings plus all self- and cross-pairs
```

Your choice? 1

Input vehicle audience weight to account for advertising
exposures or other communication effects. For example:

```
1.000 = Unweighted (vehicle exposures = ad exposures)
 .525 = Typical weight for CONSUMER MAGAZINES
```

Enter weight? .525

Describe basis of weight (e.g., awareness, recall, knowledge).

Communication effect? exposure

How many vehicles in your CONSUMER MAGAZINES schedule? 12

For each CONSUMER MAGAZINES vehicle, enter:

Vehicle Number/Name	Ad Cost	Ads(#)	Rating	1=OK 2=no
1? Reader's Digest	? 104600	? 1	? .266	? 1
2? TV Guide	? 95900	? 5	? .254	? 1
3? Family Circle	? 75280	? 1	? .208	? 1
4? Good Housekeeping	? 80025	? 1	? .208	? 1
5? Better Homes & Gar	? 95400	? 1	? .204	? 1
6? Woman's Day	? 66960	? 1	? .194	? 1
7? McCall's	? 60800	? 1	? .168	? 1
8? People	? 61345	? 5	? .152	? 1
9? Ladies Home Journ	? 61300	? 1	? .147	? 1
10? National Geographic	? 117715	? 1	? .129	? 1
11? Time	? 114955	? 5	? .109	? 1
12? Redbook	? 55255	? 1	? .102	? 1

(Output similar to Figure 12-2 is presented here for all magazines in
the data base.)

Press any key to continue.

```
 1 = Review LAST schedule
 2 = Modify LAST schedule
 3 = Create NEW schedule using parts of LAST schedule
 4 = Create NEW schedule from scratch
 5 = Combine two or more schedules
 6 = Save raw data on disk file
 7 = Get raw data on disk file
 8 = Save table on disk file
 9 = Print table
10 = Select optimum schedule
11 = Return to DOS
12 = Stop, return to DOS
```

```
Your choice? 6

Enter drive letter:output data file (e.g., B:TV.DAT)?  B:MAG.DAT
    (Type DOS to return to system)

 1 = Review LAST schedule
 2 = Modify LAST schedule
 3 = Create NEW schedule using parts of LAST schedule
 4 = Create NEW schedule from scratch
 5 = Combine two or more schedules
 6 = Save raw data on disk file
 7 = Get raw data on disk file
 8 = Save table on disk file
 9 = Print table
10 = Select optimum schedule
11 = Return to DOS
12 = Stop, return to DOS

Your choice? 10

Select Optimum Schedule
-----------------------

Total schedules in data base:       110592
Total schedules to be run:          110592

    1 = Change min/maximum ads per vehicle
    2 = Change total schedules to be run
    3 = Sort vehicles by CPM
    4 = Select optimum criteria/schedule
    5 = Return to main menu

Your choice? 4

Budget constraint (maximum =  2078335)?

     Lower budget limit (e.g., 1000000)? 475000
     Upper budget limit (e.g., 1250000)? 500000

Optimize which weighted factors?

     1 = Reach (1+)
     2 = Effective reach (3+)
     3 = Average frequency
     4 = Gross rating points (GRPs)
     5 = Cost-per-thousand impressions (CPM)
     6 = Return to optimization menu

Your PRIMARY choice? 1
Your SECONDARY choice? 5

     Optimizing ADPLAN schedules, please stand by.
     ----------------------------------------------
     Total schedules to be run:          110,592
     Now evaluating schedule:              2,000
     Primary maximum reach (1+):           36.52
     Secondary minimum CPM:               $10.20
     Elapsed time (hh:mm:ss):           00:00:12
```

(Status reports are provided for every 2,000 schedules.
The first and last status reports are presented here.)

Optimizing ADPLAN schedules, please stand by.

Total schedules to be run: 110,592
Now evaluating schedule: 110,000
Primary maximum reach (1+):   36.52
Secondary minimum CPM: $10.20
Elapsed time (hh:mm:ss):   00:07:25

(Output identical to Figure 12-2 is presented here.)

                            Press any key to continue.

 1 = Review LAST schedule
 2 = Modify LAST schedule
 3 = Create NEW schedule using parts of LAST schedule
 4 = Create NEW schedule from scratch
 5 = Combine two or more schedules
 6 = Save raw data on disk file
 7 = Get raw data on disk file
 8 = Save table on disk file
 9 = Print table
10 = Select optimum schedule
11 = Return to DOS
12 = Stop, return to DOS

Your choice? 12

CHAPTER THIRTEEN

Summarizing the Advertising Media Plan Using *ADFLOW*

Advertising media plans can be complex and difficult to communicate. So it is useful to summarize them from a variety of perspectives. Two typical approaches include a recap of an advertising flowchart and the budget, showing at a glance the timing and intensity of the entire campaign. This chapter introduces an interactive computer program that incorporates each approach. ADFLOW is a flowchart program that identifies the monthly placement of all advertisements in the campaign and summarizes media evaluation factors on a month-by-month basis. It also includes a budget summary designed to highlight the uses of the advertising appropriation in terms of targets, geographic weight, product lines, seasonality, distribution channels, and media categories, among others. The remainder of this chapter is devoted to introducing this program and examining its capabilities.

OVERVIEW OF *ADFLOW* OUTPUT

ADFLOW offers the opportunity to flowchart a media plan so that it is clear where the media insertions will be placed and when they will appear. The final printout will show the yearly media schedule at a glance. Pulsing and flighting schedules are displayed too. This gives a comprehensive overview of the media plan created, containing much of the relevant information that management would be interested in. Most of the required data come from the results of the other media models that already have been explained. A sample flowchart developed using ADFLOW is presented in Figure 13.1.

ADFLOW will also create an advertising budget summary, showing how the total advertising appropriation will be allocated across targets, regions, media categories, distribution channels, product lines, seasons, the contingency, as well as any optional category that the user might wish to specify. An example is illustrated in Figure 13.2.

ADFLOW FLOWCHART PROCEDURES

First, the program will list what the user must have before proceeding, which includes information from ADPLAN. This list can be seen in Figure 13.3. Once ready, one can continue by typing "1."

FIGURE 13.1 **Presenting a Flowchart of the Media Schedule:**
Sample ADFLOW Output

```
----------------------------------------------------------------------------------------------------
                       Kellogg's All-Bran Media Schedule For Fiscal Year 1987-88

Target Audience:  Female Homemakers                        Advertising Media Budget:  $12,412,500  ( 90.0%)
Target Audience Size:   69,405,000                         Contingency:                $1,379,167  ( 10.0%)

                                              Number of Insertions per Month
Media          Yearly  Yearly  -----------------------------------------------------------------------------
  Vehicles      Ads    Cost(000)  JAN   FEB   MAR   APR   MAY   JUN   JUL   AUG   SEP   OCT   NOV   DEC
----------------------------------------------------------------------------------------------------

Consumer Magazines  72  $6,422.9   6     6     6     6     6     6     6     6     6     6     6     6
                                  ---   ---   ---   ---   ---   ---   ---   ---   ---   ---   ---   ---
   Reader's Digest   12  $1,305.6   1     1     1     1     1     1     1     1     1     1     1     1
   TV Guide          48  $4,286.4   4     4     4     4     4     4     4     4     4     4     4     4
   Good Housekeepin  12    $830.9   1     1     1     1     1     1     1     1     1     1     1     1

Network TV           96  $5,989.6   8     8     8     8     8     8     8     8     8     8     8     8
                                  ---   ---   ---   ---   ---   ---   ---   ---   ---   ---   ---   ---
   Young and Restle  24    $540.2   2     2     2     2     2     2     2     2     2     2     2     2
   All My Children   24    $515.7   2     2     2     2     2     2     2     2     2     2     2     2
   Dallas            24  $2,580.7   2     2     2     2     2     2     2     2     2     2     2     2
   Bill Cosby Show   24  $2,353.0   2     2     2     2     2     2     2     2     2     2     2     2
                         ----------
   Total                 $12,412.5

Consumer Magazines  ($000)  $535  $535  $535  $535  $535  $535  $535  $535  $535  $535  $535  $535
Network TV          ($000)  $499  $499  $499  $499  $499  $499  $499  $499  $499  $499  $499  $499
Monthly Totals      ($000) $1034 $1034 $1034 $1034 $1034 $1034 $1034 $1034 $1034 $1034 $1034 $1034

Effective Reach            27.7% 27.7% 27.7% 27.7% 27.7% 27.7% 27.7% 27.7% 27.7% 27.7% 27.7% 27.7%
Gross Rating Points        169.8 169.8 169.8 169.8 169.8 169.8 169.8 169.8 169.8 169.8 169.8 169.8
CPM Impressions           $8.78 $8.78 $8.78 $8.78 $8.78 $8.78 $8.78 $8.78 $8.78 $8.78 $8.78 $8.78
----------------------------------------------------------------------------------------------------
```

☐ Company and Brand Names

The company and brand names that have been used throughout this text are Kellogg's All-Bran. When entering the name one should not use commas.

☐ *ADFLOW* Data File

The program will ask the user if there is already a data file available from which to work. If not, all the information must again be entered.

☐ Fiscal Year of Media Schedule

Next, the fiscal year for the media plan is inserted. If it is 1987, as in the example, one would enter "1987," but if it goes across years, say from July 1986 through June 1987, then one types "1986-1987." The program also asks if the first year starts in January or July.

☐ Target Audience

Now the target audience and its size should be identified clearly, both decisions having been made in previous programs. In the example here, Kellogg's target is female homemakers. Once again, the number is entered without commas. In this case, the target size is 69,405,000.

FIGURE 13.2 Summarizing the Advertising Budget: Sample ADFLOW Output

```
----------------------------------------------------------------
     Kellogg's All-Bran Budget Summary for Fiscal Year 1987-88
----------------------------------------------------------------
```

	Amount	Percent
Target Audience: Female Homemakers	------	-------
Target Audience Size: 69,405,000		
Advertising Appropriation	$13,791,667	100.0%
Media Budget	$12,412,500	90.0
Contingency	$1,379,167	10.0
Marketing Regions		
Northeast	$2,556,975	20.6
East Central	$1,849,462	14.9
West Central	$2,259,075	18.2
South	$3,624,450	29.2
Pacific	$2,122,537	17.1
	-----------	------
	$12,412,500	100.0%
Media Categories		
Consumer Magazines	$6,422,940	51.7
Network TV	$5,989,560	48.3
	-----------	------
	$12,412,500	100.0%
Quarterly Expenditures		
JAN-FEB-MAR	$3,103,125	25.0
APR-MAY-JUN	$3,103,125	25.0
JUL-AUG-SEP	$3,103,125	25.0
OCT-NOV-DEC	$3,103,125	25.0
	-----------	------
	$12,412,500	100.0%
Products		
Regular	$3,723,750	30.0
High Fiber	$3,723,750	30.0
Fruit and Almonds	$4,965,000	40.0
	-----------	------
	$12,412,500	100.0%

FIGURE 13.3

The following are required to use ADFLOW:
1. Company and brand name
2. Fiscal year (FY) of advertising plan
3. Target audience and its size
4. Percent of media budget for contingency
5. Media categories, vehicle and insertions
6. Cost of each insertion
7. Monthly ADPLAN results
   Effective reach
   Gross rating points
   Cost-per-thousand impressions

☐ **Contingency**

ADFLOW next asks what percent of the total advertising appropriation is to be set aside for contingency purposes, such as speculative buys and competitive response. Usually this percentage ranges between 10 and 15. Using the figure provided, ADFLOW will determine how much to add to the media budget for the contingency.

☐ **Number and Type of Media Categories**

Now the program will ask for the number and the type of different media categories in the *entire yearly* schedule. For this media plan, two different media categories were used, network television and magazines.

☐ **Names and Costs of Vehicles**

For the entire fiscal year, and for each media category, the user must now identify the vehicles included in the media schedule, as well as the cost of a single insertion. One should note, however, that the number of insertions requested per vehicle is for the first month of the fiscal year. Each media category will be handled in a similar manner. A sample interaction appears below.

FIGURE 13.4

For each FY 1987-88 vehicle used in Consumer Magazines, enter:

Name	Cost/Ad	Number of JAN Ads	(1=OK, 2=no)
1 ? Reader's Digest	? 108800	? 1	? 1
2 ? TV Guide	? 89300	? 4	? 1
3 ? Good Housekeeping	? 69245	? 1	? 1

In this example, three different magazines are used. The costs and insertions entered come from the ADPLAN results illustrated in earlier chapters.

☐ **Media Evaluation Factors**

ADFLOW then asks for effective reach, gross rating points, and the cost-per-thousand for the first month of the fiscal year. The example below shows the necessary inputs.

FIGURE 13.5

For the month of JAN, enter:

Effective Reach	? 27.7
Gross Rating Points	? 169.8
CPM Impressions	? 8.78

The numbers here come from the ADPLAN results for combined schedules: magazines and television. For effective reach, one enters the number as a percentage and not a decimal. For instance, an effective reach of 16.38 percent would be entered as 16.38. GRPs should also be entered as a number, without commas. And the CPM for the combined schedule should not include commas or the dollar sign. Thus, if the CPM is $11.51, it would be entered as 11.51.

The media evaluation factors included in the flowchart summarize the likely effects of that schedule on the target. These figures, along with the flowchart itself, are extremely valuable since they are used to summarize the major characteristics of the media plan.

☐ Matching Schedules with Months

The next section asks the user to identify other months that will also require this schedule. ADFLOW will list the months, one at a time, and one simply types "1" if the schedule will be used that month or "2" if not. This is where the concept of pulsing and flighting can be used. If a planner wishes to have heavier advertising in the winter months, then she or he can put more insertions there and leave the others with lighter schedules.

The process is repeated until a schedule has been assigned to each month of the fiscal year. Figure 13.6 shows a sample interaction.

☐ The Flowchart

ADFLOW then presents the comprehensive flowchart in a single table. Because of its large size, it will be split up on the screen into two parts, unless the screen can be set to 132 characters. However, it will be clearly presented in the compressed mode on the printer attached to the PC. ADFLOW will allow the user to review or change the flowchart or go on to develop the budget summary.

ADFLOW BUDGET SUMMARY PROCEDURES

Once users have satisfactorily completed a flowchart only a few more steps are necessary to create a budget summary.

☐ Target Market Regions

The decision of whether to allocate money across marketing regions or census regions deserves some thought. Marketing regions separate the country into five

FIGURE 13.6

```
Which plans are identical to JAN (1=same as JAN, 2=different)?

    FEB?  1
    MAR?  1
    APR?  1
    MAY?  1
    JUN?  1
    JUL?  1
    AUG?  1
    SEP?  1
    OCT?  1
    NOV?  1
    DEC?  1
```

sections: Northeast, East Central, West Central, South, and Pacific, whereas there are four census regions including northeast, north central, south, and west.

The choice varies across different product types. For example, cereal is eaten by almost everyone, so broad census regions may be chosen. On the other hand, if the product were a hot cereal, one would probably want to concentrate attention more on the northern regions. For this purpose, marketing regions might be used because the areas are smaller, enabling the planner to be more specific as to where the budget is allocated.

Once this decision is made, the percentages are all that need to be entered. Those used here can be found in SMRB, Volume P-20. In Figure 13.7 the marketing percentages are given for the example problem.

☐ Optional Categories

One can select up to six optional categories in order to create custom budget groups. First, one must decide how many categories to add. As seen in Figure 13.8, each must be named and the number of sub-categories specified. The program can handle up to six sub-categories. In the example, the category is entitled "Product Lines." The term refers to different types of the same product that might need individual attention. For example, Kellogg's All-Bran is available in regular, high fiber, and fruit and almond varieties. ADFLOW will ask for the name of each product line and the percentage of the budget to be allocated to it.

☐ Return to Re-evaluate

After the budget summary is printed, one may choose to return to any of the previous sections of the program (see Figure 13.9). If a mistake is made or changes are needed, one simply enters the appropriate number and returns to any section.

The output of the sample interaction described here will appear as depicted in

FIGURE 13.7

```
Select regions (0=skip, 1=marketing, 2=census)? 1

    Percent spent in Northeast region (e.g., 18.5)       ? 20.6
    Percent spent in East Central region (e.g., 18.5)    ? 14.9
    Percent spent in West Central region (e.g., 18.5)    ? 18.2
    Percent spent in South region (e.g., 18.5)           ? 29.2
```

FIGURE 13.8

```
How many additional budget categories? 1
Name of Category 1 (e.g., Products)? Products
Number of Category 1 subgroups (e.g., 3)? 3

    Name of Subgroup 1 (e.g., Regular)? Regular
    Budget percent of Subgroup 1 (e.g., 33.3)? 30

    Name of Subgroup 2 (e.g., Regular)? High Fiber
    Budget percent of Subgroup 2 (e.g., 33.3)? 30

    Name of Subgroup 3 (e.g., Regular)? Fruit and Almonds
```

FIGURE 13.9

What next?

```
1 = Review flowchart
2 = Change flowchart
3 = Save flowchart data on disk file
4 = Save flowchart table(s) on disk file
5 = Print flowchart table(s)
6 = Do budget
7 = Return to DOS
8 = Stop, return to DOS
```

Your choice? 3

Figures 13.1 and 13.2. The program is relatively fast and easy to use, so users should not be reluctant to experiment with alternative schedules.

With the help of this program, media planners need no longer worry about how to communicate all the objectives and financial implications of their work. Instead, they can apply themselves to obtaining the most efficient and effective use of their clients' money and leave the computer to present all the information clearly, coherently, and in detail.

CHAPTER FOURTEEN

Developing Advertising Planning Models

Media vehicle audience data are limited and expensive. Therefore, media planners and researchers have been ingenious in their efforts to project available audience data into areas where they either seldom exist or where the benefits of obtaining them are not perceived to be worth the cost. To be sure, estimating audiences with limited information is a risky activity, particularly when expensive media buying decisions hang in the balance. Nevertheless, there is a surprising degree of simplicity and stability in the relationships that exist within and between media vehicle audiences. Consequently, many audience estimating procedures are of considerable value to media planners because they save time and the expense of buying certain kinds of audience data. Even if the vehicle estimating procedures have a certain level of error, it is probably quite small *in relation to the gap between vehicle audiences and advertising audiences*, as was shown in Chapter Three.

In this chapter, these points will be illustrated quite clearly, by demonstrating how network television self-pair audiences can be approximated using only single-insertion ratings. The procedures will be described in sufficient detail so that you should be able to duplicate the results presented here. Furthermore, you should also be able to apply the techniques to network television cross-pair audiences, and to self- and cross-pair audiences of other media categories.

THE RANDOM COMBINATION METHOD REVISITED

The random combination method was explained in Chapters Eight and Nine because it is the basis for estimating self- and cross-pair audiences for several media categories using the interactive media planning model ADPLAN. You might wish to refresh your memory, at this point, by reviewing relevant sections of Chapter Nine. Equation 9-1 is presented again as Equation 14-1.

$$R_{2i} = 2(R_i) - (k_{wm})(R_i)^2 \tag{14-1}$$

This should be recognized as the general form of an equation for estimating self-pair audience size using single insertion ratings. Equation 14-1 is general because its parameters, particularly k_{wm}, must be specified to suit particular media categories and audiences. In contrast, once the form of the equation is made applicable to a particular situation, it is no longer general, but specific.

Researchers use a number of techniques to adapt equations such as this to particular circumstances.[1] The most common method includes the use of *multiple regression* analysis.[2]

MULTIPLE REGRESSION ANALYSIS

Regression analysis is a statistical method used by researchers to explain relations among two or more variables, often using lines or curves with reference to two or more axes. There is a huge body of literature which supports this technique, and to conduct it properly requires considerable experience in statistics, econometrics, and the like. This chapter cannot begin to cover the topic with any breadth or depth. The goal here simply is to provide an intuitive appreciation of the capabilities and limitations of regression analysis.

Planners are interested in fitting curves like Equation 14-1 to the data that exist for individual advertising media categories. The focus will be on network television audiences for adults. The aim is to know whether one can predict accurately self-pair network television audiences given only single-insertion audience ratings. If this can be done precisely, then a great deal of work can be saved when evaluating network television schedules against adults. Also, if the relationships hold across several other targets, such as males, females, and female homemakers, for example, then one might be able to estimate self-pair audiences for other broad targets as well, with little sacrifice in precision.

Now the question to answer is, what is the relation between self-pair and single-insertion network television audiences? Equation 14-1 suggests that, in general, self-pair ratings will equal GRPs for one insertion in each vehicle, minus duplication between the two insertions. On the basis of chance alone, one would expect duplication to be equal to the product of the two ratings. But if actual duplication is greater or less than would be expected on the basis of chance, then k_{wm} would be greater or less than 1.00.

If self-pair and single-insertion network television audience data are accessible for adults, then one could actually estimate what k_{wm} would be, on average. It turns out that such data are readily available. In SMRB, Volume M-12 (1982), there are self-pair audience sizes, in thousands, listed for 84 network programs covering all dayparts. These are shown in Table 14.1, along with corresponding single-insertion ratings.

This table presents a great deal of audience data to deal with. As one might expect, however, there are personal computer software packages to help one evaluate them quickly and easily. The first step is to create a raw data file that can then be accessed, read, transformed, and analyzed using multiple regression subroutines.

Using LOTUS or EDLIN, for example, one could create a data file called TVKWD, a file containing network television data that will allow estimations of within-vehicle correction factors.[3] Initially, TVKWD would have three fixed fields. One field (vehicle number) is two characters wide; two fields are six characters wide (R_i and R_{2i}).

TABLE 14.1 One-Time (R_i) and Self-Pair (R_{2i}) Network Television Audiences (000) for U.S. Adults (Base = 161,656 (000))

#	Program R_i	R_{2i}	#	Program R_i	R_{2i}
1	3,413	5,156	43	16,458	26,405
2	8,771	11,875	44	11,234	18,453
3	4,895	6,478	45	16,119	26,344
4	6,832	9,162	46	8,625	13,480
5	3,913	5,190	47	15,432	23,913
6	8,071	10,357	48	12,088	20,027
7	3,030	4,078	49	13,833	22,422
8	4,118	6,076	50	6,980	11,535
9	8,768	11,956	51	22,397	35,417
10	5,207	7,650	52	18,694	29,198
11	5,282	7,718	53	7,921	13,988
12	7,525	9,808	54	14,046	22,509
13	4,162	6,541	55	15,166	25,168
14	7,312	9,875	56	19,962	32,051
15	6,478	9,392	57	20,228	32,625
16	6,406	9,224	58	18,611	30,961
17	4,099	5,812	59	9,410	15,883
18	3,449	4,610	60	9,046	15,777
19	4,924	6,836	61	13,255	24,406
20	4,249	6,257	62	7,115	11,466
21	3,396	5,080	63	7,387	11,875
22	7,057	9,519	64	15,865	27,661
23	12,186	18,151	65	16,104	26,369
24	16,053	22,576	66	6,554	10,985
25	12,193	17,381	67	20,566	33,056
26	5,477	8,939	68	18,434	29,391
27	5,883	9,235	69	28,292	42,310
28	4,892	8,588	70	17,350	27,468
29	16,872	27,475	71	11,992	19,821
30	10,311	16,329	72	15,979	27,011
31	17,091	26,667	73	21,568	33,983
32	12,847	20,219	74	20,402	31,366
33	8,600	14,593	75	19,425	31,719
34	8,217	13,269	76	19,302	29,829
35	11,182	19,853	77	9,274	15,192
36	4,105	7,187	78	7,531	12,976
37	12,358	22,410	79	4,479	8,208
38	14,922	23,787	80	3,772	7,257
39	19,080	28,042	81	3,423	5,812
40	16,272	24,612	82	4,069	7,165
41	15,285	23,055	83	3,927	7,384
42	14,636	23,211	84	3,801	5,589

Source: SMRB, Volume M-12, 1982.

To analyze this data file, the graph and regression subroutines from LOTUS or SHAZAM, for example, can be used.[4] Those who have used such programs should have little difficulty following the logic of the procedures. After entering the data, one must instruct the program to convert the variables in TVKWD to percentages or ratings by dividing by total U.S. adults, in thousands (161,656). Then GRPs ($2R_i$) and random duplication (R_i^2) are created and regressed on R_{2i}.

The LOTUS Print Graph utility was used to create Figure 14.1 to show the relation between actual self-pair ratings and those estimated using single-insertion ratings.

By examining Figure 14.1, one can see that there is a strong positive relation between the two variables. The coefficient of determination is .985 (that is, $R^2 = .985$), meaning that GRPs and random duplication together explain 98.5 percent of the variation in the self-pair audience ratings. Figure 14.1 also suggests that it will be possible to accurately model the relation between self-pair and single-insertion ratings.

The specific form of Equation 14-1 can be seen in the multiple regression output generated by LOTUS or SHAZAM presented in Table 14.2.

You will notice that the equation has the same general form as Equation 14-1, except for the intercept, which though statistically significant, is not much different from zero. For the sample of data, k_w turns out to be 1.33. That is, actual duplication is approximately 1.33 times greater than that expected on the basis of chance alone. Also, k_w is significant at the .05 level ($p = .024$). Overall, the entire equation fits the data extremely well, since $R^2 = .985$. Therefore, this equation can be used as a substitute for actual self-pair audience data, with little loss of accuracy, when dealing with adult network television program audiences obtained from SMRB, Volume M-12, 1982.

FIGURE 14.1 Estimating Self-Pair Ratings

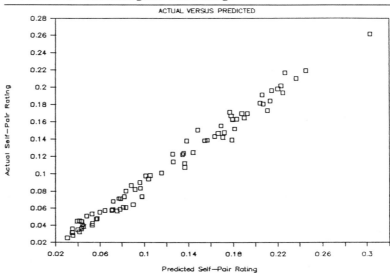

Although this equation is not based on current SMRB data, the authors have estimated similar equations for other consumer groups using 1982 SMRB data. These groups have included males, females, and female homemakers. Statistically, there are no differences between the equation presented in Table 14.2 and those estimated for the other groups. Therefore, this equation can be used for these other broad targets as well. In the absence of better data, one might also use it for broad product-user groups, such as female homemakers who use cold breakfast cereals. This, of course, introduces unknown levels of error into the estimates. But it is the authors' belief that such inaccuracy is inconsequential when compared to the gap between vehicle and advertising audiences, for instance.

The equation presented in Table 14.2 is included in the ADPLAN model in similar form. When a television schedule is evaluated, the user provides AD-PLAN with single-insertion ratings for various television programs. These are then used in the equation to estimate the self-pair ratings for each program. You may wish to refer to Chapter Nine to observe how this is done. As a test of a full understanding of these concepts, you could calculate the self-pair rating for a particular program. What, for example, would be the estimated self-pair rating for a program with a single-insertion rating of 10? Using the equation presented in Table 14.2, one should get approximately 16 percent (.1596).

TABLE 14.2   Multiple Regression Results

Dependent Variable	Intercept	Independent Variables
$R_{2i} =$	$-.0065^b$	$+$ $.8973^a(2R_i) - 1.3308^b(R_i^2)$
	$(.0030)$	$(.0456)$ $(.5784)$
	$R^2 = .985,$ $F = 2672.71^a,$ $N = 84$	

Note: Standard errors are in parentheses; "a" and "b" indicate .01 and .05 levels of significance respectively.

SUMMARY

This chapter has presented a broad-brush approach to the use of multiple regression techniques for estimating self- and cross-pair audience ratings in the face of limited data. You may not have sufficient background to deal with many of the concepts presented at anything other than an intuitive level. Nevertheless, this general approach may help you grasp a sense of the overall process and not get tangled in the infinite detail and complexity that surrounds the professional application of multiple regression analysis.

The ADPLAN subroutines based on limited information are based generally on self- and cross-pair audience estimating equations that were developed using the methods described here. In the process of this research, the authors came to a number of interesting conclusions.

First of all, there exists a surprising level of simplicity and stability in the data that were used to estimate the various equations. The simplicity arose from the observation that the random combination method was an excellent general estimating form. With a few modifications, such as hyperbolic transformations, and specifying the within- and between-vehicle correction factors as dependent variables, the estimated curves fit the data at hand well. The stability observed is due to the very high R^2 coefficients that were found to be associated with the estimated equations. Nearly all of the equations used in ADPLAN have R^2 coefficients at .99 or better.

These results suggest that there is a great deal to be gained from this approach in terms of savings in media planners' time and in costly audience data. Furthermore, a fruitful line of research would be the systematic documentation of such equations within and across a large variety of media categories and target audiences. A chapter in this book easily could be devoted to explaining the derivation of all of the equations used in ADPLAN. At this point, the goal is simply to stimulate others into following this line of inquiry further.

The appendix to this chapter introduces BASIC programming for readers interested in developing further their own interactive advertising planning models.

ENDNOTES

1. John D. Leckenby and Marshall D. Rice, "A Beta Binomial Network TV Exposure Model Using Limited Data," *Journal of Advertising*, 3 (1985), pp. 25-31; and Marshall D. Rice and John D. Leckenby, "Estimating the Exposure Distribution of Magazine Schedules in Limited Data Situations," *Proceedings*, American Academy of Advertising (March 1985).

2. M. Dutta, *Econometric Methods* (Cincinnati: South-Western Publishing Co., 1975); George G. Judge, Carter Hill, William F. Griffiths, Helmuth Lutkepohl and Tsoung-Chao Lee, *Introduction to the Theory and Practice of Econometrics* (New York: John Wiley and Sons, 1982); Harry H. Kelejian and Wallace E. Oates, *Introduction to Econometrics: Principles and Applications* (New York: Harper and Row, 1976); G. S. Maddala, *Econometrics* (New York: McGraw-Hill Book Co., 1977); and Kenneth J. White, "A General Computer Program for Econometric Methods—SHAZAM," *Econometrica* (January 1978), pp. 239-40.

3. IBM Corporation, *Disk Operating System*, Version 3.0, 1985; and Lotus Development Corporation, *123 Reference Manual* (Cambridge, Massachusetts: Lotus Development Corporation, 1985).

4. Lotus Development Corporation, ibid; and White, op. cit.

APPENDIX 14-A PROGRAMMING ADVERTISING MODELS USING THE BASIC LANGUAGE

There is an array of excellent texts and reference manuals on the market that will provide an overview of BASIC programming. The purpose of this appendix is to introduce you to some of the fundamentals on the IBM Personal Computer (PC) in the context of the advertising planning models that are used throughout this text.

Several objectives are served by introducing BASIC programming here. One is to provide a sense of closure by taking you through basic media planning concepts, the use of interactive media models, and an overview of the media model development process. The goal is to give you a sense of confidence that you can not only understand the entire process, but can even contribute to it and control it.

A second objective is to prepare you as fully as possible for the computerization of planning, among other advertising decision making systems. One day you may be in the position of introducing the use of media planning models and computers to your own organization.

There are a number of other computer languages that could have formed the basis for the programs here, such as Fortran, PASCAL or Lotus, for example. BASIC was chosen because it can be learned easily and mastered in a short time. Also, you may have learned the language previously. Therefore, using BASIC minimizes the computer language barrier and allows users to get on with a model building agenda.

This appendix, then, is designed merely to get you started. If a greater intrigue with computer model building develops, one will quickly acquire a voracious appetite for additional information and insights. To go beyond this material, you can look at some of the references listed at the end of this appendix.

The remainder of this appendix will prepare you for programming. You will learn how to use BASICA, the IBM-PC Advanced BASIC Language, including its functions, programming terminology, and commands. You will also see a simple program demonstrating most of the concepts that have been introduced. By the time this appendix is finished, you will have a "dangerous" level of knowledge of BASIC programming on the personal computer.

☐ DOS Commands

COPY

To make a copy of a program one must boot DOS. After the A >:

1. Insert the diskette with the program to copy into DRIVE A.
2. Insert the diskette that will receive the program copy into DRIVE B.
3. Type: COPY program1 B: program2

   program1 is the name of the program to copy, **program2** is the name of the program on the disk in DRIVE B. If the name is the same as the name of Program 1, then it may be omitted.

DIR

This command gives a directory of the files on the given diskette. It will allow the user to look at the file names on the screen and then proceed with whatever he or she was planning to do. Once the A > appears

1. Type DIR <CR>.
2. A list of files which are on the diskette in the specified drive will be shown.

FORMAT

New diskettes must be formatted using DOS. Once the A >: appears

1. Type FORMAT B: <CR>.

2. Insert new diskette into drive B, <CR>.

3. Computer response:

```
Formatting... format complete
XXXXXXXX bytes total disk space
XXXXXXXX bytes available on disk
Format Another (Y/N)?
```

4. If Y, <CR> then go back to #2.

5. If N, <CR> then the diskette is formatted.

☐ **BASICA Functions**

BASICA

The programs used here are written in ADVANCED BASIC. In order to begin programming, one must be using the ADVANCED BASIC interpreter which is on the DOS diskette. To do this:

1. Type BASICA when the A> appears after booting DOS.

2. The screen will show "OK" and programming can begin.

EDIT

This function uses the BASIC program editor, which is a "screen line-editor," meaning that it can edit any line on the screen, one line at a time. When editing, the numeric datapad is used (located on the right side of the keyboard), the backspace key, and the control key (<Ctrl>), located on the left side of the keyboard above the shift key.

<Home>	This key is located on the #7 key in the numeric datapad. When depressed, it will return the cursor to the upper left-hand corner of the screen.
<Ctrl> <Home>	This combination clears the screen and returns the cursor to the upper left-hand corner of the screen.
<↑>	This key is located on the #8 key in the numeric datapad. It will move the cursor up one line.
<↓>	This key, located on the #2 key in the numeric datapad, will move the cursor down one line.
<←>	This key, located on the #4 key of the numeric datapad, will move the cursor one space to the left. If the cursor is at the leftmost position of that line, it will move to the rightmost position of the previous line.
<→>	This key, located on the #6 key in the numeric datapad, will move the cursor one position to the right. If the cursor is at the rightmost position of that line, it will move to the leftmost position of the following line.
<Ins>	This key is located under the numeric datapad. It will activate the insert mode if OFF or deactivate it if ON. When inserting, the characters will appear above the

cursor. If inserting continues past the end of the line, wrap around will occur and the insertion will continue at the leftmost position of the next line. When <Ins> is depressed a second time to turn the insert mode off, any characters typed will replace the ones at the cursor's position.

<Del> This key is located beneath the numeric datapad to the right of <Ins>. It will delete the character at the current cursor position. All characters on the same line will move one space to the left to fill the empty space(s).

<←> This is the backspace key. It is located at the top of the keyboard on the right side. This key IS different from the move-cursor-back-one-space key located on the #4 key in the numeric datapad. The backspace key moves the cursor one position to the left and deletes the last character typed.

In order to use the BASIC program editor one must be in the BASIC command mode (anytime after OK and before RUN) and have a list of the program on the screen or be typing the program into the computer.

1. Move the cursor to the position where the modification is desired.
2. Perform the desired modification.
3. Move the cursor to the position of the next modification, or to the end of the listing.

LOAD

This command loads the specified program from disk into memory. It can be executed either by:

1. <F3> program name, or
2. Typing LOAD ''program name''

   Program name is the name the user wishes to load into memory.

RENUM

RENUM is short for renumber. This command renumbers the program lines of the BASICA program in memory.

RENUM newnum, oldnum, increment

Newnum is the first line number used in the new numbering sequence. If no number is specified, then 10 will be used.

Oldnum is the line in the program where the renumbering is to begin. If it is not stated, renumbering will start with the first line of the program.

Increment is the increment to be used in the new sequence. If no number is specified, 10 will be used.

RUN

RUN begins execution of the current program in memory. It can be activated by:

1. <F2>, or by
2. Typing RUN.

SAVE

This command saves the BASICA program that is currently in memory onto a diskette. The command is executed either by:

1. <F4> program name, or by
2. Typing SAVE "program name"

Program name is the name of the program in memory.

☐ **Programming Terminology**

Array

An array is a variable that can hold many values at the same time. It must be dimensioned at the beginning of the program (see DIM below). For example, suppose that the planner wants to keep track of how much is spent on advertising each month, in millions of dollars.

```
10   DIM AD(12)
....
50   AD(1) = .75
60   AD(2) = 1.30
70   AD(3) = 1.35
....
160  AD(12) = 2.40
```

AD is the variable name, and 12 is the number of slots (one per month) in the variable. Now, to know how much is spent in March, all one has to do is enter:

```
PRINT AD(3)
```

The computer will print 1.35.

Constant

A constant is a number that does not change. It is a good idea to assign a variable to a constant used often. For example:

```
KWTV = 2.66,
KBTV = 1.46.
```

Later in the program the names (KWTV, KBTV) can be used instead of the numbers. It is easier to follow and to change their values if necessary. This can also be called a fixed variable.

Initialize

Initializing a variable gives it a starting point. One uses it to establish a variable or change its value before using it again. For example:

```
COUNT = 0
```

When COUNT is used later in the program one need not worry about its previous value.

Loop

Loops are used to repeat a series of steps for a specified number of times in a row. The way to program this is with a FOR...NEXT loop (see FOR...NEXT below). For example:

```
10 FOR COUNT = 2 TO 5
20     PRINT COUNT;
30 NEXT COUNT
40 NEXT PROGRAM LINE
```

This will execute as follows:

Line Number	Count Value	Output
10	2	
20	2	2
30	3	
10	3	
20	3	3
...		
20	5	5
30	6	

10 transfers control to line 40, loop complete.

Matrix

A matrix is a two-dimensional array. This means that it has a value for each row and column. It must be dimensioned in a DIM statement at the beginning of the program (see DIM below). The following multiplication table provides an example.

```
10  DIM MULT(5,5)      (this is a 5x5 table called MULT)
.....
50  FOR COLUMN = 1 TO 5
60      FOR ROW = 1 TO 5
70          MULT(COLUMN,ROW) = COLUMN * ROW
80      NEXT ROW
90  NEXT COLUMN
```

The values of this table are filled by two nested loops. This means that the inner loop will be completed before the exterior loop is incremented. The following table results.

MULT	1	2	3	4	5
1	1	2	3	4	5
2	2	4			
3	3	6	etc.		
4	4	8			
5	5	10			

String

A string is a variable that is filled with alphanumeric data. This means that it has characters besides numbers. It is represented by a "$," the last character in the variable name. For example:

```
60    AD$ = "ADVERTISING EXPENDITURES"
```

Subroutine

A subroutine consists of a series of lines called from the main program. They are not executed in the normal top to bottom flow of the program, but must be called with a GOSUB statement within the main program (see GOSUB...RETURN below). For example:

```
10    GOSUB 40
20    PRINT "BACK IN MAIN PROGRAM"
30    END
40    PRINT "SUBROUTINE ";
50    PRINT "IS AT END OF ";
60    PRINT "MAIN PROGRAM"
70    RETURN
```

The flow of the program begins at 10 and then jumps to 40 to execute the subroutine consisting of lines 40, 50, 60, 70. Line 70 sends the statement back to the main program to the line immediately following the GOSUB statement, which is line 20, and then to line 30 to end the program. The output looks like this:

```
SUBROUTINE IS AT END OF MAIN PROGRAM
BACK IN MAIN PROGRAM
```

Variable Names

A variable name can be up to 40 characters in length. It is best to be as descriptive as possible when naming a variable as this will make the code easier to read and follow. For example:

COUNT would be a counter variable

KBTV would be a between-vehicle correction factor for TV

☐ BASICA Commands

DATA

The DATA command stores the values of numeric and string constants that are to be used by the READ statement.

DATA constants

constants are the numbers or string values. Several values can be separated by commas.

This statement is not executed by the program and can be placed anywhere within it, although it is usually put at the end.

DIM

DIM is short for dimension and is a statement used to specify the sizes of arrays and matrices. This must be done to distinguish the variable as an array or matrix instead of a one-dimensional variable. Here is the format of a DIM statement.

DIM var(subscript)

var is a variable name used for the array or matrix.

subscript is an integer that is the maximum number of elements in the array or matrix.

If there are several arrays or matrices in the program, additional variables and subscripts can be added to the single DIM statement, separated by commas. A DIM statement might look like this:

```
DIM VAR1(17), VAR2(9,6)
```

Here VAR1 is an array with 17 possible elements, while VAR2 is a nine by six matrix, or two-dimensional array.

END

The END command terminates the program. It also closes all open files and returns to the BASICA prompt. It should be placed as the last statement of the program.

FOR...NEXT

This procedure requires both FOR and NEXT statements to make a loop. The format of the FOR...NEXT procedure follows.

```
FOR var = int1 TO int2
...
NEXT var
```

var is the name of the variable that is used as the loop counter.

int1 is the beginning value of the variable in the loop.

TO is necessary to put an upper bound on the loop.

int2 is the ending value of the variable in the loop.

GOSUB...RETURN

This procedure is used to branch to a subroutine and then continue execution with the statement following the GOSUB statement in the main program. Here is the typical format.

```
GOSUB line #
...
RETURN
```

line # is the first line of the subroutine which can be located anywhere in the program.

It is a good idea to put all subroutines at the end of the main program after the END statement. RETURN is the last line in the subroutine, transferring control back to the line immediately following the GOSUB statement.

GOTO

The GOTO statement assigns control unconditionally to another section not in the normal flow of the program. Here is the format.

```
GOTO line #
```

line # is the line to which one wants the program to go.

It is NOT good programming style to use many GOTO statements. Therefore the fewer the better.

IF...THEN

This statement has many forms used to branch the flow of the program to another point depending on the quantifier. Here are some samples.

```
IF exp THEN clause1
IF exp THEN clause1 ELSE clause2
If exp GOTO line #
If exp GOTO line # ELSE clause1
```

exp is any numeric expression that can be evaluated as true or false, **clause1** and **clause2** are BASICA statements (single or multiple) that will be executed upon the value of the expression, **line #** is the line where the program is to branch to after the evaluation of the expression.

If the expression is false, then the flow of the program goes to the ELSE clause, if present, or the statement following THEN.

INPUT

The INPUT statement is used to receive data from the keyboard during execution. Here is the format.

```
INPUT var
```

var is the variable which will receive the data.

A question mark will appear on the screen and the program will wait for the user's response.

PRINT

The PRINT command is used to display something on the screen.

```
PRINT var
PRINT "exp"
```

var is the variable name for which the computer will display (output) its value at the time the PRINT statement is executed.

exp is an expression that will be displayed. It MUST be enclosed in quotation marks. The computer will display (output) whatever is written within the quotes.

If a comma or semicolon is placed at the end of the line, the next PRINT statement will continue printing on the same line, either a field or a few spaces after the point where the last PRINT statement stopped.

PRINT USING

The PRINT USING command prints strings or numbers using a specified format statement.

```
PRINT USING var; exp
```

var is a string constant or variable which consists of special format characters.

exp is the string of numbers which are to be printed, separated by commas or semicolons if there are multiple items.

String Fields. Here are two useful formats for the string field.

/n/   2 + n characters from the string are to be printed. If there are no spaces between the backslashes, only 2 characters will be printed.

&   a variable length string field. The string is output exactly as input.

Numeric Fields. When printing numbers, the following format characters are often used to format the numeric fields.

\#   represents each digit position. The positions are always filled. If the number has fewer digits than allocated by the format, it is right justified (printed on the right side of the field). A decimal point may be inserted at any position in the field.

\$\$ placed at the beginning of the format string causing a dollar sign to be printed to the immediate left of the formatted number.

,   placed to the left of the decimal point in a format string, it causes a comma to be printed to the left of every third digit to the left of the decimal point. If it is located at the end of the format string, it is printed as part of the string.

READ

The READ statement reads values into variables from the DATA statement. The format is as follows.

```
READ var
```

var is the variable which is to hold the value assigned in the READ statement from the DATA statement.

Several variables can be read by a single READ statement. When this is done, the variable names are separated by commas. A READ statement cannot be used without a DATA statement.

REM

REM is short for remark. This is used to insert comments into the program to help explain it. The format follows.

`REM remark`

remark may be any sequence of characters.

The REM statement is not executed by the program. It is only seen when the program is listed.

☐ Sample Program

Below is a sample program written in BASICA. This program uses many of the commands described in this chapter. You should follow the program "by hand"; in other words, pretend to be the computer. If the same results are obtained as those listed below the program, then one can assume that the commands are understood and users are ready to begin writing their own advertising programs. If the calculations are different from the output, one should try again, but not get discouraged. Most of the time spent programming is trying to figure out what the computer is doing.

You might want to type the program in to run your own data and change the output format. If there are any problems, one should not be afraid to use the *IBM Basic User's Manuals*. These manuals should be available at the same place where DOS was obtained.

BASICA program

```
10 REM THIS PROGRAM WILL CALCULATE CPM FOR EACH VEHICLE
20 REM AND FOR ALL VEHICLES TOGETHER
30 TOTALCOST=0:TOTALGI=0
40 INPUT"HOW MANY VEHICLES DO YOU HAVE";VEHICLE
50 DIM VNAME$(VEHICLE),TOTVEHCOST(VEHICLE),GI(VEHICLE),NUMINSERT(VEHICLE)
60 INPUT"WHAT IS THE TARGET SIZE";TSIZE
70 PRINT"TYPE VEHICLE NAME, NUMBER OF INSERTIONS, COST/INSERTION, RATING"
80 FOR COUNT = 1 TO VEHICLE
90    INPUT VNAME$(COUNT),NUMINSERT(COUNT),COST,RI
100   GRP=NUMINSERT(COUNT)*RI
110   TOTVEHCOST(COUNT)=NUMINSERT(COUNT)*COST
120   GI(COUNT)=TSIZE*(GRP/100)
130   CPM(COUNT)=(TOTVEHCOST(COUNT)*1000)/GI(COUNT)
140   TOTALCOST=TOTALCOST+TOTVEHCOST(COUNT)
150   TOTALGI=TOTALGI+GI(COUNT)
160 NEXT COUNT:PRINT:PRINT
170 PRINT"          CPM TABLE":PRINT
180 FOR COUNT=1 TO VEHICLE
190   PRINT VNAME$(COUNT);
200   PRINT USING"$$####.##";CPM(COUNT)
210 NEXT COUNT
220 PRINT:PRINT
230 PRINT"TOTAL SCHEDULE CPM=$";(TOTALCOST*1000)/TOTALGI
240 END
```

Program output

```
HOW MANY VEHICLES DO YOU HAVE? 3
WHAT IS THE TARGET SIZE? 18451000
TYPE VEHICLE NAME, NUMBER OF INSERTIONS, COST/INSERTION, RATING
? HART-HART,2,88162,16.8
? 3-COMPANY,1,88162,16.5
? SOAP DIGEST,2,7270,3.3


        CPM TABLE

HART-HART    $28.44
3-COMPANY    $28.96
SOAP DIGEST   $11.94

TOTAL SCHEDULE CPM = $26.671
```

This appendix is only an overview of some important BASICA commands and functions. There are several others that execute different and more complex commands and functions. To learn more about what is possible, you may wish to examine some of the following references.

ADDITIONAL READING

BASIC HANDBOOK, International Business Machines, Third Edition, 1984.

BASIC Quick Reference, International Business Machines, First Edition, 1984.

BASIC Reference, International Business Machines, Third Edition, 1984.

Microsoft QuickBASIC 4.0, Microsoft Corporation, 1987.

Quasney, James S. and John Maniotes, *BASIC Fundamentals and Style* (Boston: Boyd & Fraser Publishing Co., 1984).

Quasney, James S. and John Maniotes, *Complete BASIC for the Short Course* (Boston: Boyd & Fraser Publishing Co., 1985).

TURBO BASIC, Borland International, Inc., 1987.

CHAPTER FIFTEEN

Recommendations for Further Research

This chapter will provide a number of suggestions on fruitful avenues for further research. Each of the proposed topics could serve as a basis for a separate line of research activity. They also provide a blueprint for the advancement of the research program that supports this text and software. The notion of a broad and systematic research program such as this is consistent with the recommendations of Lancaster and O'Guinn[1] for developing an Advertising Research Center. This work will provide a focal point for faculty and student energy and resources which have the potential to accumulate into research output of substantial value to advertising education and practice.

BASIC MEDIA CONCEPTS

A number of important media planning concepts have not been introduced in this text, although several will be worked into future editions. For example, the material presented here does not explain how to develop media plans for top U.S. markets on a market-by-market basis. What are the problems and opportunities introduced by such complexity? You should be acquainted with the concepts of brand and category development indices and then be provided with the software to take the tedium out of the calculations required to evaluate market potential across the top 20, 50, or 100 U.S. markets, for example. As advertisers shift their marketing emphasis increasingly to a regional strategy, it is likely that this will become an important aspect of future media planning.

You should also be exposed to both the strengths and limitations of the methodologies used by the various audience measurement services. It is difficult to present this extremely complex topic during classroom hours, and to fully appreciate the diverse sources really requires the solving of some media planning problems using them; for this, a sourcebook such as the one prepared by Barban et al.[2] is one of the better ways of handling the problem. This text did not take that approach, however, in the belief that it is better to have a solid view of the entire media planning process, using just a few sources, rather than try to cover innumerable sources at the expense of a sound media planning philosophy.

Another useful research project would involve evaluating media plans on a monthly or quarterly basis and comparing the media evaluation factors to corresponding tracking study estimates of awareness and recall, for example. The goal would be to learn which media evaluation procedures are most predictive of market place results. The raw data for this kind of research already exist in the files of most major advertising agencies or advertisers who conduct systematic media plan evaluations and also do quarterly or semi-annual or annual tracking studies of consumer reaction to advertising activity.

ANALYZING THE SITUATION

The focus on a situation analysis, including the competitive advertising spending analysis and development of measurable marketing, advertising, and media goals, still needs additional work. For instance, one should consider several complicating factors, such as the possibility of widely dispersed and multiple geographic markets; two or more target markets; the distinction between heavy, medium, and light product users in terms of their differential impact on monthly sales; and the linkage between message frequency and measurable communications impact.

EVALUATING MEDIA SCHEDULES

Several possibilities for future research arise with regard to the evaluation of comprehensive advertising media plans. ADPLAN, for example, must be tested using alternative data sources. The program at the moment is most trustworthy using SMRB audience data, and then only when they involve rather broad targets such as adults, males, females, and female homemakers. The models should be adaptable to A.C. Nielsen, Arbitron and MRI audience data, among others.

Media plans usually involve more than one media category, thus the models must be developed further to account for duplication among media categories. The circumstances when it is appropriate to develop effective reach estimates for the combination of two or more media categories should also be identified. Can television, magazine and newspaper advertisements, for example, ever be treated equally in terms of target impact, even if the same general communications effects criteria and different weights are used across all media categories? And if not, how can the inherent differences in the characteristics of the various media be taken into account?

It would also be desirable to have better methods to estimate the size of advertising as opposed to vehicle audiences. While this text advances one procedure, numerous others are available and potentially useful in the absence of better data. The disparity between advertising and vehicle audiences continues to be one of the most challenging tasks for media planners and researchers to consider.

USING INTERACTIVE MEDIA MODELS

Considerable emphasis has been placed throughout this text on the use of interactive advertising models. While some may see this as too great a reliance on technology, the authors feel that carefully developed personal computer programs extend the classroom experience for students and enhance the media planning process for all users. This approach ensures that the planner has a complete, accurate, and thorough knowledge of media planning concepts and theories before he or she is exposed to the intricacies of computer models. Furthermore, rather than simply talking about the reach/frequency tradeoffs under various budget constraints, the user can actually experience them by re-evaluating media plans in an attempt to develop one that will achieve particular media goals.

DEVELOPING INTERACTIVE PLANNING MODELS

One of the most challenging aspects of this material is to etch an advertising planning philosophy into such a form that routine decisions and calculations can be handled by a machine, freeing planners to do more creative work. It will also provide a sense of closure in that users will not only understand the concepts but put them in the highly precise form of a computer program. In this way one can come to understand how such models work, and learn that the models merely embody whatever philosophy is programmed. One discovers too that imagination and energy are really the only limits to what can be achieved.

ENDNOTES

1. Kent M. Lancaster and Thomas C. O'Guinn, "Developing an Advertising Research Center," Workshop *Proceedings* of the American Academy of Advertising, Charleston, South Carolina, March 1985, pp. NR152-56.

2. Arnold M. Barban, Donald W. Jugenheimer, Lee F. Young and Peter B. Turk, *Advertising Media Sourcebook and Workbook* (Columbus: Grid Publishing, Inc., 1981).

Using Advertising Models
on IBM and Macintosh Microcomputers

Throughout this text, you have been exposed to four different advertising media planning microcomputer programs. These are compatible with both IBM and Macintosh equipment (and with IBM compatible machines). This appendix is designed to provide enough background information to get you started. After some standard terminology is explained, you are directed to one of two sections, depending on the type of equipment used.

PRELIMINARY TERMINOLOGY

You should become familiar with the following microcomputer terms.

INPUT: Data entered into the microcomputer using the keyboard.

OUTPUT: The tables or data that the computer produces after performing an operation.

DATA: Pieces of information, usually numeric, but sometimes alphanumeric.

<CR>: Carriage return or Enter key.

RUN: A complete interaction with a program.

BOOT: This means to ''start up'' the computer to run programs.

HARDCOPY: A paper copy of either an entire run or the final output tables or data.

DEFAULT: Built-in features in the computer and software that will operate unless changed.

CURSOR: The flashing box or line that tells you where the next character will be positioned on the screen.

USING IBM (AND COMPATIBLE) EQUIPMENT

IBM (and compatible) equipment users must become familiar with the following additional terms and concepts before proceeding.

DRIVE A: The disk drive usually located on the left-hand side or above. It is often the default drive.

DRIVE B: The disk drive located on the right-hand side or below.

DRIVE C: If available, this is often a RAM disk or a hard disk.

A>: "A" prompt. This means that the computer is operating from drive A.

B>: "B" prompt. The computer is operating from drive B.

C>: "C" prompt. The computer is operating from drive C.

DOS: Disk Operating System. This software system controls the movement of information into and out of the computer.

You are now ready to begin using the personal computer. Most keyboards have over 80 keys. Some of these perform special functions on their own, while others do particular functions when used in conjunction with another key. The braces "< >" will denote a key on the keyboard. You should NOT type the word within these braces. Rather, press the key that is indicated, and if more than one is listed, then they should be pressed simultaneously. For example, <x> means press the key "x."

ON/OFF: This is the main power switch. It is usually located on the back right side of the disk drives.

BREAK: To terminate a program or stop a command before it finishes its run, hold down <Ctrl> and press <Break>.

BACKSPACE: This key allows one to move the cursor backwards, thus correcting a mistake before pressing <CR>. It is denoted by <←>.

BOOT: This command returns the computer to DOS. In most cases, put the DOS diskette back into Drive A, then press <Ctrl>, <Alt> and <Del> simultaneously. Machines with hard disks generally boot directly from them, requiring you to leave the drive A door open.

PRINT SCREEN: With this feature, you can send the information on the screen to the printer, although it will print the screen displayed. To accomplish this, simply turn the printer ON, then hold down <Shift> and press <PrtSc>.

☐ Getting Ready

1. First obtain a DOS diskette or boot it from a hard disk if available.

2. Turn on and adjust the screen (knobs to right of screen).

3. Finally, if a hardcopy is desired, make sure the computer is attached to a printer.

☐ Running Programs

1. Gently insert the DOS diskette into Drive A, without forcing it, then close the drive door. Available versions of DOS include 1.1, 2.0, 2.1, 3.0, 3.1, 3.2 and 3.3. It is better to use 3.0 or higher.

2. To boot the system:
   a. insert DOS into the computer while it is turned OFF and then turn it ON, or
   b. press <Ctrl> and <Alt> and <Del> once the computer is on.
3. The screen will display:

   ```
   Current date is xxx x-xx-xxxx
   Enter new date:
   ```

4. Enter the date or enter <CR>
5. The screen will display:

   ```
   Current time is x:xx:xx.xx
   Enter new time:
   ```

6. Again, enter the date or enter <CR>
7. Next will appear:

   ```
   The IBM Personal Computer DOS
   Version x.xx  (c)Copyright IBM Corp.
   ```

8. Remove DOS from drive A and insert the diskette with the media planning programs (ADCOMP, ADGOAL, ADPLAN, ADFLOW, and BRUN40).
9. To run ADPLAN (or any of the three other programs) on it, after the A>, type ADPLAN <CR>.
10. You are now ready to begin running the media programs.

☐ **Using the Printer**

Each of the programs include instructions for preparing the printer attached to your system. Nevertheless, the following instructions provide additional control and flexibility.

1. Make sure that the personal computer is attached to a printer.
2. The printer can be turned on at any time.
   a. The "power," "ready," and "on-line" lights should all be on.
   b. If one of these lights is not lit, check:
      "power" - to ensure the printer is on;
      "ready" - in case someone else is using the printer;
      "on-line" - the <on-line> button next to the light.
   c. If the PC shares a printer with others, then turn the dial on the connecting box to the letter (A, B, C, D) of the computer.
3. To advance paper, with power on press <on line> then either:
   <LF> line feed, one line at a time, or
   <FF> form feed, one page at a time, about 66 lines.
4. The Print Screen (<Shift> <PrtSc>) command allows you to print the information displayed on the screen.

5. Each of the four programs allows you to print tables only instead of the entire interaction. Simply turn the printer on, adjust the paper, and select the option for printing tables. Tables can also be saved on disk files for later printing. This is done by saving the table file, activating the printer, getting the DOS prompt, A >, B >, C >, etc., then entering TYPE (filename.extension), where "filename" is the name of the file and "extension" is a three letter extension (for example, A > TYPE ADPLAN.TAB).

Users are now ready to begin working with any of the programs included with this text.

☐ How to Install DOS onto a Media Planning Diskette

Installing DOS onto the media planning diskette allows you to put all programs necessary for media plan evaluation on a single diskette, saving time if the system is used frequently. More importantly, it will free a drive and allow you to make a permanent disk file of any interactions with the system. This is useful if the PC is attached to a printer shared with other users. You can complete a media analysis in the usual fashion without regard to printing a hard copy. Then, as soon as a printer becomes available, simply print the output file that is saved on the working diskette in an available drive.

First you need to format a blank diskette using the "/B" command. This will create space for IBMBIO.COM and IBMDOS.COM to occupy the first two directory entries on the media planning diskette. You can follow these steps to install the available version of DOS onto that diskette.

1. Begin by booting DOS, version 3.0 or higher, in Drive A.

2. Insert a blank diskette in Drive B.

3. After A >, type FORMAT B:/B, and follow instructions to format the blank disk in drive B.

4. After A >, type: SYS B:. This will transfer IBMBIO.COM and IBMDOS-.COM to the first two directory entries on the media planning diskette.

5. After A > again, type: COPY COMMAND.COM B:. This will transfer COMMAND.COM to the media planning diskette.

6. Now, remove DOS from drive A and replace it with the disk labeled "Advertising Media Planning and Evaluation." Next enter COPY BRUN40.EXE B:. Also enter COPY AD____.EXE B: for each program desired, substituting the program letters for the blanks shown.

7. After the A > prompt, enter B:.

8. After B >, it is a good idea to type DIR for "directory" to see a listing of files, such as the following.

```
COMMAND.COM
BRUN40.EXE
AD____.EXE
AD____.EXE
AD____.EXE
```

The number of media planning programs that will fit on the diskette will depend on the diskette size and density, the version of DOS used (the more recent the version of DOS, the larger the COM file), and the choice of media planning files. You will probably have to create two diskettes to accommodate all of the media planning programs, following steps one through eight above for the second diskette.

You now can boot the system with the media planning diskette and run any of the media planning programs chosen from Drive A. But since there will be very little room remaining on the diskette, it is advisable to write-protect the diskette at this time to avoid the possibility of erasing any of these files.

If you want to save the interaction table or data as permanent diskette files to be printed later, at a more convenient time or location, place a working diskette, which has been formatted using the FORMAT command, in Drive B. Then follow these steps.

1. First boot the system with the media planning diskette created using steps one through eight above.

2. After A >, enter ADPLAN

    This will LOAD and RUN ADPLAN immediately. Write the output data or table files to Drive B on a file called ADPLAN.OUT. Any of the media planning programs can be run in place of ADPLAN. The output file can have any name, as long as there is not a duplicate file name on the working diskette in Drive B. It is a good idea to number them sequentially (for example, ADPLAN1.OUT, ADPLAN2.OUT) so that you can keep track of several different interactions with the same program. Using the extension ''.OUT'' will also remind you that the file is an output file if there are several types of files on the working diskette in Drive B.

    You can be sure that the interaction is being saved on the diskette in Drive B by observing the red light flashing on that drive as the memory buffer fills and is emptied onto Drive B. If B: is not specified as the output drive, output will be written instead to Drive A, or the default drive, if there is sufficient memory.

    Once you have finished executing a particular program, the program instructions can be followed to stop the run. The DOS prompt A > will then appear. You can choose to run another program in a similar fashion.

3. To get a hard copy of the output files, set up and activate the printer (by pressing <Ctrl> <Shift> <PrtSc> simultaneously) attached to the PC. After getting A >, enter TYPE B:ADPLAN1.OUT <CR>. Print any file chosen using this procedure by substituting the selected file name for ADPLAN1.OUT.

If you are familiar with EDLIN, MULTIMATE, VOLKSWRITER, WORD PERFECT, or other word processing systems, you can also edit your output files before having them printed. You should experiment on some small files to gain experience doing this before tackling more demanding ones.

USING MACINTOSH EQUIPMENT

Users of Macintosh equipment should become familiar with the following additional terms and concepts before proceeding.

Mouse: The mouse is a mechanical tracking device attached to the keyboard or machine which operates the pointer displayed on the screen. Moving the mouse moves the pointer. To select an item from the screen display, move the mouse pointer over the item, then click and release the mouse button. To move or drag an item, move the pointer over to it and hold down the button, then shift the pointer to the new location and release the button.

Menus: Menu bars appear at the top of most Macintosh displays. They often include an apple icon, File, Edit, View, and Special, among others. To select an item on a menu, place the pointer over the appropriate menu heading, press the mouse button, then move down to the desired item and release the button.

Windows: Disks and files are represented as icons on the screen. To open a file and display its contents, place the mouse pointer over the file, press the mouse button twice (that is, double click it), and a window will open displaying file contents. To close a window, click the close box in the upper left hand corner on the title bar. To change window size, click the zoom box in the upper right hand corner or click and drag the resize box in the lower right hand corner. Scroll bars are located at the bottom and on the right hand side of most windows; click the arrows or drag the thumb box to the desired position. Several windows can be open at once, with the active window on top. One click in an inactive window will make it active.

Files: There are three basic file types. *Application* files are executable programs, such as ADPLAN, and have the file extension ''.APL'' at the end of their name. Double click application files to execute them. *Document* files will not execute as they are usually created by an application file. *Folders* are directory names. When opened or double clicked they will display another window with their contents. Files can be moved from one location to another by dragging their icon to the destination folder or disk icon. Files can also be erased or disposed of by dragging them to the trash icon.

☐ **Running Advertising Programs**

To execute any of the advertising planning programs, readers should follow these steps.

1. First turn the machine ON.
2. Next, insert the ''System Tools'' diskette provided with the machine. This does not have to be inserted if the machine is equipped with a hard disk drive.
3. The screen will display a menu bar, the System Tools (or hard disk) icon,

and a trash bin. If the machine has only one disk drive and no hard disk, eject the System Tools disk by selecting ''Eject'' from the ''File'' menu on the menu bar.

4. Now, insert the AD MODELS disk into any available disk drive.

5. When the AD MODELS disk icon is displayed on the screen, double click it to open a window displaying its contents. The window will display the icons for each of the application programs included with the disk as well as any documents created by using them.

6. To run a program, simply double click its icon.

7. Document files can be created by the programs. These usually will be data or table files that you designate. They will be saved on the AD MODELS disk if you do not designate another disk name (e.g., MAG.DAT might be the name of a magazine data file that would be saved on the AD MODELS disk). Each table and data file will have its own icon.

8. To stop a program before arriving at its main menu, simply select ''Quit'' from the File option on the menu bar. Selecting the stop option from the program menu will return control to the system. To turn the machine OFF, select ''Shut Down'' from the Special option on the menu bar.

☐ **Printing Tables and Document Files**

Tables can be printed directly from most ad model interactions by selecting that option from the program menu. Once selected, the program provides instructions for activating the printer and printing tables.

Alternatively, table files may be saved on disk and printed separately after the program is executed. Simply select the table file desired by clicking its icon. Choose ''Print'' from the ''File'' menu on the menu bar. You may follow the instructions displayed on the print windows that appear to prepare the printer and print the file.

ADDITIONAL READING

IBM Disk Operating System (Various versions).

Lu, Cary. *The Apple Macintosh Book*, 2d ed. Microsoft Press, 1985.

Glossary

A. C. Nielsen A syndicated data service that provides media audience ratings for network and spot television. See also: Media audience data.

ADCOMP An interactive media planning model that aids the planner in preparing a competitive advertising spending analysis for a particular product class using Leading National Advertisers (LNA) expenditure data as a basis.

ADFLOW A flowchart program that identifies the monthly placement of all advertisements in a campaign and summarizes the media evaluation factors on a month-by-month basis.

ADGOAL An interactive planning model that allows the planner to develop measurable media goals to direct the overall media plan. They are developed as a complement to marketing and advertising goals.

ADPLAN An interactive advertising media planning program designed to provide estimates of reach, gross rating points, gross impressions, average frequency, total schedule cost, cost-per-thousand impressions, frequency distributions and effective reach, among others, for a variety of major print and broadcast media categories and target audiences.

AdTel A syndicated data service that provides retail purchase information.

Advertising audience The number or percentage of target audience members exposed to a particular advertising message, as differentiated from the vehicle audience which includes those exposed to a particular vehicle that delivers the advertising message. The vehicle audience often is larger than the advertising audience.

Agate line A unit of space for buying newspaper advertising. One agate line is one column wide and 1/14 of an inch deep.

Annual rate of change A dimension of competitive advertising spending analysis that describes how each brand is allocating advertising expenditures to various media categories from one year to the next.

Arbitron Ratings Company A syndicated data service that provides television and radio audience data. See also: Media audience data.

Area of Dominant Influence (ADI) Geographic market definition that assigns counties to one television or radio market as defined by Arbitron. Arbitron divides the U.S. into approximately 220 ADIs.

Audience duplication The overlap between audiences of various media.

Audience factors Dimensions for making specific media decisions that include consideration of the interaction of the medium with the viewer or listener, such as the audience size of prime time network television or the characteristics of the readers of a certain magazine.

Average frequency   Estimate of the average number of times those reached by a schedule are likely to have been exposed to the advertising campaign.

Average-Quarter-Hour rating (AQH)   The rating in broadcast media which measures the number of homes or persons tuned to a program for an average quarter-hour.

BARCUME   A syndicated source of competitive advertising expenditure of spot television advertising activity for national advertisers covering the top 75 U.S. markets.

BehaviorScan   A syndicated data service which provides purchase data from retail stores that use electronic scanning systems.

Beta Binomial Exposure Distribution (BBD) Model   A statistical procedure for estimating the likelihood of a target's exposure to a schedule a given number of times. The beta distribution estimates the number of different ways target members can be exposed to the schedule 1, 2, 3, to N total insertions in a schedule. The binominal distribution estimates the average probability of exposure to the schedule 1, 2, 3, to N times. The product of the beta and binominal distributions is the schedule exposure distribution.

Birch Reports   A corporation that provides radio audience data to the advertisers and stations in markets smaller than those typically measured by Arbitron. See also: Media audience data.

Boot   Another word for activating DOS when preparing the computer for running programs.

Brand Cumulative Audience (BCA)   A syndicated data source that provides detailed information on competitive network television advertising schedules for selected brands.

Broadcast Advertisers Report (BAR)   A syndicated source of competitive advertising expenditure data on the network television activity of national advertisers.

BAR network radio service   Report on network radio activity of national advertisers.

Burke   A syndicated advertising message measurement company which provides broadcast advertisers with ''day-after-recall'' scores, among other services.

Business magazine   Publications directed at a particular industry or profession, such as *Advertising Age*, *Chain Store Age*.

Cable Audience Measurement Profile (CAMP)   Arbitron's local cable audience measurement service based on the telephone recall method.

Cable television   Television channels available for an additional monthly fee in areas wired with cables to relay programs.

Carry-over effects   The proportion of communication effects due to advertising that continue from one period to the next. Also called advertising retention rate.

Churn rate   The proportion of cable subscribers who drop their subscription in a given time period.

Cognitive advertising communication effects   The initial stages of the communication effects hierarchy, such as attention, awareness, knowledge, etc., as differentiated from attitudinal and behavioral advertising communication effects, such as liking, preference, conviction, trial, purchase.

Contingency budget   The percent of the total advertising appropriation that is set aside for contingency purposes, such as speculative buys and competitive response. Usually this ranges from 10 to 15 percent.

Continuity   A measurement of advertising activity that asks how often the audience would see the ads at regular intervals, such as once a day or monthly.

Controlled ad placement   The advertiser's control over when and where an ad will appear. Television and outdoor allow strong control on placement whereas magazine ads are often controlled by the editors.

Controlled circulation   Distribution of a publication to audience members meeting certain minimum requirements.

Cost-per-effective-reach point (CPEP)   Total schedule cost divided by the total effective reach (n+) delivered.

Cost-per-rating point (CPP)   The total cost of a schedule divided by the gross rating points delivered.

Cost-per-thousand impressions (CPM)   Cost to achieve every thousand impressions using a particular vehicle or schedule.

Cross-pair rating   The reach of a pair of different vehicles or media.

Cumulative audience (CUME)   The net unduplicated audience of a schedule.

Designated Market Area (DMA)   A Nielsen term for those counties in which the home stations have a plurality of the counties' share of television viewing or the largest average quarter-hour audience. Similar to Arbitron's ADI.

Disk Operating system (DOS)   A software system that controls the movement of information into and out of IBM and compatible microcomputers.

Direct Broadcasting by Satellite (DBS)   Expansion of Television Receive Only. Signals from the cable or broadcast network are transmitted up to a communication satellite, scrambled, and sent back to homes of individual subscribers, each of whom is supplied with a 2-foot wide rooftop dish antenna and a decoder box.

Dual audience   The various aggregates of the upper quintiles or terciles of two different media categories. For example, SMRB defines the dual to be those target persons in the upper two quintiles of each media category plus those who are in the third quintile of both media categories.

Effective reach   The percent of the target exposed to an advertising schedule some minimum number of times or more in order for the message to have some measurable impact on the audience.

Efficiency factors   A dimension for making a specific media decision that deals primarily with cost, in terms of time or space, production, and in relation to the target reached.

Exposure distribution   The percentage of the target exposed to each frequency level of a schedule. Also called frequency distribution.

Full information   A schedule evaluation based on single-insertion, self-pair, and cross-pair ratings. Differentiated from limited information evaluations based on single-insertion ratings only.

Geographic flexibility   Ability to place ads in several regions, such as on spot TV or in a magazine's regional editions.

Gross impressions   Gross rating points expressed as the potential number of target impressions delivered.

Gross rating points (GRPs)   A crude or gross measure of audience potential expressed as the sum of the rating points delivered by a particular schedule. It does not account for audience duplication.

High definition TV A TV screen that uses 1,125 lines instead of the present 525 to improve the picture quality.

Interactive Market Systems (IMS) A media software house that provides a variety of audience data and media models to subscribers.

Interconnect System that sells local advertising on cable TV. With a "hard" interconnect, the systems are linked by cable or microwave relay to ensure simultaneous transmission of the ads, while the "soft" interconnect allows the operator to insert ads on videotape into the local avails in that system.

Leading National Advertisers (LNA) A syndicated source of competitive advertising expenditure data. It provides estimates of advertising expenditures in seven media categories for most major national advertisers.

LNA-PIB (Publishers Information Bureau) It provides data on brand, product, and company expenditures by magazine and type of advertisement.

Low Power Television (LPTV) A pay TV service that amplifies and rebroadcasts signals of distant full-power stations in a range of five to 40 miles. The operator chooses the programs, and whether to use UHF or VHF signals. The services are advertiser-supported.

Media audience data The size and characteristics of mass media audiences expressed as a percentage of a particular segment of the population, such as adults, males, females, or female homemakers. Some of the corporations that provide audience data include Arbitron, A. C. Nielsen Company, Simmons Market Research Bureau, Mediamark Research Inc., RADAR, The Birch Report, and Monroe Mendelson. The data often cover the full range of mass media categories, demographic groups and product categories, among other breakdowns.

Media imperative data Measure of media category audiences that show duplication as well as exclusive coverage.

Media mix Brand or segment advertising expenditures by media category expressed as a percentage of its total. The purpose is to see how strong the competitors are across media categories, removing differences in advertising scale.

Media Records A syndicated data source that provides extensive product and brand data on advertising volume and expenditure in major newspaper markets.

Mediamark Research Inc. (MRI) A service that provides audience data on a variety of media categories and target audiences. A competitor to Simmons Market Research Bureau (SMRB).

Message factors Media decisions based on the advertisement itself in terms of its likely impact on consumers.

Monroe Mendelson A service that provides audience data on "upscale" target groups.

Multichannel Multipoint Distribution System (MMDS) A version of the multipoint distribution system that allows up to eight channels of programming, picking up satellite signals from both broadcast and cable to redistribute them through microwave relays.

Multipoint Distribution Services (MDS) An alternative to pay cable TV that offers one channel by closed-circuit microwave within a 25-mile range of the originator.

National Audience Demographic Report Cable audience report that shows monthly cable/non-cable breakouts for network programs and various time periods.

Newspaper supplements Any printed material inserted in newspaper editions, such as comics and magazine sections.

Nielsen Cable Status Report Cable audience measurement service that gives quarterly penetration rates and audience viewing trends based on metered samples.

Nielsen Home Video Index Cable audience measurement service that tracks basic cable networks.

"Noted" score, Starch Percentage of the Starch sample of readers of a given magazine that can recall having looked at a particular advertisement. See also: Starch.

Outdoor Advertising Expenditure Report A syndicated source that provides outdoor advertising expenditures for major brands.

Pair-wise audience rating The average of all possible self- and cross-pair ratings in a given schedule.

Pay-per-View (PPV) A pay cable service that lets subscribers purchase individual programs when they want.

People meter A TV audience rating measurement device. It is a box attached to the TV set, accompanied by a hand-held device similar to a channel selector. Viewers push a button every time they watch TV to record their actual viewing.

Production flexibility Ability to make last-minute changes in ads. Spot radio and local newspapers offer this advantage. Also refers to the variety that a medium allows, such as cable TV and direct mail.

QUBE The first two-way interactive service, set up in Columbus, Ohio by Warner Cable Communications, Inc., employing both TV and computers.

Quintile Five equal-size groups of the population ranging from the heaviest to the lightest in terms of the amount of exposure to the medium.

RADAR (Radio All-Dimension Audience Research) Research provided for network radio audiences.

Radio Expenditure Report (RER) A syndicated data source of national brands' use of spot radio advertising.

Random combination method A method of estimating self- and cross-pair audiences when data are limited. Net audiences are estimated by taking GRPs for a pair of ratings and subtracting duplication.

Rating point The audience size of a particular vehicle expressed as a percentage of a given population. One rating point is equivalent to one percent of a particular population or base.

Reach Estimate of the total universe of individuals who may receive an advertiser's messages. It accounts for vehicle duplication.

Regression analysis A statistical method used by researchers to explain relations among two or more variables, often using lines or curves with reference to two or more axes.

Satellite Master Antenna Television (SMATV) A mini cable system in which each household is hooked up to a private satellite antenna located on the roof of the building, or adjacent to it, in order to receive multichannel programs. The signals are picked up from the satellite, amplified, and sent through the cable wires.

Self-pair rating The reach of two issues of the same magazine. Also called "cume."

Seasonality Seasonal characteristics that pertain to each medium or vehicle; for example higher radio listenership during the summer months.

Secondary data Data that have been gathered previously for other purposes or general consumption.

Selectivity Ability of a medium to focus on the audience type to whom ads are intended to appeal.

Share-of-voice (SOV) Advertising expenditures for a brand divided by the product category or segment total expenditure. It indicates which brand has what percentage of the advertising in each medium.

SHAZAM An econometrics package designed for the microcomputer based largely on regression analysis; it can be used to help develop media models.

Showing The number of illuminated and non-illuminated outdoor posters required to reach a specified percentage of the mobile population of a market each day.

Simmons Market Research Bureau (SMRB) Provides audience data for a variety of target groups and all major media categories. A competitor to Mediamark Research Inc. (MRI).

Spot television Television programs bought by national advertisers in specific markets.

Standard Advertising Unit (SAU) A unit of space sold in newspaper advertising. One SAU consists of 14 agate lines, or one column inch.

Standard Metropolitan Statistical Area (SMSA) A geographical division in which a unit consists of one or more counties that are defined by certain criteria regarding population, metropolitan character, and economic and social integration between central and outskirt counties.

Standard Rate and Data Service (SRDS) A service that provides the rates, including discount structures, of all major media categories.

Starch/INRA/Hooper A syndicated service that provides magazine and newspaper advertising readership by measuring various levels of recognition, such as "noted," "associated," and "read most."

Subscription television (STV) Television program system that offers a broadcast version of pay cable TV for those without access to cable. A scrambled signal is transmitted electronically over the air to subscribers, on the UHF band.

Task-objective method A method of deciding on an advertising appropriation in which the budget is allocated by the advertising objective established in advance.

Teletext Data transmission using the vertical blanking interval of the television screen.

Television Receive Only (TVRO) A private earth dish erected to receive cable or satellite programs at no charge by aiming it at appropriate satellite locations.

Telmar Media software house that provides a variety of audience data and media models. A competitor to IMS.

Tercile Media category audiences broken into thirds.

Turnover rate The percentage of a program audience that tunes in and out of a program in a specified time period.

Vehicle Individual publications or broadcasting programs in each media category, such as *Reader's Digest* and "60 Minutes."

Vertical Blanking Interval (VBI) Unused picture linage of the television screen through which data can be transmitted for Teletext and Videotex.

Videotex An interactive service that allows the viewer to respond to the information transmitted through the vertical blanking interval. Subscribers can access the information using phone lines or two-way cable systems.

Weight The percentage used to adjust vehicle audience ratings in order to get an estimate of advertising audience ratings or other desired communication effects. They can be obtained from Starch/INRA/Hooper, Burke Marketing Research, Gallup and Robinson, among others.

Zapping The tendency of television viewers to switch channels during commercial breaks.

Zipping The fast-forwarding of tapes by VCR users to avoid ads in previously broadcast programs.

Index

BRIEF BIOGRAPHIES OF THE AUTHORS

KENT M. LANCASTER is Associate Professor of Advertising, College of Journalism and Communications at the University of Florida, where he had served as the Gannett Distinguished Visiting Professor of Advertising. Previously, he was Associate Professor of Advertising in the College of Communications at the University of Illinois, where he taught for ten years. His Ph.D. in Mass Media and M.A. in Advertising are from Michigan State University. His current research focuses on advertising media and on the economics of advertising. Kent has written more than fifty research reports, some of which have appeared in the *Journal of Business, Journal of Macromarketing, Journal of Advertising, Journal of Advertising History, Journalism Quarterly, Journal of Marketing Education, Journalism Educator,* and in the *Proceedings* of the American Academy of Advertising, the American Marketing Association, the European Marketing Academy, and the American Statistical Association. Kent also serves on the editorial boards of the *Journal of Advertising* and the *Journal of Media Planning.* He is a consultant in advertising media planning, budgeting, and market analysis to a variety of public and private organizations.

HELEN E. KATZ is Assistant Professor of Advertising at Michigan State University. She received her Ph.D. in Communications and M.S. in Advertising from the University of Illinois. While at Illinois, she was a Teaching Assistant of Rhetoric and a Research Assistant in the Department of Advertising. Her primary teaching and research interests are in mass media research, management, and international advertising and media. Her work has been published in the *Proceedings* of the American Academy of Advertising, the European Marketing Academy, and the University of Illinois Advertising Research Center *Advertising Working Papers* series. She has also been cited in the *Journal of Marketing Education* and has presented papers at international conferences in London and Edinburgh. Helen has also served as a Faculty Intern in the Media Department of DDB Needham Worldwide in Chicago.

NTC Publishing Group

4255 West Touhy Avenue • Lincolnwood (Chicago) Illinois 60646-1975 • USA
Phone: 312/679-5500 • Telex: TWX 910 223 0736 (PATGROUP LCWD) • FAX 312/679-2494

NATIONAL TEXTBOOK COMPANY • PASSPORT BOOKS • NTC BUSINESS BOOKS • CRAIN BOOKS • VGM CAREER HORIZONS • VOLUNTAD PUBLISHERS

NTC Publishing Group

4255 West Touhy Avenue • Lincolnwood (Chicago) Illinois 60646-1975 • USA
Phone: 312/679-5500 • Telex: TWX 910 223 0736 (PATGROUP LCWD) • FAX 312/679-2494

NATIONAL TEXTBOOK COMPANY • PASSPORT BOOKS • NTC BUSINESS BOOKS • CRAIN BOOKS • VGM CAREER HORIZONS • VOLUNTAD PUBLISHERS

NTC Publishing Group

4255 West Touhy Avenue • Lincolnwood (Chicago) Illinois 60646-1975 • USA
Phone: 312/679-5500 • Telex: TWX 910 223 0736 (PATGROUP LCWD) • FAX 312/679-2494

NATIONAL TEXTBOOK COMPANY • PASSPORT BOOKS • NTC BUSINESS BOOKS • CRAIN BOOKS • VGM CAREER HORIZONS • VOLUNTAD PUBLISHERS